Industry Experts Praise *Beyond 2000: The Future of Direct Marketing*

This book is a marketer's dream come true. Jerry's gathered some of the great minds of the direct marketing industry and packaged them for us. Imagine being able to look into the future with the likes of Bob Stone, Ron Bliwas, Herschell Gordon Lewis, Alan Rosenspan, Leon Graham, Murray Raphel, Jim Rosenfield, Tom Collinger and the rest! Wow! A time like this only comes along once in a millennium! Reitman has made this "must reading" for any marketer who's heading into the 21st century with an eye for business.

> **John J. Flieder**
> **Vice President**
> **Allstate Insurance Company**

If direct marketing is part of your future, then *Beyond 2000* should be part of your present. I've read many books about direct marketing strategy, techniques, and even books containing lots of DM rules. *Beyond 2000* fills a void by providing a view of direct marketing's future as perceived by a distinguished list of co-authors.

> **John T. Kuendig**
> **Director, Direct Marketing**
> **Kraft General Foods USA**

What a line-up of co-authors! Only someone like Jerry Reitman, with all his worldwide contacts, could put together a group of superstars like this to share their expertise on the future of our business.

It takes someone who is a real visionary to be able to step back from today's challenges and "see around corners" to predict what's ahead. Jerry Reitman has always been such a person. And in this volume, he's assembled an all-star cast of visionaries to guide you on an exciting journey into the future.

> **Jim Kobs**
> **Chairman**
> **Kobs Gregory Passavant**

I found this book very informative and recommend it highly. I built a successful company because I learned how to communicate effectively with my customers. That basic premise has not changed, but the technology certainly has. In order to thrive in this constantly evolving industry, it is vitally important to keep up with the latest technology.

Lillian Vernon
Founder and Chief Executive Officer
Lillian Vernon Catalog

Direct Marketing is evolving so quickly, that the only way to stay abreast is by following the experiences of the leaders in the Industry. *Beyond 2000* compiles years of practical knowledge in a manner that will bring its readers into the 21st century with a perspective that will provide them with a real marketing advantage.

James Spector
Director, Consumer Promotions
Philip Morris, USA

This book is not just about the future of a marketing discipline or even a business industry. It's about the future of our daily life!

Erik Van Vooren
President
Montreux Symposium
Switzerland

The trouble with discovering and exploring new worlds is that one never knows exactly what to pack. *Beyond 2000* calls on some of the best minds in direct marketing to take their best shot at predicting just what might be needed in the way of luggage, as we direct marketers set sail for the new world of exploding technology . . . .

Beyond 2000 not only sets the historical context for what is happening but explores the possible impact it will have on our lives as marketers.

Mike Slosberg
Executive Creative Director
Bronner Slosberg Humphrey

With direct marketing accelerating at warp speed, *Beyond 2000* is the seat belt for anyone taking the ride. It's certainly a "wake-up" call for industry traditionalists.

Jim Reilly
General Manager
IBM Communications Services

Beyond 2000 is the seminal work which promises to propagate the thinking of the next generation of direct marketers.

Like studying a map before beginning a journey, reading this book will increase your chances of arriving at your chosen future destination safely, with your profits intact and your business secure.

Stephen Lloyd
President & Publisher
Canadian Direct Marketing News

Beyond 2000 helps us get closer to understanding the accelerating pace of change and closer to our customers by bringing together some of the best thinking by the best participants in the selling process. This book provides an invaluable road map for successfully navigating the emerging new world of integrated marketing management.

James N. Desrosier
Vice President, Advertising
MasterCard International

. . . essential reading, not only for us in the industry, but for anyone in the marketing landscape . . . This is an important book full of enlightening predictions.

Ian J. Kennedy,
Chairman
K & D Bond Direct International

This book is highly recommended for the classical marketer or advertiser, and for general managers as well . . . . It will be considered a milestone.

Georges Van Nevel
Managing Partner
DVN-De Visscher & Van Nevel

If you plan to continue earning your living in the direct marketing business, here's your navigational beacon. It's been said that everything is simpler than you think, and more complex than you can imagine. Direct marketing is no different, and looking into it's future takes special insight. Jerry Reitman brings the seers of the business together for a provocative look at what lies ahead.

Chuck Tannen
Chairman
Direct Marketing to Business Conference

It's not too early to start thinking about the direct marketing involvement in the year 2000. Jerry Reitman's *Beyond 2000: The Future of Direct Marketing* provides critical insight on what to expect and how to prepare for these new challenges and opportunities.

Pat Corpora
President
Book Division-Rodale Press

Beyond 2000 is a fine idea turned into a thought-provoking text well worth reading. The book challenges rather than purports to provide a blueprint for the future. Jerry Reitman deserves kudos for giving his profession something to think about—it truly lights up opportunities for those who are smart enough to grasp the brass ring.

Robert F. DeLay
Editor/Publisher
The DeLay Letter

Change is the one constant force in direct marketing and in every direct marketer's life today. Only those who adapt to the new and constantly changing realities of doing business will survive. *Beyond 2000* is one of the essential survival guides to success for all marketing and advertising decision makers.

Walter Schmid
Former President of the Montreux
Symposium
President, Walter Schmid, AG

For someone who grew up in the mail order business—where the emphasis was on "mail" and "order"—the year 2000 and beyond is a daunting challenge. The "electronic highway," "virtual reality," "interactive marketing," "evolving media," "integrated marketing"—all are terms not used by marketers as little as 10 years ago.

It's axiomatic that the one single thing to avoid in business is surprise. Jerry Reitman has assembled an extraordinary roster of consummate professionals to create a wiring diagram that will enable direct marketers to deal successfully with the complex changes that will be taking place in the coming years and decades. Must reading for every direct marketer.

> **Denny Hatch**
> **Editor/President**
> *Target Marketing/Who's Mailing What!*

There is no doubt that a revolution in direct marketing is in full swing. Many forces are involved, but increased use of technology by other direct marketers, much more retail competition, rapidly increasing costs of doing business combined with lower profit margins . . . these are the key elements driving the revolution now. Today.

There are some nerve-wracking changes ahead. It could be fun. It should be exciting. But it is also going to be tough for many of those brought up in the old ways.

But on the other hand, as we are forced to really think about our businesses—think hard about them—we are finding many new and great opportunities. *Beyond 2000* provides invaluable food for thought about where we are headed and how we are going to get there.

> **Jack Miller**
> **President**
> **Quill Corporation**

Beyond 2000

The Future of Direct Marketing

Beyond 2000
The Future of Direct Marketing

Jerry I. Reitman

Foreword by James G. Oates
Group President/Leo Burnett Company, Inc.

Printed on recyclable paper

NTC Business Books
NTC a division of *NTC Publishing Group* • Lincolnwood, Illinois USA

To Monica, Jennifer, and Sarah.
Each of you, in your own way, has enriched
my life. Thank you for sharing the joys,
the disappointments, and the adventure
. . . there's more to come.

**Library of Congress Cataloging-in-Publication Data is available from
the Library of Congress**

1996 Printing

Published by NTC Business Books, a division of NTC Publishing Group
4255 West Touhy Avenue
Lincolnwood (Chicago), Illinois 60646–1975, U.S.A.

67890 VP 9876543

CONTENTS

FOREWORD   James G. Oates   xv
ACKNOWLEDGMENTS   xvii
INTRODUCTION   Jerry I. Reitman   xix

Part I / Strategic Challenges for Beyond 2000

1   The Natural Evolution of Direct Marketing: 3
     Integrated Marketing and Integrated Marketing
     Communications
     Don E. Schultz

2   Integrated Marketing: Uncertain Today, Less   15
     Certain Tomorrow
     Carol Nelson

3   The Future Is International: A Guide for Growth   21
     Drayton Bird

4   What Direct Agencies Will Need to Succeed: 33
     Coping with the Forces of Change
     Tom Collinger

Part II / Technology and the Consumer

5   Consumer Privacy: The Saga Continues—And Will   45
     Not Go Away
     Lisa A. Petrison, Paul Wang, & David M. Messick

6   Back, Back, Back to the Future: How Quantum   57
     Leaps in Technology Bring Us Back to the
     Days of Old—Personal Service to Every Customer
     Stephen A. Cone

7   New Heights for the List Broker: The Top Ten   69
    Challenges
    Linda McAleer

8   A Media Planner's Guide to the Future: More   79
    Choices, More Tools
    Jack Klues & Jayne Zenaty Spittler

9   The New Media Company: What Magazine   97
    Companies Need to Offer Direct Marketers
    Hershel Sarbin, William Duch, & Toni Apgar

Part III / Messages for All Media

10 Looking Back Is Looking Ahead: Every Syllable   109
    Counts in Making Creative Messages Stand Out
    Herschell Gordon Lewis

11 Is There a Future for Direct Mail? Problems   115
    and Prognosis
    Alan Rosenspan

12 Catalogs: New Technology, New Markets,   131
    New Horizons
    Maxwell Sroge

13 Integrated Telemarketing: Sheathing the   139
    Double-Edged Sword
    Ernan Roman

14 Sales Promotion and Trade Incentives: 149
    New, Electronic Horizons
    H. Robert Wientzen

Part IV / Special Applications

15 Direct Response TV: Keeping an Eye on the Prize   159
    Ron Bliwas

16 Business-to-Business Direct Marketing: 165
    The Fundamental Forces of Change
    Donald R. Libey

17 Retail Direct Mail: Comes the Revolution   195
    Murray Raphel

18 Clubs: Old, Now, and New   209
    Leon Graham & Worth Linen

19 Financial Services Direct Marketing: Investing   217
    for the Future
    James R. Rosenfield

20 Book Publishing and the New Consumer: 227
    Providing Information and Entertainment
    for the Year 2000 and Beyond
    John D. Hall

21 Finding the Direct Marketers of the Future: 233
    Accomplishments and Challenges

    John D. Yeck

AFTERWORD

    The Past, Present, and Future of Direct Marketing   243
    Bob Stone

ABOUT THE CONTRIBUTORS   251
INDEX   263

FOREWORD

JAMES G. OATES
Group President/Leo Burnett Company, Inc.

Beyond 2000: The Future of Direct Marketing reads like the future of the advertising industry, covering topics vital to how we will plan and execute marketing strategies in years to come. The contributors, 28 of the most well-regarded names in the profession today, provide thought-provoking, pointed insight into what has become a critical part of the new marketing landscape.

To fully understand the relevance of direct, we must first look at the current state of today's marketplace, society, and industry, all of which have invalidated old assumptions and strategies.

Take a glance at media: they are vastly different. The idea of a mass market is outdated. And what used to be a simple trip to the grocery store to pick up a few items is now a journey into a supermarket of technology.

For starters, over the last two decades we went from being primarily a three-medium household—radio, TV, and print—to a household of over 150 media forms providing countless options. Some 500 TV channels are on the horizon.

Ironically, direct originally grew out of a lack of mass media. Now the importance of direct is due to an *explosion* of mass media, and a host of other factors.

At the same time, our culture has become more diverse . . . more fragmented. Instead of a single mass market, an idea that took hold in the 1950s and prevailed until recently, nontraditional life-styles and the increase of Hispanics, Asians, African-Americans, and women in the work force have caused a fragmented marketplace.

And then there's scanner data, which has opened up an entirely new world of information. With this technology, we are able to determine who is buying what, when, how often, and in what quantity.

That's where the advertising and marketing folks enter. Taking the data and turning it into direct marketing campaigns, among other communication vehicles, has become a key part of the marketing profession.

New technologies, including interactive media, enable us to segment what was once a gray and faceless mass market. It's feasible today—with scanner data and interactive media—to pare down that mass market, tailoring messages to one person, one household, or one specific, targeted group of people.

Consistent with these changes has been an avalanche of new products that, like media options, are tailored to a specific group of consumers. Line extensions offer different tastes, features, price points, and attributes to address the needs of a diverse society. The notion of one ad for one product communicated via one medium is absurd, given today's market-place.

But that doesn't mean that the idea of a cohesive brand image is lying by the wayside. It's possible to integrate each part of the communications plan with each other part.

For example, there are four different varieties of Marlboro cigarettes sold in over 16 different packages. The advertising and marketing of each is geared toward different consumers wanting different attributes in their cigarettes. However, care is taken to make sure that each element of each ad is consistent with the overall image of the brand, which has been carefully cultivated over time.

Part of maintaining that image, and the image of any brand, is ensuring that whether print or out-of-home, sales promotion or direct, a cohesive tone and message is communicated.

Explored in the following pages is how direct marketing plays a major role in communicating those unique but integrated messages. I now turn to 28 experts whose insights and knowledge make this book an important tool for understanding and executing what has become a vital part of our industry.

ACKNOWLEDGMENTS

This book was a collaborative effort in every sense. It was made possible by the generous contributions of the 28 people who co-authored its 22 chapters. They include colleagues, past and present, a few competitors, and a couple of second-generation direct marketers. What they all have in common is vision.

When I invited each of these distinguished professionals to join in the writing of this book about direct marketing's future, not one declined. Each of us, in our own way, and in our own segment of the industry, has been an active participant in and beneficiary of what came before us. The history of direct marketing is rich with innovative and creative individuals, many of them contributors to this book.

The world of direct marketing has changed. What started as a method of selling by Richard Warren Sears and Aaron Montgomery Ward in the 19th century has been enriched by countless other individuals and companies. People like John Caples of BBD&O gave it a creative style in print. Henry Cowen, Walter Wentz, and Herschell Gordon Lewis brought imagination to direct mail. Companies like Time/Life Books, the *Reader's Digest*, and Publishers Clearing House gave it credibility. Visionaries like Lester Wunderman and David Ogilvy recognized, early on, its inherent potential and importance, and their agencies served as the professional model many others were to follow.

But its heart and soul remains innovative practitioners in virtually every industry who applied direct marketing to their businesses and their problems. And it is for these professionals, as well as for the future contributors of direct marketing—in all its many aspects—that this book is written, with the hope that the spirit of innovation will continue to be part of the fabric of direct marketing. If direct marketing is to continue to serve an ever-increasing number of industries, it must continue to evolve. It must move further ahead into the marketing mainstream. Its strategic role must be understood by the next generation of marketing generalists.

Some special appreciation is also in order. To my friends Murray Raphel, Herschell Gordon Lewis, and Ian Kennedy, who have for so many years been a source of support and inspiration. To Tom Collinger, my friend and colleague, who has given new meaning to the word "partnership," and who has inspired the next generation of folks at Leo Burnett, an agency dear to both of us. To Janette Gleed, who has been there in the best and worst of times, always providing a helpful hand and encouragement. To Lee Graham, who by his example taught me about true humanity and personal courage.

And, finally, to all my colleagues at Burnett around the world who provided ideas and encouragement, thank you. Many U.S. "Burnetters" gave unselfishly of their own time to edit, correct, and promote this book. Ella Strubel, Wally Petersen, Lisa Lagger, Joe Silberman, and Miss "Docent," I am deeply grateful to each of you. It all started with a vision and some special folks who were committed to it: Cap Adams, Bill Lynch, and Jim Oates, who continue to make it an adventure. I am especially indebted to Rick Fizdale, whose passion, patience, and enthusiasm made it happen in the first place . . . thanks, Rick.

Jerry I. Reitman

INTRODUCTION

It all began some years ago when a group of friends formed a club called Odyssey. This was no ordinary club. No monthly meetings, no dues. Not even a newsletter. Rather, each year, these friends journeyed to an exotic place to discuss the changes in the area of direct marketing and how those changes would affect their business.

This was important, for these friends were leaders in their fields of advertising, publishing, media and related areas. Their business interests were as diverse as their hometowns—from Saõ Paolo to Toronto, Sydney to Zurich, Tokyo to London. But they all had a common bond that led them on *this* odyssey: better understanding the use of direct marketing as one of the many, but a critical aspect of achieving success.

I was not a member of ODYSSEY, but occasionally they would invite a guest or two to their annual meeting. As one of those guests, I saw first hand this special group in action.

They asked questions that required thoughtful, reflective answers:

- How would a less literate society impact the use of traditional direct marketing tools?

- Would the worldwide industry be able to self-regulate, or would governments dictate the terms of doing business?

- How would issues such as privacy and ecology affect their future?

- What were the major trends that would affect them and their companies?

- Where would the next generation of professionals learn the skills needed to manage and build companies?

- What were the emerging technologies, and how would they impact communications forms as we knew them?

- How would the media evolve?

- Who would be the "winners and losers" and why?

These and countless other questions were the grist of their informal yet impassioned discussion.

I would think back to some of the things that had been discussed, and how they influenced me, how focusing on the future shaped my present thinking. I also recognized that many others in advertising and marketing might benefit from taking time from the issues of today to think about the future. All of us tend to be consumed by the pressures of today that too little time is actually spent thinking about and preparing for the issues that are part of our future.

That odyssey led to this destination: The Future of Direct Marketing. That was the beginning of this project, I thought of the many professional conferences, in all forms of communications, that contain segments dealing with future trends. They partially addressed the issue of the future of direct. However, I concluded rather quickly what made Odyssey unique was the special nature of this small collection of trusted friends and colleagues. I recognized that a large public forum was not the answer. But I remained interested in the idea and talked to friends and colleagues who shared the view that a look into the future of direct marketing was of keen interest.

I also realized that as direct marketing grew it became increasingly difficult for any person to have the knowledge to cover the entire subject, whether in a seminar or in a book. Only by compiling the views of a number of gifted people and giving them the opportunity to discuss their specific expertise in a broad context could some useful glimpse of the future be made.

As I discussed the preliminary idea with several of the co-authors, they would suggest other topics and people to co-write their chapter, adding to the perspective and coverage.

Reinventing Direct Marketing

In their provocative and insightful book, *Reinventing the Corporation,* John Naisbitt and Patricia Aburdene describe companies that have truly reinvented themselves. These companies recognized the fundamental changes that were necessary to be able to compete more effectively in a contemporary society. They point out, however, that the "reinvention" of a company, as with all things, begins with the individual: someone prepared to make changes in themselves. Only then can a new process begin.

Direct marketing is changing too. In many ways, it has already reinvented itself. In the late 1970s, Stanley Marcus, the innovative retailer and Chairman Emeritus of Neiman Marcus, predicted that by the year 2000 as much as one-third of all retail sales would take place in a *nonstore setting.* This was before the Home Shopping Channel, QVC, and others appeared on cable television. It was before services like Prodigy filled computer screens. It was before there was talk of a superhighway of 500 channels. It was before the full implementation of 800 numbers and other advances that have fueled direct marketing's continued growth.

And while Mr. Marcus' prediction may indeed be accurate, in a strange way he did the broader aspect of direct marketing a mild disservice. His views simply reaffirmed in the minds of many that direct marketing meant mail order (even if those sales were initiated by an electronic medium and not direct mail itself).

In less than 15 years, direct marketing has been discovered as having qualities long known to many, but practiced by only a few true innovators: that is, that the heart of direct marketing is its ability to deliver, in all of its forms, highly relevant communications based on the known behavior of individuals. Direct marketing was not simply a means by which one could sell subscriptions, records, books, vitamins or food products, but it could also be a useful tool to build and sustain relationships for almost any product or service in any category, particularly via direct mail.

Early on it was the Very Important Traveler program for American Airlines, which was created by Ogilvy & Mather Direct. Today it's the AAdvantage Program. Meanwhile, in Chicago, long before frequent flyer clubs became an industry norm, United Airlines had a simple and effective program recognizing flyers who had flown 100,000 miles or more. This was introduced in the '60s and ultimately became United's Mileage Plus Loyalty program. However, it was years before other mainstream marketers could make the leap from advertising in measured media to direct marketing.

In the 1930s, the automotive industry used direct mail to remind owners of servicing time. They discovered some forty to fifty years later that the imaginative use of direct marketing could help successfully introduce new models. And a few have understood that customer loyalty, while ultimately a product of consumer satisfaction with the car and its dealer, could be enhanced through personally relevant communications.

In the late 1970s and early 1980s, General Foods used direct marketing to introduce a Swedish coffee called Gevali. Using both stylishly written print and direct mail, GF and its agency Wunderman, Ricotta & Klein (now Wunderman Cato), found an audience eager to buy this quality product through home delivery at prices that would make the average coffee broker envious. It is this kind of spirit of innovation that transforms an industry and broadens perspective.

Direct Marketing Is Just in Its Infancy

Depending on which publication you read or how you measure the size of direct marketing, it is between $30 billion and $300 billion in annual revenues. The actual number may never be known, and, frankly, it's unimportant. Whatever the number, it is only a fraction of the relative importance of direct marketing.

Direct marketing's growth has been driven by a number of factors that have also changed its character. In its early days, the best indicator of who might be interested in a particular product or service was based on the simplest of judgments. If the marketing effort was made in direct mail, the criteria was usually a prior mail-order action in that category. Audiences were sometimes selected by the magazines to which they subscribed. Today, the nature of direct marketing has become increasingly enhanced with the development of behavioral databases. When these databases are augmented with other databases, helping to select people most likely to respond or react to a given communication, both the marketer and the consumer benefit. It results in better targeting for the company and less unwanted mail for the consumer—something that will only continue in the future, as you'll read in the following pages.

Our Future is not Direct Marketing but All Marketing

For most of its history, direct and general marketing lived in separate rooms, separated from their colleagues in other forms of communication by perceptions of second-class citizenship and "junk mail." Where there were opportunities for collaboration, they were usually not realized.

The purpose of this book is not only to point out where collaboration can occur. We have a common future that requires that we think about a new marketing landscape where all the issues and the appropriate strategic solutions regardless of form, need to be understood.

Pages written by the likes of Hershel Sarbin, Bill Duch and Toni Apgar, who talk about the new media company. Media companies that understand the future is a concept they call media neutrality, a view that goes beyond audience or ink on paper to recognize the special relationship the media has with its audience.

In his direct and candid style, Drayton Bird speaks to the growing international nature of direct marketing; its challenges, its pitfalls, and its potential. He provides a recipe for international growth in a multicultural world by following some hard-won advice: *Profit from similarities but allow for differences.*

This book will explain that some lessons of the past remain part of its future. Ron Bliwas writes about how direct response television has changed and will continue to change, but that certain qualities long associated with direct response television will remain unchanged.

What advertising agencies will need to succeed in a broadened and more complex environment is discussed in detail by Tom Collinger in his chapter, followed by a unique media perspective from Jayne Zenaty Spittler and Jack Klues. No easy answers here . . . the future will challenge the media and its media planners, perhaps becoming the golden age of media as options expand and interactivity becomes commonplace.

It's the Software, Stupid! is how Steve Cone begins his look at how technology will affect most modern marketing decisions and their companies. He describes a concept he calls "Right Time Marketing" that reaches the consumer with the right message at the right time to fit their needs at that specific moment. And the key to this ability is information that will be effective only if used creatively.

Herschell Gordon Lewis explores why we as marketers must understand the craft of communication rather than rely on "tricks" and gimmicks. He speaks about some of the basic tenets of good writing that will surely be as much a part of our future as they are of our present.

Few areas have grown as dramatically as business-to-business marketing. In his view, Donald Libey takes a thorough and critical look at some of the fundamental forces of this area: economics, technology, social and cultural issues. He explores the impact of global competition on all business marketers and puts forth his ideas on the strategic focus that the successful companies will have employed.

This book also discusses the issues that face specific aspects of the direct marketing community. From Linda McAleer's highly specific discussion of the future role of the list broker, to Carol Nelson, who sees both opportunity and threats in integrated marketing for those who only see its superficial benefits.

Murray Raphel writes of the impact of direct on the way all retailing will take place and provides case histories that support a basic strategic imperative: Only those retailers who understand database marketing will inherit the future. John Hall looks at the issues facing book publishing and intellectual properties and how they can be applied to a host of new technologies.

In their chapter, Lee Graham and Worth Linen consider the ever-changing of marketing through "clubs." They see a marketing landscape in which the traditional method of the negative option will be under pressure, but they also see a bright side, as interactive technologies form a new relationship with the record and book consumer.

Ernan Roman challenges us with his review of integrated telemarketing, finding new solutions that speak in a single voice to the consumer while respecting the privacy and other personal concerns of people. This is an important and expanding area for all in direct marketing.

The co-authors will explain the issues as they see them. They will frame the industry according to their perspective.

Beyond 2000: The Future of Direct Marketing provides some thought-provoking insights into how a diverse industry of direct marketing experts sees the future.

Direct Marketing during a Cultural Revolution

In a highly provocative and informative chapter, James R. Rosenfield looks at the future of financial marketing. His comments focus on the impact of deregulation and a shrinking financial services world. He raises issues and provides ideas that can be applied to any industry that must better understand its customer.

Alan Rosenspan heightens our understanding of the very real threats to direct mail if the issues of privacy and responsible communication are not observed. Maxwell Sroge presents a fascinating case for a new dimension of catalog marketing, some of it a natural evolution of where we are today, some of it breathtakingly new and innovative.

Few people have spent as much time thinking about writing and teaching *integrated marketing communications* as Don Schultz. His chapter is filled with a concise and focused understanding of this emerging viewpoint. He makes the case that *direct marketing was part of the evolution towards integrated marketing communications*. He explains that the same forces that were important to the development of direct marketing were also important to *mass marketing* but that both are less likely to survive in their purest form as a result of technology and changes in the consumer and our ability to identify and communicate with them.

To communicate effectively in the future, marketers must not only understand technology, but the related concerns of consumer privacy. Lisa Petrison, Paul Wang, and David Messick review the privacy concerns of the public and our institutions, particularly as they relate to the inappropriate use of data. They examine the tools that can not only bring us close to the customer with relevant communication, but address what happens if insensitive marketers misuse information. Can consumers control their own information and under what circumstances? How will that impact effective communication and the availability of information sources in a free society? These and other areas are explored with care and candor.

Every industry, including direct marketing, has had its innovators. And among those who have most shaped the learning and education of at least two generations of marketing people has been Bob Stone. In a short, but important Afterword, Bob Stone describes the *Past, the Present, and the Future* by summarizing just a few of the things we all take for granted in all forms of marketing.

Does this book provide all the answers? No. It does, however, raise questions that can only be answered by us as individuals as we create our own vision of the future. The future of all marketing is full of new complex challenges that are new to all companies. Those who flourish will be challenged but not overwhelmed by what they encounter, will embrace change, and with it find exciting opportunities for responsible communication.

Many people today, not just a select group of friends, take an odyssey everyday . . . a journey into the cyberspace of direct marketing. It's a trip that's full of complex challenges that can be applied to companies as diverse as health care to automotive products. Those who return from the odyssey wiser and ready to embrace the changes we face in the future of direct marketing will ultimately find exciting new opportunities for creating successful communication programs and successful businesses.

PART I

Strategic Challenges for Beyond 2000

The Natural Evolution of Direct Marketing

Integrated Marketing and Integrated Marketing Communications

Don E. Schultz

Don E. Schultz is a Professor of Integrated Advertising/Marketing Communications at the Medill School of Journalism at Northwestern University. Schultz has consulted, lectured, and held seminars on marketing, sales promotion, advertising management, marketing strategy, and integrated marketing communications in Europe, South America, Asia, and the United States. His latest book is *Integrated Marketing Communications,* (NTC Business Books, 1993, with Stanley I. Tannenbaum and Robert F. Lauterborn), the first text in this new field.

What is integrated marketing? What is integrated marketing communications? How do they fit together? Or *do* they fit together? Perhaps, more importantly, how do they relate to direct marketing? Or *do* they relate to direct marketing at all? These questions and more are being raised in the mid-1990s about these concepts and ideas. And few good answers are being provided. At least, there are few that satisfy the concerns of the functional specialists who have developed traditional direct marketing to its current level.

In this chapter, the argument will be made that integrated marketing (IM) and the integrated marketing communications (IMC) approach are the natural evolution of the principles on which traditional direct marketing has been based. Indeed, just as database marketing has developed as a higher, more sophisticated level of direct mail and direct response marketing, so too, integrated marketing and integrated marketing communications are essentially more advanced forms of direct marketing. Both have been brought about and will grow as a result of increased and enhanced technology. In this view, traditional direct marketers have nothing to fear from IM or IMC. Indeed, they should embrace it, for these concepts will form the basis on which all types of organizations will conduct their marketing activities in the 21st century.

Understanding the Evolutionary Chain

Direct marketing has always been driven by technology. From electronic pagination to selective binding to USPS bar coding to the toll-free 800 number to overnight UPS and Federal Express delivery, traditional direct marketing has changed as technology has evolved. In this section, we look first at how direct marketing developed in the second half of the 20th century. Then we can more accurately predict what will happen in the first half of the 21st century.

Direct marketing began with lists. Lists of people. Lists of what they bought or didn't buy. Lists of what mailing efforts they responded to or didn't respond to. Lists. Lists are the basic history of direct marketing.

Initially, direct marketing developed because merchants had merchandise to sell, and they needed someone to sell that merchandise to. They developed a mailing package. Obtained a list. Mailed to the list and waited for response. Then they mailed again and perhaps again. And, thus, the direct marketing industry was formed.

In the beginning, and even today, many direct marketers still rely on these traditional approaches. They buy merchandise or create a product or develop a publication, and they mail to lists. Their business grows as they find better lists or as they refine the lists they have. But still, they work from lists.

Because of this history, many traditional direct marketers are internally focused. Certainly, most catalog marketers still are. They buy products in advance. They then try to sell those products to persons they have on a house list or can find on an external list. In other words, they practice inside-out marketing. They buy first, then try to sell what they have bought or acquired or manufactured or created.

This inside-out approach to marketing worked well in the middle of the 20th century. There was a constantly increasing population. New products were entering the market at a rapid rate. Credit was easy. There was demand for almost anything the marketer could make available. As a result, direct marketers prospered. And some continue to prosper under the same paradigm.

Enter Electronic Marketing

In the mid-1970s, electronics entered the marketing arena. Not electronics in the sense of television or radio or recorded music. Electronics in the form of computers and lasers. Electronic technology changed the direct marketing business. Changed it in ways that some current direct marketers are still struggling with. Electronic marketing, in the form of databases, gave the direct marketer incredible amounts of new information on consumers and exciting ways to manage and manipulate that data. With electronic marketing, direct marketers knew what people bought, what mailing efforts they responded to, and what inventory they had purchased from the marketer in the past. And with sophisticated new forms of statistical analysis and modeling, direct marketers knew what they might buy in the future.

Electronic marketing thus allowed the direct marketer to move from inside-out marketing to outside-in. In other words, with the advent of electronic marketing, the direct marketer could forecast what customers might buy. They could start to tell who were the best customers. They could identify prospects similar to the customers they presently had. In short, they could start to market to customers and their needs, rather than to lists and their addresses. Truly, it was electronic marketing in the form of databases, instant ordering and delivering, instant payment and credit, instant sourcing, and instant information that has changed the practice of traditional direct marketing.

A Similar Track in Mass Marketing

Mass marketing developed on a similar track to direct marketing, only a bit earlier. Manufacturers developed products. Mass produced them. Sent them into distribution channels such as mass retailers and merchandisers. Then they mass advertised and mass promoted to mass audiences, which they believed they could reach with various forms of mass communication. Mass marketing worked in the middle-to-late 20th century for the same reasons direct marketing worked: Lots of new products. Increasing population. Instant and easy credit. Increasing availability of products and services. Sophisticated communications channels.

But in the 1970s and 1980s, all this mass marketing broke down. Technology in the form of UPC codes, point-of-sale scanners, and sophisticated new research techniques combined to give the retailer and the marketer more and more specific information on their individual customers. New media forms developed. Databases were constructed and filled with purchase behavior data. Micro-marketing was in. Mass marketing was out. That was true whether you sold men's slacks, women's perfume, automobiles, or potato chips. Technology, just as it had been used to create the mass market, destroyed it.

Interestingly, the same thing happened to traditional direct marketing at about the same time and also as the result of new technology. The electronic database created massive changes in the heart of traditional marketing, the list business. While the list is still a critical element of traditional direct marketing, the overuse of many lists, mailbox clutter, and the entry of inexperienced marketers caused response rates to tumble. This has caused major questions about what will happen to traditional direct marketing in the future.

Figure 1 shows how marketers in the 1990s are moving from mass or "historical marketing" to targeted or customized "new marketing." Today in the United States, we have the capacity and capability to do one-on-one marketing to every household in the country. While it's still very expensive, the important thing is, it can be done.

As marketers move from marketing on the averages to marketing on the differences and as they move from broad, undifferentiated marketing programs to more targeted, selective, measurable approaches, the walls that formerly separated the direct marketer from the mass marketer are crashing down. Both are trying to do the same thing. Both are using the same concepts, the same approaches, and even, in some cases, the same techniques.

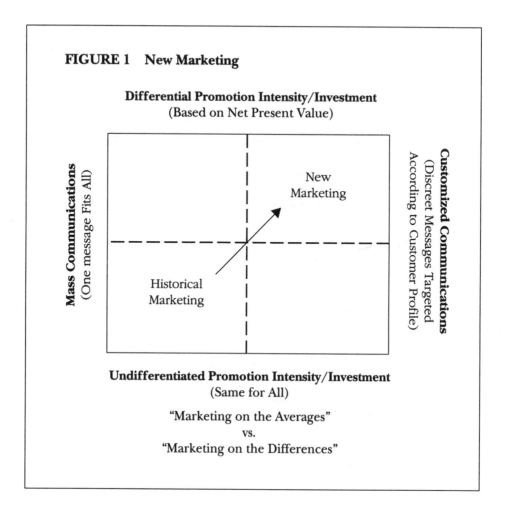

FIGURE 1   New Marketing

Differential Promotion Intensity/Investment
(Based on Net Present Value)

New Marketing

Historical Marketing

Mass Communications
(One message Fits All)

Customized Communications
(Discreet Messages Targeted According to Customer Profile)

Undifferentiated Promotion Intensity/Investment
(Same for All)

"Marketing on the Averages"
vs.
"Marketing on the Differences"

Voilà! Integrated Marketing Communications

The availability of the consumer database, with individual household product and brand purchase information, has led to the development of integrated marketing communications. The IMC process, as it has been developed at the Medill School of Journalism at Northwestern University, is an attempt to move from mass marketing to customized or individualized marketing, not just for traditional or even database-driven direct marketers, but for what traditionally have been mass marketers as well.

The primary difference between traditional marketing and the new, integrated form of marketing and marketing communications is outside-in planning. By having considerable information about every customer or customer segment, the marketer can start to plan from the customer back to the product or organization, rather than focusing on the product first and then moving toward the consumer.

The IMC concept, as it has been developed, is rooted in database marketing. It uses behavioral data for purposes of segmentation. But it also combines traditional attitudinal data, to provide a better understanding of that consumer behavior. The process developed at Northwestern University is illustrated in Figure 2. We will not spend much time explaining the IMC process. Most of it is self-evident. It relies on setting behavioral objectives for specific market segments. Then communication tactics are selected to achieve those objectives.

As can be seen, the critical ingredient in the IMC process is the thinking used in the planning process. The thinking is about the consumer and the customer. About what the customer needs or wants from the marketing organization, not what the organization wants to make or sell. This is a prime differentiating feature between the IMC approach and that used by traditional direct mail and direct marketing organizations and, indeed, by mass marketers as well.

The question is, what is next? Integrated marketing communications, as we have described and illustrated it, is simply a more sophisticated approach to general marketing. It is, however, based on many direct and database marketing concepts. What follows that? Is IMC what will be used in most marketing scenarios in the 21st century? Our answer is: Yes, but only up to a point. That point is the need to truly re-think the entire concept of marketing using the technology and information that is already available and that will become more prevalent in the future.

The New Marketing Paradigm

Starting today, a new approach to marketing is not only possible, it is practical. It is database driven. It is individual and customer focused. It is outside-in marketing taken to the next step. The term we have given this new approach is *customized mass marketing*. The process is illustrated in Figure 3.

As with IMC, customized mass marketing (CMM) starts with a database. Behavioral segmentation is then used to understand and identify specific groups of customers or prospects. From there, CMM varies significantly from traditional marketing planning approaches. Once the target market has been selected, traditional marketing methods commonly start to iden-

FIGURE 2 Integrated Marketing Communications Planning Process

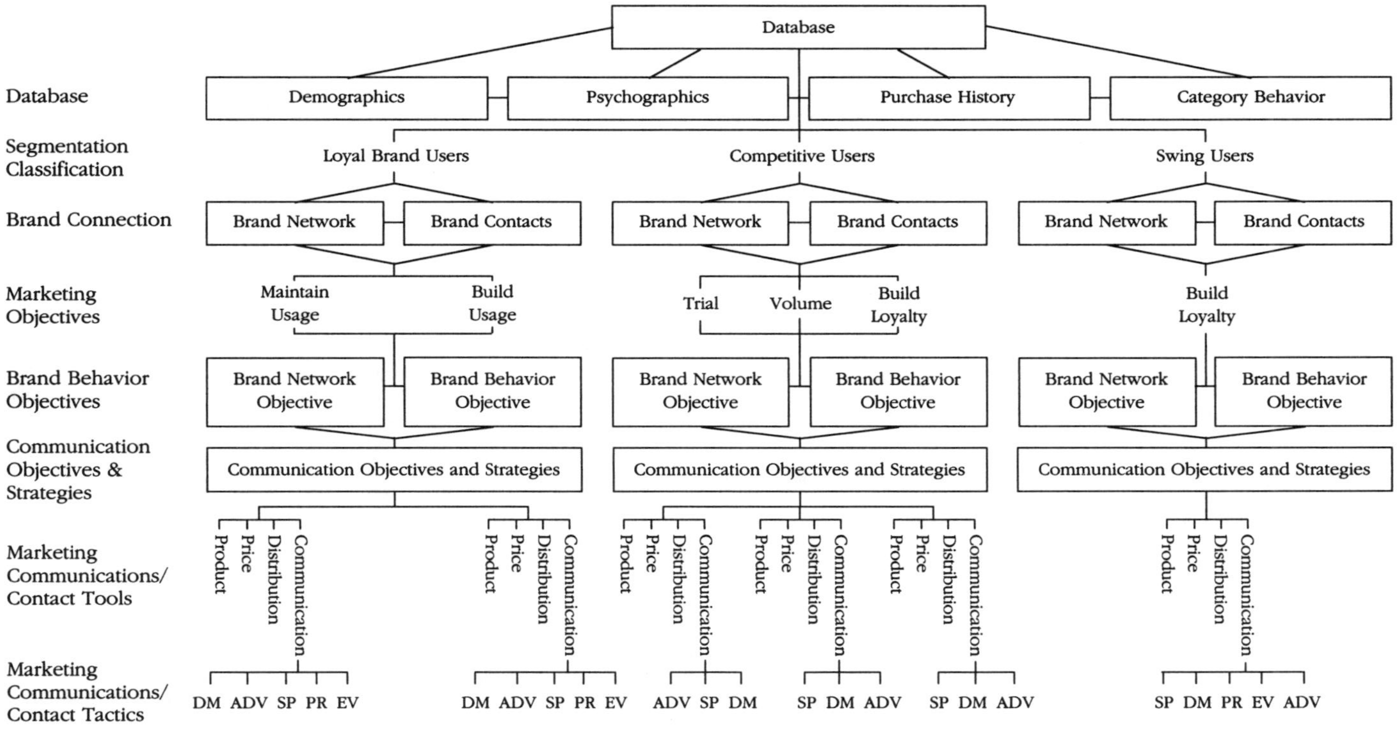
Database
Segmentation Classification
Brand Connection
Marketing Objectives
Brand Behavior Objectives
Communication Objectives & Strategies
Marketing Communications/ Contact Tools
Marketing Communications/ Contact Tactics
Database
Demographics
Psychographics
Purchase History
Category Behavior
Loyal Brand Users
Competitive Users
Swing Users
Brand Network
Brand Contacts
Brand Network
Brand Contacts
Brand Network
Brand Contacts
Maintain Usage
Build Usage
Trial
Volume
Build Loyalty
Build Loyalty
Brand Network Objective
Brand Behavior Objective
Brand Network Objective
Brand Behavior Objective
Brand Network Objective
Brand Behavior Objective
Communication Objectives and Strategies
Communication Objectives and Strategies
Communication Objectives and Strategies
Product
Price
Distribution
Communication
DM ADV SP PR EV
Product
Price
Distribution
Communication
DM ADV SP PR EV
Product
Price
Distribution
Communication
ADV SP DM
Product
Price
Distribution
Communication
SP DM ADV
Product
Price
Distribution
Communication
SP DM ADV
Product
Price
Distribution
Communication
SP DM PR EV ADV

DM = Direct Marketing ADV = Advertising SP = Sales Promotion PR = Public Relations EV = Event Marketing

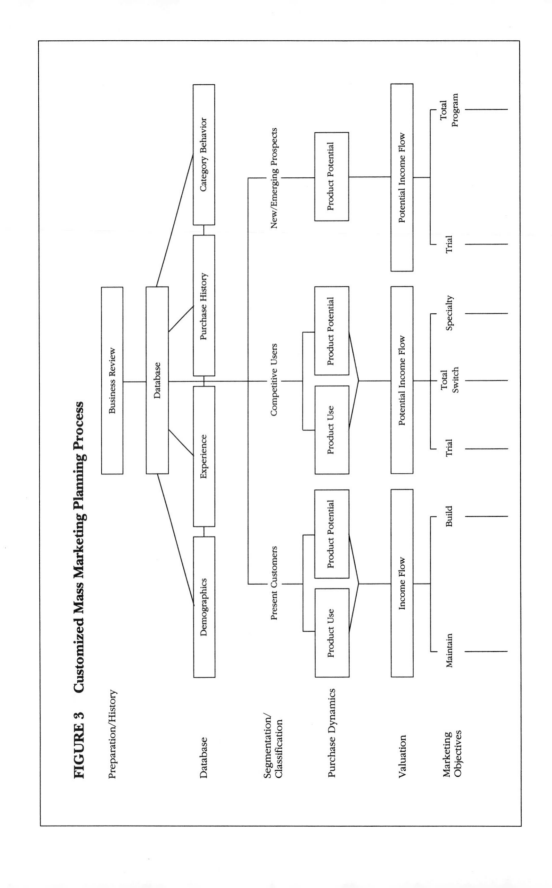

FIGURE 3 Customized Mass Marketing Planning Process

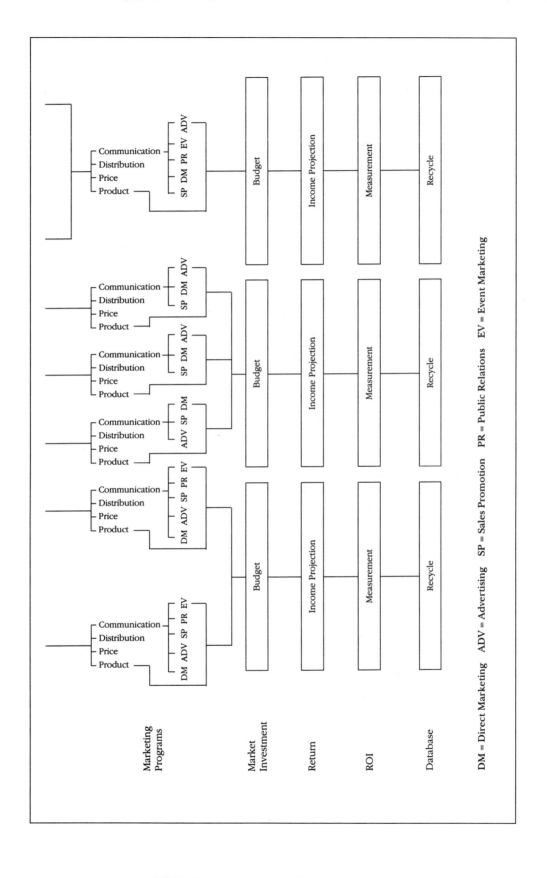

tify marketing objectives and develop a marketing mix. It is focused on what the marketer wants to achieve in either volume, units, dollars, share of market, or the like. It is inside-out marketing.

With a customized mass marketing approach, the consumer or customer segments are first valued in some way. Generally, this can be done based on present purchases by item or on total projected income flows over time. In other words, with the CMM approach, the marketer looks at how much a customer is actually worth to the organization, not just how many purchases have been made or what share of market has been obtained or what volume has been shipped. This calculation can be done at the gross or even net margin level.

The next step in the CMM process is to set marketing objectives. As is illustrated in the example, the only two objectives possible with existing or present customers are either to maintain their purchases and income flow at the current level or to try to build their use of the product or service. This decision is critical, for it determines the marketing mix to be used and the communications tactics to be employed.

The next step varies substantially from traditional marketing planning. The budget is determined based on the potential income flow for the target segment selected. By using income projections from either households or target segments, the CMM marketer can determine whether to investment spend or to plan a break-even level on the marketing program or somewhere in between. Obviously, lifetime customer value, which is a critical element of the process, helps in this decision.

Finally, the proposed marketing spending budget is tested against the income projection, assuming varying levels of success with the plan. From that, the final marketing program is developed along with the measurement system. Measurement, in the CMM approach, is a rather simple process. The marketer knows the current income flow from the customer or prospect and can estimate the potential. From that, information on the specific spending in terms of a marketing program can be developed. This can be tested against incremental income flows and a calculated return on investment (ROI). Indeed, ROI is a primary feature of the CMM approach.

What Will It Be in the 21st Century?

Will integrated marketing and integrated marketing communications be followed by the even more sophisticated approaches of customized mass marketing in the 21st century? Most likely. Mass marketing is over, but the economies of customized mass marketing are still evident. In truth, IM and

IMC are marketing approaches that deal with the individual or household. There are, however, major advantages in some type of aggregation of these individuals into groups or segments that provide manufacturing or processing economies to the marketing organization. So our scenario consists of a flow from database marketing to integrated marketing and integrated marketing communications and finally to customized mass marketing. Will the market and the industry evolve that way? Buy the next edition of this book and find out.

2

Integrated Marketing

Uncertain Today, Less Certain Tomorrow

Carol Nelson

Carol Nelson is Executive Vice President of Communicomp, based in Plantation, Florida. Previously she was General Manager and Creative Director for
Cohn & Wells, Chicago, a full-service international direct marketing agency.
She has held staff positions in both general advertising and direct marketing
agencies and has written and created advertising campaigns for a variety of
consumer, business-to-business, financial, and fund-raising clients. She is
author of *Integrated Advertising*.

Two terms have become more than buzzwords in the waning years of the 20th century; they've become religious icons. Those terms are:

1. Database

2. Integrated marketing

Others will, in these pages, write about the pros and cons of databases, a far more historical fact than many of its more recent admirers accept. My contribution will be an analysis—and, yes, the analysis may be cold, but the very word *analysis* demands a cooling of ardor—of integrated marketing.

As the author of one of the first books describing integrated marketing, I am, of course, its fan. I am also a savage critic of its misuse.

Misuse comes at the hands of those who use the term and discard the practice. Many advertising agencies give lip service to integrated marketing and privately curse its birth, because integrated marketing demands fields of expertise to which the typical agency had not been privy before the 1990s. Not been privy? Let's make that stronger: Many agencies "touted" clients away from any type of marketing that varied from traditional media advertising.

And this is what smart lobbyists should do; on the other hand, it isn't what a statesmanlike attitude demands.

Components of Integrated Marketing

Direct marketers, in turn, have a skewed view of integrated marketing. To them, integrated marketing means adding direct marketing to conventional advertising, backing up (or replacing) media advertising with mail or telemarketing.

For years, direct marketers have sat in the dim afterglow of marketing, with crumbs as their budgets. They seize the term *integrated marketing*, and their chests expand to accept the self-thumping: "Now it's our turn."

Sales promotion agencies have been content to accept their inclusion in this new "royal court." And so they should. Integrated marketing surely includes sales promotion. It also includes telemarketing . . . advertising specialties . . . handing out circulars in stores and on street corners . . . demonstrations and sampling . . . and the often-missing component, ongoing contact such as newsletters to the names you've captured.

Integrated means *integrated*. And—uh oh—it means leaving both your ego and your greed at the door. Therein lies the problem integrated marketing has had and probably will continue to have, until advertising agencies change their structures.

Academicians Love It

At least half the seminars on integrated marketing are delivered by academicians. There is nothing wrong with that, except that academicians are by their nature theoreticians and not hands-on practitioners.

This enables them to, well, to theorize

Since the theory of integrated marketing is totally sound, these lecturers are totally safe. But value lies in the application under battle conditions, where a "Get off my turf!" attitude too often results in intramural squabbling, and theory vanishes under the repeated pounding of insecurity and what insecurity does to the fragile egos of advertising practitioners.

So integrated marketing parallels integrated society: It's completely sound, as a theory; it has yet to be proved workable as an operating strategy.

For integrated marketing to take hold and not just be a buzzword, a functional change has to take place in corporate marketing philosophy. That change has to be superimposed on all the "Get off my turf!" kids in the various heavily armed gangs.

Successful Integrated Marketing

As we approach the 21st century, to the surprise of many who fully expected integrated marketing to be universal by the year 1995, protectivism seems stronger than ever. Conventional advertisers say they're applying integrated advertising because they're amassing databases—and databases are usable only through direct marketing and telemarketing, aren't they?

No more.

With fiber optics and desktop publishing, media exist to reach deep individual crannies of target groups. But so what? Specialized media have always existed.

A store announces it's sending "targeted" mailings to specific segments of its database, based on what a customer bought and when that customer bought it. But so what? This is about as new as "Run, Dick, run."

What we haven't seen is a rush to plan, from Day One, a comprehensive integrated marketing campaign in which each facet feeds into and benefits from the other facets.

The theory couldn't be more logical. Test after test has shown that when a mailing to a subscription list is exquisitely timed to coincide with a space ad in the publication, response to *both* increases. Synergy in action!

We've learned from Publishers Clearing House and the *Readers' Digest* that using television as an ancillary medium gives a boost to direct mail, in excess of the cost of television time. (And relating additional results to additional cost is a factor more television-worshippers should check with each exposure.)

Cigarette companies, under siege from many attacks, are, curiously, consummate masters of integrated marketing. They'll combine space ads, couponing, outdoor advertising, sweepstakes or contests requiring name registration, and free handouts. Then, from the names acquired, they'll publish a newsletter and offer "member" incentives. No, they can't use broadcast media (which is why so many "definers" of integrated marketing can't see them as candidates); but multi-exposure and multi-use of names *is* a working example of integrated marketing.

Coexistence Isn't Integration

We've proved in society as well as in advertising that coexistence isn't integration. In fact, society is moving away from integration, with inward-directed ethnic groups isolating themselves more and more from mainstream integration as they coexist within their own enclaves. Can you see the parallel in the world of advertising, where "specialists" tout their specialty regardless of marketing validity?

I've made this statement before, and it's a truism, in my opinion:

> Every time you sit down to create an advertising message—any advertising message, whether it's a space ad, a mail piece, or a broadcast commercial—always keep in mind *who* the target of your message is, *what* message they'll respond to, and *which* sales medium is the most efficient to reach them.

How many advertising agencies have the statesmanship to make a decision based *totally* on what's right for this campaign? Not at the exalted top levels, but down in the trenches, where account people have their shibboleths . . . and copywriters specialize (and feel comfortable) in one medium . . . and art directors think of their portfolios first and salesmanship second . . . and media people respond to free lunches by media representatives.

The art director who thinks of winning an award before thinking of *selling* and the copywriter who thinks of an addition to the sample reel before thinking of *selling* are the exact equivalent of those ethnic enclaves that keep a nation from being the "melting pot" of its claims. They coexist without integrating. My point is this: Don't regard the two terms *coexisting* and *integrating* as synonymous. They aren't. During America's Civil War, the North and the South coexisted.

The Next Act?

As we peer into the cloudy crystal ball, vainly trying to see even a trace of what the future holds, a few self-evident truths do form within the clouds.

The first is recognition that true integration has to spread from the top through all the echelons of marketing. What a difficult job that is. A media person wants *media* or the job itself is in jeopardy. A copywriter specializing in broadcast needs broadcasting assignments or food disappears from the table. A slogan-saturated account person is bewildered by the thought that "awareness" or "recall" aren't the counterparts of an order.

So what marketing organizations need is an ombudsman. Not just a listener and evaluator; an ombudsman with *power*. A dangerous job? Of course. Power with the potential to corrupt? Of course, but only on a short-term level, because an unwise marketing decision shows up quickly where it counts—on the bottom line.

The ombudsman would, in fact, *integrate* a campaign. Petty fiefdoms would have to turn in their swords for plowshares or else face dissolution.

The other self-evident truth is that because specialization is, in fact, a move away from integration, the earliest moves toward seamless, totally integrated marketing seem to come from smaller, not larger, advertisers and their agencies. This is because fewer people suffer when their pet method of communication gives way to a greater whole.

Will integration become a fact and not a mistaken twin for coexistence in the 21st century? Of course it will.

The arrival may be grudging, but of course it will.

The birth may be messy, but of course it will.

The youngster may fail some of its courses as it gains the painful education, but of course it will.

Of course it will . . . because in the 21st century, when the buyer has the last word and the tiny buyer enclaves are harder and harder to penetrate, those marketers who can't or won't adapt their selling techniques to use specific weapons designed to reach specific enclaves will perish in favor of those who do.

3

The Future
Is International

A Guide for Growth

Drayton Bird

Drayton Bird has 34 years' experience as copywriter, client, creative director, and Vice Chairman and Creative Director of Ogilvy & Mather Direct. Today he runs Drayton Bird Direct, a consultancy working with national and international clients. He is a columnist for *Direct* magazine and Britain's *Marketing*.

Nothing is as it seems in Hollywood, so I wasn't surprised to learn that Sam Goldwyn never said those loopy things attributed to him: somebody else wrote them. However, I always liked this one "Predictions are difficult, especially about the future."

Remember these prophesies? Records would kill large concerts; TV would end book reading; video catalogues would be the death of printed catalogs. All wrong. When a novel is serialized on TV, up go the book sales; when a record climbs up the charts, thousands jam stadiums to hear the artist; and although Sears and Montgomery Ward have had their problems, others thrive in the catalog business.

Accordingly, I will make only *one* confident forecast here: international direct marketing will continue to grow. Everything else you can file under the word "premonition," rather than "prediction."

Your Best—and Worst—Prospects

The practical purpose of chapters like this is to help you plan. So I will first review your opportunities around the world and second give you the principles for success.

You can conveniently divide the world up as follows:

1. United States and Canada

2. Central Asia and Siberia

3. Africa and the Middle East

4. India and Pakistan

5. Latin America

6. Western Europe

7. Eastern Europe and Russia

8. Southeast Asia, including China and Japan

9. Australasia

I shall dismiss the United States and Canada swiftly, partly because this is most likely to be read by North Americans and partly because North America has a better infrastructure than elsewhere: superior list availability, technology, quality of service and range of services offered, and far more providers of advice and information to help you.

For opposite reasons I shall deal quickly with some other areas. Central Asia, Siberia, and Africa above southern Africa possess neither the infrastructure nor the potential. You certainly can make money in Africa, but pervasive corruption and incompetence do not make it easy. I gather that much the same, with neo-Communist variations, applies in Central Asia.

South Africa and its satellite economies are more advanced than their northern neighbors. There is a direct marketing industry catering to both black and white and a good infrastructure, including agencies of sufficient calibre to be recognized in the Echo awards regularly. There again, though, there are many political imponderables.

The Middle East certainly has the money and, particularly in the Lebanese, some brilliant entrepreneurs. But there are fearful political problems, and the infrastructure—the postal service and the telephone service, especially—is variable. The concept of direct marketing is unknown to most people in the Arab world, as I learned a couple of years ago when addressing a large conference in Cairo. Israel, I confess, I know nothing about.

In India and Pakistan there is a small middle and upper class, about 10 percent, who are literate and have money. Ten percent doesn't sound like a lot till you realize that the population of India is around a billion. I helped Ogilvy & Mather set up its direct marketing agency there, and it enjoys considerable success acting for typical clients such as banks, retailers, watch manufacturers, an office equipment company, and the like. But here again, there are byzantine difficulties, especially regarding corporate ownership and the transmission of currency.

Latin America, once a gold mine (almost literally), plunged into decline in the middle of this century. In some countries it is still extremely difficult to do business. I recall a Brazilian explaining to me how they coped with a rate of inflation which was at the time 300 percent a month. This is not conducive to successful trading, unless you are very clever—and Brazilian.

Other countries, however—Mexico, Chile, and Argentina, especially— show more promise. Their governments are coming to grips with economic problems; there is a substantial educated middle class with money. Interestingly, Neiman Marcus has decided that its primary export focus will not be Canada, but Mexico, which is closer to Texas and has a larger population than does Canada.

Western Europe is very appealing, with the next best infrastructure after the United States, and the bonus that England is a congenial place to start, with a well-developed direct marketing industry, good agencies, and a long mail order tradition. Western Europe is in recession and has been for some time, but it remains a wealthy market. Do not imagine, though, that trade barriers between countries have been completely removed, or will be any time soon. And don't forget, these nations speak different languages; indeed, sometimes different languages within a country, as in Belgium, where the Flemings and Walloons not only speak different tongues, but have different attitudes and religions as well.

Some have been seduced by the rather dramatic way Eastern Europe has emerged (or semi-emerged) from Communist rule. However, this is not a homogeneous whole, any more than is Western Europe. Russia, for instance, is infinitely less promising than Czechoslovakia, which has always looked west and been more advanced in every respect. Four years ago I met a Russian in charge of an ad agency there. What was his biggest problem? "Getting typewriters," he said.

The pace of change in that area is so bewildering that it is hard to give sound advice. Poland, for example, is beginning to look much better. You have to research country by country or have close connections over there to enter with any confidence.

I think the most intriguing area is Southeast Asia, including China and Japan. You have the world's fastest-growing economies, industrious people, cultures that respect money and education, and relative stability. The language problems are there, true, but English and Mandarin between them meet most needs.

A friend indicated the enormous potential China offers. "They sell 40,000 television sets there . . . a day." The Chinese have a deep thirst for products of all types and love brand names. China is a good medium-term bet, but you need strong nerves, good connections, and endless patience.

The wealthiest market on earth outside the United States and Germany is Japan, where mail order was surprisingly slow in taking off, although the *Reader's Digest* and Franklin Mint have been there for many years. According to an American Express financial expert I once quizzed, "It took far more money than we planned—but it makes more, too."

Australia and New Zealand are culturally closest to the United States and the United Kingdom, respectively. In Australia the recession has been longer and deeper than in any country I know of. Competition is ferocious. New Zealand, however, is climbing out of its slough thanks to a courageous government. Remember, though, that the two countries offer you a market of fewer than 20 million people between them.

I went to Australia in 1971 intending to set up in business. I asked everyone about mail order. "It doesn't work here," I was assured, and indeed I saw few signs of mail order. Yet it seemed to me that Australia was ideal. It is extremely large, so many of the population can't get hold of products easily. And the urban areas (though few realize it, the population is largely urban) are spread out, so you have to travel a long way to buy things.

I listened to my Australian friends and went home, only to see Australia emerge some ten years later as one of the fastest-growing mail order markets. I ignored an important principle, which I shall now discuss.

The Guiding Principle

What does it take to succeed internationally? Confucius gave the best clue: "Men's natures are alike; it is their habits that drive them far apart."

If you have a successful product in one market, it can do well elsewhere as long as the motivation in that market is the same and no local conditions exist to distort that motivation or your marketing. If you read no further, and act upon that principle, you will do better than most, including me in Australia.

Not only can the same product succeed internationally, but also the same creative approaches work. Most people in the world want to be healthy, happy, rich, beautiful, and successful. Most people want ease, speed, convenience. That's why companies like Avon prosper universally. That's why Book Clubs flourish worldwide. That's why the credit card succeeds everywhere. Companies like the *Reader's Digest,* the Franklin Mint, the *National Geographic,* American Express, and the *Economist* conduct their businesses all over the world and have done so for decades. Their appeal crosses frontiers.

To discover whether what you sell has that appeal, go and look. My associate Gordon Ellis-Brown, former INMAC International Creative Director, now advises companies considering export from the United States to Europe. "Amazingly some people don't even visit their prospective markets," he reports. It's not enough to send juniors; you must see the market for yourself. Failure to do this can cost you dearly.

A Simple Recipe

People who fail do so because they ignore one or another part of a simple recipe I concocted in 1982: profit from similarities, but allow for differences. Some believe foreigners are so different that their product cannot possibly appeal; others believe everywhere is like home. Neither are right. And each belief leads to an expensive mistake.

The first mistake (often encouraged by local agencies) is to change the product or the creative radically to meet cultural differences in the market. This is often unnecessary, and, in the process, the factors that made the original product or the appeal successful are eliminated and the marketer is surprised to have a flop on his or her hands.

First, test what works for you at home, if the appeal seems right, with minimal changes. I have lost count of the times I have asked somebody to run some copy, translated as closely as possible from the successful United Kingdom or United States original, only for them to go away and make needless changes based on their own judgment.

However, beware of the opposite: assuming everywhere is exactly like home and people have the same attitudes. Read this from the journal of the Euro-Asia Centre, a division of my client's, INSEAD, the top European business school:

> Australians think that because they are casual, more easy going people, Asians like them better. Then they slap Chinese on the back, drink beer in the office in a Moslem country . . . and wonder why there is a conflict. Americans want to get in there, negotiate the contract and get out again. It's quick, it's clean and it's easy. It just isn't Asian. (*Euro-Asia Center News*, Issue 24, 1992)

I encountered cultural arrogance (and other errors) when Mutual of Omaha approached my agency with the intention of taking the British market by storm. They discounted the existence of powerful, entrenched companies in the United Kingdom. They would have ignored, if we had not persuaded them by research, the fact that their name was unknown—and misleading—to prospects. Fatally, they did ignore the lead-time, effort, money, and patience required. When they gave up, they even ignored the fact that, as we had pointed out, they had actually established the basis for a viable business.

Proper reconnaissance pays, as does listening to the locals. Remember, too, that usually not only are there domestic companies entrenched in any market, but also there are other multinationals moving in to compete with you.

In fact, the most valuable reconnaissance is to find out who are the real experts in a market and to spare no time or effort in doing so. Contact the appropriate trade association: the United Kingdom Direct Marketing Association or the European Direct Marketing Association, for instance. Whom do they recommend? Study the local direct marketing press, if any, to see who talks sense. If there is a direct marketing conference in that country, go and observe or send observers. All of this is obvious and all too often neglected.

Allow yourself time to get your back-up and logistics right. Check on the people you are proposing to work with. Who else have they dealt with? Have they any experience with overseas marketers? Do they have other clients you can refer to for validation of their claims? In fact, do the sensible things you would do at home. Don't settle for the first supplier you meet, which is tempting in a strange country because you are so delighted to encounter somebody who seems helpful and informed. Above all, test—don't jump in with both feet.

Beware Linguistic Traps

Bill McNutt III, who has been leading United States direct marketing delegations to Europe, Canada, and Mexico for some time now, believes that English-speaking companies enjoy an advantage because 750 million people around the world speak English. True, but English can take on strange guises.

We all know the old joke that Britain and America are two countries divided by a common language. However, when I visit India, for instance, it is not always clear that people are addressing me in my own language. Over the years they have developed not merely their own accent but also their own figures of speech.

In some countries, they have even formed hybrids. Recently the president of the Philippine direct marketing association, Yoling Sevilla, revealed that while the upper classes might speak English, a new linguistic omelette called Taglish works when targeting the middle- and lower-class markets. The native Filipino tongue is Tagalog; Taglish is half English, half Tagalog.

Be careful about claims to English fluency. A client in southeast Asia was mailing his Chinese prospects and customers in English, as their stated preference. I suggested that, nonetheless, they would find it easier to read their own language. A test proved it was so. They got more replies from Chinese mailings. It is seen as a sign of status by Chinese to be able to read English properly. The solution, however cumbersome, was to run mailings printed in both English and Chinese.

Advantage for the United States Marketer

The United States exporter enjoys a huge advantage from the vast home market, which allows great manufacturing economies. Even allowing for shipping and duties, a United States marketer can be highly competitive. Prices elsewhere are usually much higher.

That's why Land's End was able to take its U.S. catalog, reprint it with little change, increase the prices by 50%, and still do well in the United Kingdom. Richard Anderson, CEO of Land's End, recently said, "We're committed to the United Kingdom," and Land's End has opened up a U.K. distribution center.

You can sell products at high prices even in countries that appear poverty stricken. In many, particularly in Latin America and southeast Asia, there is an impoverished majority but a small and wealthy minority, just as in India, with a thirst for Western products.

But don't imagine the growth of international direct marketing is driven entirely by U.S. exporters. Companies like Bertelsmann are spreading their wings. An insight into direct marketing in Europe itself is given by a Euromonitor market analysis, which in 1993 observed: "Mail order's growth over the next five years will be driven by the expertise of operators such as Otto Versand and La Redoute."

How Sophisticated Is the Market?

When I was working with American Express, Taiwan was a cash society. A bank account was a sign of prestige. The most effective way to sell the American Express Card was to link it with a bank account that gave you a check book.

Sometimes people are not familiar with techniques we take for granted. Some time ago, Damart, which sells thermolactic clothing, sent out a personalized mailing in Spain. I would hardly have thought Spain cold enough to merit thermolactic clothing, but there are some very chilly parts of Spain, and Damart did very well.

The mailing was a copy of a best-selling gossip magazine. The headline was personalized: "Señora Bird wins it big at Damart." The cover cleverly featured a Señora Bird lookalike entering a store, shot from the side and behind so you couldn't see the face. Inside the brochure, interspersed with stimulating tales about Damart, was the story of how Señora Bird won an exquisite silver-plated rhinestone ring. At that time, the Spanish population was not used to personalization. Hundreds of irate women wrote in asking why their name and picture was being sent to all the households in Spain. They wanted either their blood, royalties, or a public apology.

Watch out for other local sensitivities. A few years ago, in a laudable attempt to save the world from rat infestation, one company created a most ingenious mail pack extolling its number-one poison. The idea was that this poison would make the rats bite the bullet. The creative execution was, guess what, a box with a bullet in it. The bullet had no gunpowder, but it was very realistic.

This mail pack was sent to people in Venezuela. Unfortunately, as those of you who follow foreign affairs may have noticed, there is a certain amount of political instability in South America. This detail was overlooked by the agency. When the shipments of bullets arrived, the customs authority took one look and dumped the whole lot in the sea. None of the fish responded.

Religion can be a problem, too. Xerox, for many years clients of mine, considered running an advertisement (an extraordinarily bad advertisement, in my view) featuring Moses. In northern Europe, where religious sensibilities are not great, this was perfectly acceptable. In southern Europe, some felt it close to blasphemy.

Keep an eye on the law. In some countries, outbound telemarketing is banned. In some, free gifts are illegal. And for some time the various European countries have been wrangling over the law on data protection. The same argument has transferred itself to the other side of the world. In southeast Asia, many countries are discussing very restrictive legislation.

Another critical element to watch is the way companies make decisions. The differences are great. One Pan-European research study revealed that in Scandinavia and northern Europe decisions are made democratically. Everyone is involved. Everyone has a fair knowledge of the product in question. Southern Europe is different. Decision making is autocratic. The managing director or some senior person makes the decision. Moreover, general knowledge is poor.

What about Lists and Media?

The direct marketing industry is young in most markets. Don't assume the level of infrastructure that you are accustomed to.

In the United Kingdom, for instance, there are pro rata only half as many lists available as in the United States. (This is the only figure I have seen, and I think it flatters the United Kingdom.) Not only are there fewer lists, but the number of possible selections within a list is generally lower. And what applies in the United Kingdom applies even more elsewhere. The less sophisticated the market, the fewer the lists.

This has practical implications. When I discuss testing in New Zealand or Hong Kong, people are bemused. These markets are tiny—under 5 million—and even where the population is large, the number with money is much smaller. And, supposing you do have the numbers to test, you won't have the facilities to conduct split runs in the press, for instance.

In some countries, the United Kingdom in particular, although there aren't as many lists, this is compensated for by a national press with enormous coverage. So direct response advertising is far more important than in the United States. As far as I know, the only country where people read more newspapers than in the United Kingdom is Japan.

One thing you can do in the United States but can't do as easily elsewhere is target competitive users. For instance, Dove is being rolled out all over the world. The original United States program for Dove targeted competitive customers, such as Ivory users. The brand is now being promoted in places as varied as England, New Zealand, and even India. In none of these countries is it easy to target competitive users. However, because of the expansion of organizations like NDL, this situation is improving.

The Biggest Problem—and the Solution

I asked a colleague who ran the direct marketing for a multinational brand what his biggest problem is. He answered, without hesitation, *cost*. In countries like the United States, Japan, and Germany you have large markets with high incomes. You can afford to invest heavily in creativity, printing, and gimmicks.

Your business must reflect economics. In the United States, a major client will invest as much as $40,000 for creative on a big mailing. Such expenditures are unheard of in small markets like Norway, Singapore, or Denmark. In poorer countries, Malaysia or Thailand, for instance, a $10,000 fee would be seen as daylight robbery.

Happily, you can often transplant what's worked in one country to another. The skill, the thought, and the talent you have applied to creating effective direct marketing programs pays off spectacularly. That's because, as Confucius said, motivations are often the same although cultures are not. For one client, linking offers to particular holidays in the United Kingdom (Christmas, Valentine's Day, or Easter) worked very well. I suggested to Chinese colleagues that they link their offers to occasions like the Moon Festival and the Chinese New Year. It worked. Same principle; different culture.

I wrote copy in the late 1970s for a product developed in England—a set of cookery cards coded for calorie content. This product, with the same creative, sold extremely well in France, Italy, Canada, and Australia. Imagine the British teaching the French how to cook! The same company sold cards to teach people how to knit. Amazingly, this did well in Japan.

Good News on People and Results

It is a cliché that ours is a people business. With talented people you can do practically anything; without them, nothing. One of our biggest challenges at O&M Direct was to find, train, and move talented people around.

Where the industry has only existed for four or five years, as in countries like Indonesia or the Philippines, there simply isn't anyone who knows what it's all about. So, incredibly, in a country where the average income might be less than $1,000 a year, and even executives would not get more than $10,000, it pays to get somebody in from the United States or the United Kingdom and pay them eight or ten times as much because of the leverage their knowledge gives.

Once again, though, watch out for cultural arrogance. All too often, expatriates, because they know more, imagine they are more intelligent. In fact, your local colleagues may not know much about direct marketing, but they can be smarter than you—and more eager to learn. In many markets the levels of intelligence and education are as high as or higher than in the United States or the United Kingdom. People are often harder working, quicker to learn, and extremely determined to succeed. You will also find high levels of creativity in many countries, reflected recently in the Echo awards in New York.

I've saved the best till last. No other country is exposed to the same weight of advertising, promotion, and direct mail as the United States. Even in England, the average consumer receives six times less direct mail than do consumers in the United States. This shows when you look at your results. Because when you transfer a United States mailing concept successfully, it doesn't just do as well . . . not even just a bit better . . . not even a lot better. It can do three or even four times as well as in the United States.

Good luck! And with careful planning and reconnaissance, you won't even need that.

4

What Direct Agencies Will Need to Succeed

Coping with the Forces of Change

Tom Collinger

Tom Collinger is Senior Vice President and Director of Direct Marketing of Chicago-based Leo Burnett Company. His responsibility spans all Burnett clients. He has been a guest speaker at the local and national Direct Marketing Association Conferences, the Professors Institute of the DMA's Educational Foundation, the Advertising Research Foundation, and Northwestern University's Kellogg Graduate School of Business.

I'm not sure many of us remember all of our defining moments, but I remember one. It was one of those nights when my parents let me stay up late because a teenage baby-sitter, a fanatic of the TV show "The Twilight Zone," was present. This particular episode featured two ne'er-do-wells who had stolen a magical camera capable of producing photographs of the future. They stole this camera from its kind-hearted inventor and began using it to win money at the race track by "seeing" the toteboard minutes before a race had been run. With their ill-gotten knowledge they kept betting and winning, but naturally the forces of good overcame these scam artists and they met their fate: they entered the Twilight Zone.

As my sensibilities developed, I grew to see other benefits to future-looking, and this is what captures the imagination of many of us. It's what drives this question about the future of direct agencies, isn't it? If we understood the future better, we'd be able to leverage that knowledge and make more money. Predict the Future and Make More Money. That's why I first looked at past results to predict the future of direct agencies. But before I share the results of this review, it's important to reflect on some of the forces that make this forecasting even more of a challenge.

Forces of Change

Direct marketers have watched their business(es) change over the last 20 years with the addition of toll-free 800 numbers, data cost reductions, and scanners. These changes have provided tremendous opportunities for us. But changes we currently face, combined with those of the next 10 years will be, in total, greater than anything we have ever seen—as if change itself has taken on its own momentum—and the velocity continues to increase.

> It takes all the running you can do, to keep in the same place. If you want to get somwhere else, you must run twice as fast.
>
> — *Lewis Carroll, Alice In Wonderland*

Successfully managing direct agencies is becoming increasingly more challenging and demanding. What, exactly, is driving this trend? It's what *always* drives increased challenges; competitive forces. I believe that there are three particularly challenging ones on the horizon; *new players, fusion,* and the *battle for the consumer.*

It's just that the environment in which direct response agencies live seems to be an area that has created a competitive feeding frenzy. According to a recent *Advertising Age* study, there are now over 95 direct response agencies in the U.S., billing over $1 million per year. That would be enough competition to move people of character to run and hide, but wait! There's even more! What's more is the first force, which I call the "new players."

The New Players

A quick review of the roster of the 1992 National DMA Conference confirms the presence of general marketing service companies and printers that now deliver turnkey creative services and database companies that do so as well and telemarketing firms. Many are horizontally integrating services either in-house or through alliances with other providers/suppliers.

And there are the consultants who are no longer just one-person operators, but are now the Big Six. All of these groups are provide services that were once the exclusive property of direct agencies. This is occurring for the obvious reasons: direct response advertising and marketing is growing at a rapid rate and will continue to do so.

What's more, this growth will add even more complexity, more competition and more challenges, because of the other *two* forces that are picking up their own momentum: *fusion,* and the *battle for the consumer.*

Fusion

Yesterday, the very reason that direct agencies were born rested on the different skills they brought to marketers. But these differences are becoming so indistinct today that all the marketing disciplines are fusing.

For example, Hal Riney and Partners, a so-called general agency, was awarded agency-of-the-year status by *Advertising Age* in part because of their "Integrated Solutions" approach. In other words, if direct-to-consumer communications is the right solution, Hal Riney will deliver it. This integrated approach is also true of the Leo Burnett Company, an agency dedicated to providing "Solution Neutrality," an approach fueled in part by this fusion of direct and mass marketing.

Said another way, what exactly is mass marketing? With the dramatic increase in television channel choices and "Addressable TV" through interactive capability, one commercial aired to one audience at one point in time will become an increasingly rare proposition, if not, ultimately, an anachronism. Doesn't that mean that all marketing will embrace segmentation and targeting? If mass marketing is dead, won't heretofore "general advertising agencies" want to play in our playground? How could they not?

Consider that as of June 1993 (according to the Leo Burnett Company Media Research Department):

- 62% of homes have cable TV, with an average of 51 channels per home.

- There are over 2,400 consumer magazine titles.

- Over 30 million homes have a personal computer.

- Over 70% of individuals have shopped by phone or mail.

- *Time* magazine now produces over 100 versions each week.

- There are over 20 different interactive systems in various stages of testing.

The entire media landscape today provides the type of segmentation and targeting options once the exclusive domain of direct mail. Fusion is around the corner, and it will provide added challenge and possibilities.

The Battle for the Consumer

Retailers and brands seem to be in the middle of a duel over the right to connect with the consumer. This battle will likely create great opportunities for database/direct marketers, but with it will come some new challenges: adjusting to the proliferation of databases by consumer marketers?

John Cummings, publisher of *DBM Scan*, reports that 275 consumer marketers built databases *in 1992 alone*. Add to this the growing number of supermarkets, department stores and even some specialty stores that are delivering frequent buyer benefits to their best customers. The retailers and consumer product companies are both pitching hard to win the favor and loyalty of the consumer.

Many of these industries (e.g. supermarkets) have not been those typically served by direct agencies, so our opportunities will grow. Our main challenge is to help them communicate to their consumers in a responsible and effective fashion.

"The Future is just like the past, only more so."

— Faith Popcorn

I agree with Faith Popcorn, so I looked at current and historic results of direct response agencies. Who has succeeded? Who has failed? Why?

I reviewed six years' worth of articles about agencies and their futures. In addition, I looked at the rankings of the top 100 direct agencies during this time. I added some other criteria, to look for some immutable facts. To succeed in the future, I wondered, what will be the key factors? Is the size of an agency a big issue? Being integrated with other skills? Being owned by a big "general" agency? Being publicly held or private? Being the fastest, the cheapest? What about having only one CEO?

While these criteria tend to be the ones that grab headlines, interestingly, they do not provide much illumination. A case can be made both for and against these criteria.

Big and Resourceful or Small and Nimble: The Size Factor

Why Big is Better

In the last five years, O & M Direct, Wunderman-Cato Johnson, FCB Direct, and Rapp, Collins, Marcoa have remained as four of the top five direct agencies in the country; their combined billings have increased 38.2%.

Why Medium Size Is Better

The most recent Lou Harris Poll conducted among agency clients indicates that they believe the best work comes from medium to small shops . . . but

Why Small Is Better

. . . Only seven of the smallest direct agencies (those ranked number 50 to 100) suffered reduced billings last year, and 30 of the remaining 43 had double-digit growth.

Net: Current size does not appear to predict future opportunity.

The Debate of the 90's: To Integrate or Not to Integrate

There have been many articles written about the right way to organize direct marketing capabilities. These views are often characterized like this:

To deliver world class direct marketing, can an agency be separate from or must they be part of the total marketing solution, planned in a synergistic fashion? If so, the debate usually goes on, can a separate independent direct agency succeed?

First, the easy part. Clients, agencies, and industry experts all seem to agree that the work for a brand must be integrated to be most effective. In fact, Laurie Spar, Vice President of the Direct Marketing Educational Foundation, wrote that "Integration is best for Direct Marketing Education" (*Proof,* June 1993). However (and this is a *large* however), there is general *disagreement* about how to do it, and whose responsibility it is . . . the agency's or the client's.

Advertising Age (January 25, 1993, p.19) featured opposing editorial views on this subject. Gary Moss, V.P. Marketing Communications for Campbell Soup, takes the position that the responsibilities of creating integrated communications belong to the client:

> True Integrated Communications is bringing to bear all forms of media, coordinated and leveraged against the consumer to create a new persuasive, larger whole (I call this TPP—Total Persuasion Process). Agencies that don't see this may find their clients taking more and more control of the entire process; not by choice but by default.
>
> Until agencies can demonstrate that they can objectively and effectively serve as coordinators for a broader range of marketing approaches, clients will continue to believe we are the best coaches for the new integrated marketing team of the 90's.

According to Moss, agencies *should* figure out a way to bring total solutions, but because he does not believe it happens today, he's comfortable selecting the skills of a direct marketing specialist *as part of their total communications package.* There is support for this view. Four of the top five largest direct agencies are all *separate* units of larger advertising companies, and the fifth, Bronner, Slosberg, is an independent. Additionally, the majority of the top 100 direct agencies are separate, "un-integrated" firms.

However, there is an opposing view supporting agencies as the integrators. Interestingly, it is eerily similar in its perspective, as articulated by Mark Goldstein, President of Earle, Palmer, Brown Advertising in Bethesda, Maryland. He challenges agencies to become integrators:

> The truly effective IMC (Integrated Marketing Communications) agency leaves its biases at the door. There is only one agenda: What's best for the client's business.
>
> The agencies who are re-inventing themselves now will have enormous opportunities. The agencies who insist on staying in the craft business will find themselves driving off an ever shorter pier. (" . . . Or Can Agencies Handle It?"*Advertising Age* [January 25, 1993] p.19.)

In other words, learn to do it all. A good example of this strategy is the one adopted by Herring, Newman, a top-25 direct agency based in Seattle that acquired a broadcast agency, McMath & Gross, in May 1993, apparently to expand their ability to deliver more fully integrated plans. Another is Wunderman's merger with Cato-Johnson, giving them more ability to deliver fully integrated solutions. There are many supporters of Goldstein's view.

Further, Leo Burnett's approach has been part of their growth and they have organizational integration, where Burnetters become direct marketing practitioners, supported by specialists.

One illustration of this struggle to find *the* very best approach to organize for integration is Ogilvy & Mather's Direct's decision to build a blended version of organizational integration in Australia, the opposite approach to the successful and *separate* one used in the United States.

The debate rages on about how to facilitate integrated marketing solutions, but there does seem to be universal support for tools working in strategic and creative harmony.

Net: Both approaches are equally viable. We can deliver fully integrated solutions including direct marketing, *or* deliver direct marketing solutions as integrated parts of total marketing plans.

To Be or Not to Be Owned by a Commications Conglomerate

On the one hand, it would appear as if being owned presents a real advantage, looking at the success of O & M Direct (WPP); Wunderman (Y & R); FCB Direct (Foote Cone-Belding); Rapp Collins Marcoa (OMNICOM); and Kobs and Draft (Saatchi & Saatchi).

On the other hand, there is a handful of independents that have flown into the top 10 in size: Bronner, Slosberg, and Humphrey: DIMAC Direct, and Barry Blau & Partners. Further, the remaining top 50 are predominantly independent operations.

Net: Ownership is not a driving factor in a direct marketing agency's success.

Other Criteria

Finally, while I was unable to rate the agencies' performance on their speed, costs, public versus private ownership, or even the number of chief executives they've all had, I'm led to little in the way of guidelines.

So, what's *the* answer? *There isn't one.* Keith Reinhard, the chairman of DDB/Needham, has arrived at the same conclusion. In the first of a series of reports on how agencies are repositioning themselves for the future, *Advertising Age* reported on Reinhard's perspective. He said:

> In a nutshell, there isn't *a* way. There are *many* ways. And that is really the point. (Pat Sloan, DDB Needham Clusters for the Future, *Advertising Age* (May 31, 1993, p.4.)

I'm in agreement. After all, we all believe in segmentation and customization in marketing. Why wouldn't we all agree that these principles apply in the delivery of direct agency services?

So, armed with the answer that there isn't one answer, I searched for *principles* with which to ensure a successful future. I looked at companies that are now leading their industries. I also looked for reasons why some former leadership companies are no longer on top of the heap. I looked for consistent themes from the articles written by management consultants discussing the success in the '90's theme. I also asked the CEOs of three of the most successful direct agencies in the world over the last 5 to 10 years why they have succeeded.

And, once I began this approach, I discovered what I believe to be the touchstones for *our* future, two qualities that are desirable today and may become necessary for our future, regardless of our agency's size, approach, or ownership.

Two Principles to Guide a Successful Direct Marketing Agency Professional to the Year 2000

Principle 1: Focus

There's a rock & roll song from the '80's that goes: "You've got to stand for something, or you'll fall for anything." Tom Peters talks about defining a mission statement that "is a clear and compelling goal that focuses people's efforts.": How can you tell if *you* are focused?

- Can you describe your agency's point of difference?

- Can you explain it in a sentence or two? Or even one word?

- Is the point of difference one that is sustainable? One that is client driven? One that is a superlative: smartest, fastest, least expensive, most responsive, most effective over the long haul, most effective over the short term, most innovative, most creative, most desirable place to work?

- Would all staff members agree on the agency's point of difference? Do your clients know what it is?

- Do you, as Jerry Pickholz, Chairman of Ogilvy & Mather Direct warns, "Say no to opportunities" that quarrel with your mission, your focus? Do you make decisions that enable the present to be comfortable, regardless of their impact on the future? Do you hire, train, and reward based on what you stand for?

- Or are you caught somewhere in the middle? Short of a superlative, but good enough?

Throughout the '80's, "Good Enough" was a very acceptable place to be, but the '90's are forcing us to plant flags in superlatives. Look at the distance that has grown between the "leaders" in consumer product categories and the non-leaders. For example, Sears has always been awfully good. But today, there are choices that are faster, less expensive, filled with more variety, and more service oriented than Sears. More importantly, consumers appear to be voting for the superlative alternatives with their pocketbooks. Focus. It is a quality quickly moving from desirability to necessity. So, my recommendation is to add a magnifying glass to your toolbox.

Principle 2: Listen

This principle is, arguably, even more challenging to use as a guidepost because listening to signals in the market will undoubtedly force a response that will require change. Of course, change usually scares people. Change is also quite difficult when the first principle, focus, is successfully addressed. However, we can take a lesson or two from Lester Wunderman, who has succeeded mightily since his agency's inception in 1958. Thirty-five years later, it is still one of the top agencies worldwide. His agency has clearly been listening. In fact, his answer to why they have been so successful deals with results of the input they get *because* they listen . . . They have innovated. As Lester put it,

> With some modesty, I think it fair for me to suggest that we here have innovated and discovered more of the principles of direct marketing than any other agency or group, and we plan to continue to do so.

Recent merger with Cato Johnson, a successful sales promotion agency, further supports its commitment to innovation. Steve Dapper is Chairman and CEO of the successful Rapp-Collins, Marcoa agency, one of only four agencies to have sustained a top-five ranking over the past five years. O & M Direct, Wunderman, and FCB Direct are the other three. Here's Steve's answer to why they've been able to sustain this success:

> I think it has to do with the ability to embrace change. You have to create change when it's needed.

His company's decision to acquire a Minneapolis-based sales promotion marketing services firm in 1992 supports this strategy. It looks as if he's another listener.

Perhaps we ought to take a page from the successful strategies written by Nordstrom's, a department store chain that has essentially redefined the concept of customer service. They are a company that could easily stick to its retail strategy and avoid risk, but it too is listening. It has decided to extend this superior level of service to innovative ways the consumer wants to shop: interactively, initially through catalogs, and soon through television shopping.

Listening. This is a quality that does not come naturally to many of us. It requies a commitment to asking questions and to learning, strategies that often feel like luxuries in the thick of a competitive business environment.

Therefore, my second recommendation is to get another new tool for the toolbox, a high-powered listening device with an antenna capable of picking up signals from all over the marketing world. Why am I so confident these tools will be so important to our future? These principles are working for successful companies today. O & M Direct is the largest direct agency in the world, and Jerry Pickholz talks about "successful management skills" and "saying no." This sounds like focus to me.

One could argue that these principles are less evident at less successful companies. Did Schwinn forget to listen to signals that the bicycle market was changing? Did Sears stop listening? Did one of the pioneering direct agencies Stone & Adler?

So Search for the Camera No Longer

So, there's no need for a futuristic camera or even a rule book. We do need to follow some principles. Of course, there may be more than two of these. And perhaps some would argue that there are others that are more important. As for me, I'll stick with my magnifying glass and antennae kit. If we work on focusing and on listening as we move forward to the 21st century, I think we'll do just fine.

PART II

Technology and the Consumer

5

Consumer Privacy

The Saga Continues—and Will Not Go Away

Lisa A. Petrison,
Paul Wang, & David M. Messick

Lisa A. Petrison is an adjunct professor at Northwestern University, and is currently working on a Ph.D. in marketing at Northwestern's Kellogg Graduate School of Management. She formerly held marketing and communications management positions in the banking and video-game industries. She is the co-author of Sales Promotion Essentials, 2nd edition (NTC Business Books, 1993, with Don E. Schultz and William A. Robinson).

Paul Wang is an assistant professor in the graduate direct marketing program at Northwestern University and the technical editor of the *Journal of Direct Marketing*. He specializes in database and direct marketing issues and serves as a research consultant to a variety of companies interested in database marketing. His Ph.D. is in communications studies from Northwestern University.

David M. Messick is the Morris and Alice Kaplan Distinguished Professor of Ethics and Decisions in Management at the Kellogg Graduate School of Management at Northwestern University. His research areas deal with decision making in social environments. He has authored more than 100 scientific papers and books on related topics.

It has become widely recognized in recent years that consumer privacy is one of the most important issues facing the direct marketing industry. Consumer privacy has become a popular topic in the news media, with numerous articles, books, and television shows addressing the methods that direct marketers use to collect and share information about their customers. A majority of Americans routinely express concern about privacy issues in polls, and most tend to agree with the view that consumers have lost control of how information about themselves is used. Numerous state and federal laws have also been passed or proposed to regulate how direct marketers can obtain and use information about consumers.

Faced with an onslaught of negative publicity and outside pressure, many direct marketers at first tried to dismiss the issue as trivial but then eventually began to make changes in the ways that they do business. Many companies, for example, are now careful to allow customers the option of requesting that information about them not be shared with other organizations. The Direct Marketing Association promotes its Mail and Telephone Preference Service, which allow consumers to greatly reduce the amount of business mail and telephone calls they receive. The major consumer credit bureaus, often a target of consumer complaints, have voluntarily agreed to refrain from releasing credit information about people without those individuals' consent, and they also have made it easier for people to obtain copies of their own credit reports.

Despite these advances, consumer privacy remains a problem for the direct marketing industry, and one that probably will not be easily solved. The issue is a difficult one to address, in part, because it is a multifaceted problem with no clear-cut "right" answers. For example, actions that are described as "invasions of privacy" may be quite disparate and may tap into a number of underlying consumer and societal concerns. It is also the case that there does not seem to be much consumer agreement about what constitutes and invasion of privacy; while a few people object to a wide variety of activities undertaken by direct marketers, others object only under specific and often idiosyncratic conditions.

Despite the fact that consumer privacy is a difficult problem, it is nevertheless important for direct marketers to take steps to address the issue. This is especially true because advances in computer technology and the increasing usage of interactive marketing is likely to increase the opportunities for privacy violations to occur in the future, making it more likely that objections will be raised. It also seems to be the case that attempts to "make the problem go away" through the use of public relations may continue to be doomed for failure. As will be apparent in the following discussion, many privacy concerns stem from deep seated fears and beliefs about what is appropriate, which cannot be easily brushed aside. It therefore is important for marketers to attempt to understand exactly why consumers are concerned about consumer privacy and to develop forward-thinking solutions in concert with consumers.

Underlying Consumer Privacy Concerns

There exist at least five reasons why consumers may object to activities conducted by direct marketers: fears of inappropriate data usage, fear of "Big Brother," irritation at inappropriate activities, wastefulness and the environment and relationship violations. While each of these is often described as a "privacy threat," the objections seem to stem from different underlying concerns.

Fears of Inappropriate Data Usage

Perhaps the most recognized consumer privacy concern is the fear that data collected by direct marketers may fall into the wrong hands, leading to unfortunate consequences. Examples of such occurrences (or potential occurrences) are commonly cited in articles or books urging stronger privacy legislations. For example, reporters managed to obtain information about the videotapes rented by Supreme Court nominee Robert Bork; although none of Bork's choices was controversial, Congress quickly passed a bill forbidding video stores from releasing such information to individuals or marketers in the future.

Farrell's, an ice cream parlor, sold its list of children's birthdays to the Selective Service, which used them to make certain that young men turning 18 registered for the draft. Rebecca Schaeffer, a TV actress, was murdered outside her home by a fan who obtained her address from public records, legislation following her death made records such as auto registrations and driver's licenses inaccessible to individuals and marketers in many states.

Stories like these understandably make people more concerned about the potential misuse of the consumer information that is collected by companies. It also seems likely that as people are faced with losses of privacy in other parts of their lives, their impatience with activities performed by direct marketers may increase. For example, many employers regularly request urine samples for drug testing, as well as credit checks and health records, from potential employees. Some employers also investigate whether potential employees have, for example, previously collected workman's compensation or filed a suit for sexual harassment; others monitor current employees' phone calls or computerized electronic-mail messages. Similarly, insurance companies have at least the potential of conducting genetic screening or family background checks and of denying coverage when there appears to be a risk of, for example, genetically influenced physical or mental health problems. Banks have been known to check the credit histories of their current customers and to recall their credit cards if they have taken on too much debt, even if their accounts have always been in good standing. Credit bureaus have also traditionally been relatively unresponsive to consumers' needs, making it difficult for consumers to correct inaccurate information in their files or even to obtain copies of their own credit reports.

Compared to these kinds of losses of privacy, the sharing of lists by mail-order companies may in some ways seem almost benign, and it may therefore be the case that some consumers will overlook direct marketers activities as they focus their attention on more important privacy concerns. However, it may also be the case that losses of privacy in other areas may sensitize consumers to privacy issues, making them more likely to object to activities performed by direct marketers. Employees may need their jobs and may therefore not openly object to losses of privacy in the workplace, even when they feel the losses are unfair. Customers of direct marketing companies, however, are likely to have no such hesitations and may therefore attempt to retain some measure of privacy by protesting direct marketers' activities.

Fears of "Big Brother"

While the blatant misuse of information gathered by direct marketers that has resulted in actual consumer harm has been relatively infrequent, the mere *idea* that companies are collecting and exchanging information about them makes many people uneasy. Such activities often conjure up, for example, the images of "Big Brother" that were presented in the novel *1984,* where an omniscient government used its knowledge of individuals to maintain tight control over their activities and thoughts.

In some cases, people have specific concerns about the potential misuse of information being collected. Databased information might have made it much easier, for example, for Germans to locate Jews or for the United States to find Japanese Americans during World War II, some people assert. Others worry that their reading material or purchases of certain products may reveal information that could potentially be used against them, or that their telephone records may be used to monitor their contacts with potential "undesirables." People fear that such collection of personal information would make it easier for individuals to be persecuted under repressive conditions, such as those experienced in the United States during the 1950s when anti-Communist feelings were common.

Even people do not have specific worries about what may happen to them, they may still object to the idea that marketers are creating "master files" of information on their personal characteristics and purchasing activities. It may be the case that even if people cannot imagine what, for example, their grocery store purchases reveal about them, they still may fear that such information may somehow be used in detrimental ways that they cannot currently imagine. This fear is undoubtedly magnified by the notion, promoted by the news media, that marketers can understand the "motivations" and "drives" of consumers simply by observing their buying patterns. This knowledge may be used either to coerce consumers into buying products they don't want, or to determine their innermost secrets, people may believe.

While few people may openly express or ruminate upon these vague fears, it is arguably the case that these types of worries underlie many of the consumer privacy objections that marketers need to address. Even if they do not wish to appear paranoid, many people simply do not like the idea that companies are collecting information about them, especially when they don't know what data is being stored or who has access to it. It therefore is the case that even when the information being collected seems completely innocuous, it is still important for marketers to be cognizant of potential privacy concerns.

Irritation at Inappropriate Direct Marketing Activities

Direct marketing is an inherently intrusive medium; unlike mass media advertising, it is difficult for consumers to ignore direct marketing messages. Mail that is received must be, at the minimum, examined and sorted; many people also make it a practice to open all of their mail to make certain that they don't throw away anything important. Telemarketing phone calls can be even more intrusive, interrupting consumers when they are eating, sleeping, bathing, or engaging in other activities. The intrusiveness of the medium makes the potential for irritation high, meaning that consumers may easily develop negative feelings toward those companies conducting direct marketing activities.

The annoyance that direct marketing activities can cause is relevant to the issue of consumer privacy for two reasons. First, consumer frequently attribute their receipt of direct mail advertising or telephone solicitations to the fact that information about their previous purchases has been sold to other companies. The response that is usually given by direct marketers, that without list rental agreements people would receive more direct mail that is less relevant to their specific interests, is usually not understood very well by consumers; they see only that whenever they buy something, they receive much more mail, most of it irrelevant to their needs. Second, privacy is often defined as the "right to be left alone." That is, people may object to information about products coming into their homes as well as to information about themselves getting out.

Of course, some types of direct marketing activities are often perceived to be more annoying than others. At the top of many people's lists are time-wasters—for example, computerized phone calls that instruct the consumer to "Please hold for an important message," or mail that pretends to be something it's not (such as a bill or telegram) in order to entice people to open the envelope. While such techniques may in some cases cause more people to be hit with the selling message, and may even lift sales, they also may succeed in alienating many consumers over the long run.

Another irritation can be when companies act overly familiar with their customers. Some people do not like it when direct mail efforts or tele-marketers use their first names, for example. Others may object to personal information being used in ways in which it was not originally intended. For example, a financial services company that sends birthday cards to credit card holders based on the birthdate information supplied on their credit card applications should expect to receive some complaints.

People may also object to the idea that when they do business with some companies, they are expected (or even "required") to share information about themselves. For example, at some national retail chains, clerks demand that customers supply their names, addresses, and phone numbers before purchases are entered into the cash register. Business magazines often send cards to subscribers who have failed to supply company or income information with the admonition, "Your records are incomplete." Even when people are willing to supply the information, the fact that it is demanded rather than requested from them may be perceived as disrespectful.

Some consumers may also be irritated by certain types of direct marketing materials, especially when those materials seem to imply that they should be living their lives in different ways or when they remind consumers of sensitive topics. Grocery store customers, for example, objected when a purchase of baby diapers triggered a coupon for condoms to be dispensed at the cash register; some took it as a rebuke for a previous moment of passionate abandon. While some people may appreciate receiving information from large-size clothing stores or dieting centers, others may perceive the receipt of such items to be indicative that "someone" perceives them to be fat. Single people may similarly be annoyed by receiving information from a dating service. More seriously, people who have suffered miscarriages or the death of infant children may be upset by receiving information targeted at parents of young children; similarly, parents whose adult children have died may be saddened when they receive, for example, recruitment information from colleges or the armed forces.

Of course, it is probably impossible for any direct marketer to totally avoid annoying all consumers all of the time, because people tend to be idiosyncratic in terms of what things they find irritating. Still, it is important for marketers to understand that such irritation can lead to additional concern over consumer privacy issues. It may therefore be the case that activities that annoy consumers will make them ultimately more impatient with direct marketers as a whole, increasing the likelihood that they will support more government regulation of the industry in the future.

Wastefulness and the Environment

The impact of unwanted advertising mail on the environment is widely recognized as a problem for the direct marketing industry. For many consumers, however, the impact of direct mail on the environment is just another example of the negative effects that the general loss of consumer privacy has brought about. As noted earlier, consumers (rightly or wrongly) blame the sharing of consumer information for the fact that they get so much unwanted mail; the subtlety of the argument that without list selling, "junk" mail would be even less relevant to their own needs and wants eludes most people. It may well be the case, therefore, that as concern for the environment grows, annoyance with direct mail practices and with perceived violations of consumer privacy may also increase.

One of the issues here is the fact that many people perceive that they have no control over the kinds of mail they receive. Most consumers are accustomed to receiving mail over and over again from companies in which they have no interest; on the other hand, they may have to pay money to receive catalogs that they do want. While the Direct Marketing Association's Mail Preference Service may succeed in reducing unwanted mail, it also may halt mail that people want to receive; for example, in a survey of people who had registered with the service, most stated that they would actually prefer to begin receiving mail again, but only from certain types of marketers.

The environmental issue, in short, seems to be largely a matter of control. It does not seem to be the case that most people want to stop receiving all direct mail; rather, they want to cut down on the amount of wasteful clutter they see in their mailboxes, and their inability to do this may frustrate them. It may also be the case that this lack of control may have a negative impact on people's feelings about privacy issues in general; if consumers feel that they have little control over their relationships with companies, they may begin to resent the fact that those companies seem to know so much about them and that they blithely share that information with other companies without getting permission.

Relationship Violations

In many cases, consumers may supply specific companies with information about themselves that they would not share with other companies or even personal friends. In some cases, such information may be supplied because it is pertinent to the relationship being developed. For example, people applying for a mortgage or credit card need to supply details about their finances in order to be considered. In other cases, people may supply information about themselves to a certain company because they like the organization and perceive that an ongoing relationship has been established. Car buyers, for example, may fill out detailed owner satisfaction surveys that include personal demographic information because they want to help the automobile company to build even better cars in the future.

Such "relationship marketing" carries certain responsibilities, however. Information shared with companies with whom customers have relationships may be viewed as similar to secrets disclosed to a friend. There may be an implicit expectation that the private information will not be shared indiscriminately with others, and a violation of that trust may result in a weakening of the relationship. It therefore may be the case that companies that have access to more personal information about their customers need to be especially attentive to potential privacy concerns. A bank, for example, may be criticized more harshly than a retailer for selling information about its customers to other companies.

Even when companies do not possess particularly sensitive information about consumers, it is still important for them to maintain reasonable policies with respect to the usage of whatever information they do have if they hope to avoid alienating their customers. For example, most consumers expect that companies' requests for information will be reasonable (guided, for example, by previous practice or "need to know"), and that those companies will make polite and honest attempts to honor their own requests for service. This may be especially important when customer requests are related to privacy issues. For example, many consumers expect that if they ask that a company not share information about them with other firms or bother them with telemarketing calls, those wishes will be politely and promptly honored. For charities, this may also mean that contact will be made only during yearly membership drives or in the event of infrequent, authentic emergencies; more frequent contacts may appear exploitive and detract from the positive feelings that people gained from donating to the organization in the first place. Many consumers may also prefer that they be informed about the fact that information about them is being sold to other companies, and about what type of information (e.g., just name and address or also purchase and payment history) is involved.

In short, creating stronger relationships with customers may help companies to avoid some problems stemming from privacy concerns, because it may decrease reliance on prospecting efforts and because customers may be more willing to share information with companies when they have established strong relationships with them. However, the formation of closer relationships also carries with it certain responsibilities, because consumers may perceive that their trust has been violated (or that they have been "sold out") if information about them is used in inappropriate ways.

Addressing Privacy Concerns

In summary, then, consumer privacy is a complex issue that is influenced by a number of core consumer concerns. It is therefore important for managers to attempt to better understand their customers' views on privacy, and to be very careful to avoid taking missteps that may lower the company's and the industry's reputation and value over the long run.

Even for companies that want to be sensitive to customer and societal concerns, however, privacy is a tricky issue. It is easy enough to state that managers should learn to think like their customers; however, those customers may be a diverse group of people with a wide range of views on the topic. For instance, some people look forward to receiving catalogs and other direct mail and may even feel rewarded when their purchases prompt the receipt of other catalogs; others object to the selling of their names under any circumstances. Similarly, some people appreciate being contacted by telephone by, for example, their dentist when it is time for a checkup or by the local theater company when season tickets are being sold; others find such contacts to be unacceptable intrusions.

Our research suggests that people tend to be more tolerant of activities performed by direct marketers when the information being supplied is relevant to their needs. For example, persons who are in poor health tend to be more accepting of being contacted by a hospital than are the rest of the population. The type of company conducting a particular activity is also very important. For example, in one survey it was perceived as much more acceptable for a hospital promoting health-related programs to target overweight persons based on height and weight information on their driver's licenses than it was for a large-size clothing store to do the same thing. (In another study, financial institutions and charities were perceived more negatively than retailers and catalog companies when they bought and sold information about consumers.) Our research also suggests that it is generally considered much more acceptable for a company to use information that it has gathered about customers for its own purposes (even when it is used in ways not originally intended) than to sell it to other firms. It also seems to be the case that the purchase of information about consumers is often perceived as more acceptable than the sale of that information.

In short, then, it is unlikely that direct marketers will be able to develop hard-and-fast rules that will cover every potential privacy violation. Indeed, consumers themselves do not seem to have established any strict guidelines that allow them to judge what kinds of direct marketing activities are or are not acceptable. Rather, they seem to evaluate each situation on its own merits, weighing the loss of privacy against the potential benefits that they may receive.

This is good news for direct marketers in one respect, because it suggests that most consumers are open to at least some direct marketing efforts and are not completely inflexible about the kinds of activities they will consider to be reasonable. On the other hand, however, the fact that privacy is not a black-and-white issue makes it more difficult for voluntary rules or legal restrictions to be set to govern the way that the industry conducts direct marketing activities; this is likely to mean that privacy will continue to be an ongoing problem into the foreseeable future

Still, if direct marketers are to successfully cope with consumer privacy concerns, a number of changes in the industry will probably need to take place. First, as companies focus more of their emphasis on retaining current customers rather than on prospecting, an effort will need to be made to understand more thoroughly how customers of specific companies feel about particular direct marketing activities. It is obviously important to consider the impact that potentially objectionable activities may have on the long-term value of the company; it generally is not worth alienating current customers simply to make a few dollars over the short run.

A second important step is to find ways to put the data back into the hands of the consumer to the extent possible. One of the main complaints that people have about direct marketers is that consumers have lost control of information about themselves (information that they may perceive "belongs" to them); giving consumers more power over what happens to that data may therefore be taken as a gesture of goodwill and may make consumers feel that they are in some small way "in charge." For individual companies, this may mean making it easier for consumers to request that information about themselves not be shared with other companies. For example, consumers may be encouraged to inform telephone order-takers or to check a box on an order form if they want information about themselves to remain confidential. It might also be interesting to test sharing with consumers some of the profits generated through the selling of names in the form of a small yearly discount; this may potentially lessen consumer resentment caused by the perception that companies with whom they do business are profiting from the exploitation of the relationship while they themselves get nothing.

On the industry level, it may be worthwhile for trade groups to consider establishing a selective mail preference service that would allow consumers to indicate the types of mail that they would and would not like to receive. While such a project might be complicated and relatively expensive to set up and run, it would certainly send a clear signal that direct marketers are interested in the concerns of consumers and that they are eager to listen to consumer input concerning the amount and type of mail that they want to receive. Such a preference service might also have the added benefit of being useful to companies who want to sell items to established direct mail buyers who are interested in products that they have not purchased in the past.

It may also be necessary or desirable at some point for the industry to agree to or even to encourage legislation that requires all businesses, no matter what their size, to obtain and use the DMA Mail and Telephone Preference Service lists before contacting prospects by mail or phone. These lists have historically been available only to DMA members; however, some of the worst offenders in the area of consumer privacy violations are often small businesses who are looking only for short-run sales to keep their companies afloat. While many small businesses operate with consideration for consumer privacy concerns, those that do not may succeed in damaging the reputation of the direct marketing industry as a whole, making it more likely that restrictive legislation such as that in Europe (which has traditionally required that companies obtain explicit written permission before sharing customer information with other companies) will eventually be passed in the United States. It therefore may be reasonable to mandate that small businesses meet the same guidelines that other, more established members of the Direct Marketing Association follow voluntarily.

Finally, it is important that direct marketers and the direct marketing industry take the offensive in protecting consumer privacy, rather than waiting until consumers complain, reporters write exposés, or legislators propose regulation. Consumers often do not complain about practices that upset them, but they may still stop buying from specific direct marketers or from the direct marketing industry in general. In addition, by the time that news stories are written or government legislation is proposed, it may be impossible to reverse the negative impression that has been created and to convince the public that direct marketers are truly concerned about privacy issues.

Attaining a greater customer focus when it comes to privacy matters can be accomplished in a number of different ways. Some companies set firm policies that they will simply not share consumer information with other companies and communicate this clearly to their customers. Other companies that do engage in data sharing practices may, for example, set up a consumer advisory board to evaluate company practices or may conduct frequent focus groups or other research projects on the topic. It also may be useful to assign an on-staff "consumer advocate" to evaluate privacy-related activities; such a person should be in close contact with consumers and should preferably not have any profit responsibility in order to avoid a conflict of interest.

Consumer privacy is a crucial issue for direct marketers, but it is one that seems to have the potential of being managed successfully *if* direct marketers act responsibly. This means being sensitive to privacy concerns (rather than simply dismissing them as unimportant), developing a better understanding of consumer perceptions and needs, giving consumers some measure of control over what happens to information about them, and erring on the side of conservatism in order to maintain long-term customer value for individual companies and for the direct marketing industry as a whole. If all direct marketers were to consistently take these stops, privacy-related problems would probably still not be totally eliminated; however, they most likely would be greatly reduced, meaning that the survival and prosperity of direct marketers in the future would be much more certain than it is today.

Back, Back, Back to the Future

How Quantum Leaps in Technology Bring Us Back to the Days of Old— Personal Service to Every Customer

Stephen A. Cone

Stephen A. Cone currently serves as Chairman of Epsilon, a wholly owned subsidiary of American Express. Epsilon is the world's recognized leader in providing state-of-the-art marketing database services. Prior to being named Epsilon's Chairman, Steve served as Senior Vice President of Direct Marketing for five years at American Express headquarters in New York.

It's the software, stupid!! My overriding purpose in explaining technological advances that affect the future of marketing is to make everything sound very simple. In fact, all good marketing ideas are simple; otherwise, they could not be executed or understood by a wide range of consumers. But just so you are crystal clear, selling a Lexus or a Cadillac or a Chevy is one thing; building them is quite a different proposition, entirely.

Indeed, using the car analogy to explain where technology is taking marketing, software is what is under the marketing "hood." Software that makes building a gasoline engine, by comparison, look like child's play.

And it is software and the folks who create it who are a truly scarce resource. A resource that, in future years and well into the next century, companies will come to fight over and throw huge sums of money at to ensure their very survival. Software experts will be on the top of the job food chain and will be haggled over like professional athletes are today.

Alvin Toffler, the well-known futurist, has been quoted as saying, "Information is the currency of the future." I agree. And software is the information printing press.

Okay, now that we all agree on the importance of software, let's see where marketing and supporting software will lead us in the near term and beyond.

Let's Pick On American Airlines

American has always been a top-notch marketing company. It started a whole new way of focusing on the customer in the late 1970s when it introduced the very first frequent flyer program and named it American AAdvantage. This customer loyalty program is still going strong and over the years has become more and more sophisticated thanks to—you guessed it—major software enhancements. These enhancements have enabled much better tracking and analysis of American's frequent customers.

About ten years after the AAdvantage program was initiated, American very smartly noted a need to better recognize the real cream of its revenue crop: the top 2 percent of its customers. For these folks American created AAdvantage Gold.

All of the 100,000 or more flyers in the top 2 percent were automatically enrolled and offered a host of ground- breaking benefits. Each received a special gold card. Every one of these flyers was thrilled with this program and the attention and benefits American bestowed on them.

My wife was one of the anointed. She flew American every chance she got and still does. But herein lies an interesting story about one of the very best marketing programs in the world and how 1980s and early '90s technology is already behind the curve.

On a summer day in 1991, my wife Faye was flying American from new York to Austin, Texas, via Dallas for a same-day business meeting—a very long day. Unfortunately, Dallas weather was stormy, and major delays kept Faye's flight from landing until it was two hours late. Her Austin connection was missed, and she had to return to New York and reschedule her Austin trip for another day. Needless to say, she wasn't happy, but one can't control the weather, and American wasn't to be blamed for summer thunderstorms in north Texas.

Weeks passed. Five, to be exact. In week six, Faye received a letter from American, signed by the Senior Vice President of Marketing.

The letter specifically referenced the flight Faye had been on and apologized for its late arrival in Dallas due to weather conditions that day. The letter noted Fay's status as an AAdvantage Gold member. It went on to say that while American could not control the weather, it wanted to do something to make up for Faye's inconvenience that day, and thus 2,500 bonus miles had been placed in her AAdvantage Gold account.

Faye handed me the letter with a smile on her face and said, "Well, I give them credit for trying." I said, "Gee, I think American did a pretty good job, keeping track of this incident and getting back to you." She said, "They did, they're just five weeks late!"

I know this is not like the Red Sea parting or the invention of electricity, but it was a defining moment in how I came to think about the future of customer marketing and the role technology has to play. Faye had raised the bar for me—significantly raised the bar.

Here was a great marketing program of great sophistication and great success, fumbling on the one-yard line and failing to score the winning points. Everything had been done right, except the apology letter program was either scheduled at that kind of interval or only ran when a certain number of apologies had accumulated. Either way, the great impact it could have had was lost because of the number-one enemy of any kind of one-to-one marketing: time.

It's the Right Time for Right Time Marketing

Right Time Marketing* is the high ground going forward that all marketing programs will be judged against. It simply means getting the right message to the right person at the right time.

*Right-Time Marketing is a registered trademark of Epsilon, a wholly owned subsidiary of American Express.

For the past 20 years, marketers and direct marketers have spent great amounts of money and time doing an increasingly better job of getting the right offer to the right person. But not at the right time.

Time is truly elusive to a company trying to do the best job it can marketing to and servicing its customers. The fact is that we rarely communicate to a customer or prospect at the right time for them, when what we have to offer fits exactly with their needs at that time.

But now the technology is within our grasp to practice Right Time Marketing with thousands and even millions of customers. I will describe this technology in more detail later in this chapter.

What technology allows a company to do is literally, on a daily basis, comb through any and all accumulated customer and prospect data to determine which existing products or services should be presented to which customer immediately—by fax or phone or computer or in the mail within 12 hours. The more data to analyze, the better! The data should be as comprehensive as possible; purchase behavior data at the detail level, any and all customer service history, survey data, even climate data and local or regional news and events data.

Here are three examples of Right Time Marketing in the near future.

You live in the near north section of Chicago. This past December you got a great bonus and bought an Armani cashmere overcoat from a major upscale retailer. On March 1 of the new year, you receive a postcard announcing a private two-week special sale on Armani spring jackets.

On May 1, you get a short letter from the store manager thanking you again for the December purchase of the cashmere coat and listing three simple things you should do right away to store this coat properly over the hot summer months. The letter also states that for a small charge, the store will pick the coat up and clean and care for it until you call to have it delivered in the late fall.

In example two, you have lived in Florida for seven years and have enjoyed a sporty convertible made by one of the major full-line auto manufacturers. You accept a significant promotion with your Fortune 100 firm. The bad news is that you will be transferred to Boston and physically move in late November—brrr!

You put your Florida home on the market, start house-hunting in Boston, and cancel some local Florida magazines and newspapers as of November 1. Several weeks before you actually move, you receive a letter from the manufacturer of your convertible. It says if you plan to keep the car in Boston you should have it winterized at an authorized dealer immediately upon arrival. Also, the manufacturer has a number of 4-wheel drive and front-wheel drive models you might want to consider at this time. A special offer is mentioned.

The letter even points out that if you buy one of these models, you can store the convertible during the winter months at one of several authorized Boston-area dealers and save it for those short but sweet Boston summers. The letter goes on to say that in the event you would rather sell your convertible before the move, the manufacturer can handle that plus delivering a new car to your new home in Boston.

Example three: Because your advertising agency has picked up several new clients in Kansas City and you are based in Los Angeles, you have just begun traveling regularly, almost once a week, between these two cities.

Suddenly, you receive a letter from your favorite credit card company detailing special hotel and restaurant highlights in Kansas City. You are told about special offers at a number of these establishments that are for you, personally, and are good for the next three months. Coupons are not necessary. The credit card company assumes you entertain clients and associates and do not wish to carry and redeem coupons, say, at a dinner with a client.

Not to worry. Whenever you use your card at any of the establishments where a special offer applies, the appropriate dollar discount will be automatically credited on your next monthly statement.

A Brief Word about Swimming in Unknown Waters

These examples of Right Time Marketing are grains of sand on a huge beach of opportunity that technology can and will support in the years ahead. However, some among us will see privacy sharks in the water and yell for every marketer to get out of the water and off the beach!

I'm reminded of a recent quote from Harrison Ford's six-year-old son, Malcolm. During a first-grade discussion of parents' jobs, when asked what his father did for a living, Malcolm answered, "My daddy is a movie actor, and sometimes he plays the good guy, and sometimes he plays the lawyer."

The privacy advocates, mostly lawyers, will undoubtedly try to scare consumers about the possible Big Brother aspects of Right Time Marketing. While debate is healthy on any issue, I am convinced that the quantum leaps in customer service that Right Time Marketing will bring will far outweigh consumers' concerns.

The fact is that companies want to help customers with their life-style and life-stage needs in a more timely and cost-effective fashion. Data accumulation and analysis for this purpose poses absolutely no threat to individual liberty or happiness.

But make no mistake, the privacy extremists will remain vocal and active and worthy of marketers' time and attention well into the next century.

I Know It's Hard To Believe, But the Government Has Spent Some of Your Money Wisely!

Well, perhaps not on purpose. But, hey, give them a break. What will make Right Time Marketing a reality are data storage capacities and processing speeds that were sheer fantasy just a few years ago at the start of the 1990s. This new leap in computer technology is called *massive parallel processing* (MPP).

MPP had its birth in the early 1980s, thanks to the Defense Department's advanced technology group, the Defense Advanced Research Project Agency (DARPA). DARPA has been responsible for handing out tens of millions to small "out-of-the-box technologists" who traditionally have had great ideas that are just too risky for the commercial world to be interested in.

One such idea is the concept of massive parallel processing. DARPA needed smart weapons and stealth technology, which, in turn, needed computing horsepower that in the early '80s wasn't even on the planning charts of IBM or Cray. Along came Danny Hillis, then a recent graduate of MIT, who had a simple yet radical concept: make computers act more like the human brain. Make them process information in parallel fashion, just like the brain does instead of passing data serially like all conventional computers do.

DARPA liked Danny's thinking and gave him and some other start-up firms development money, and, presto, after a lot of hard work, Danny and friends developed exactly what DARPA wanted: computers with blindingly fast processing speeds that could be increased indefinitely.

Sitting by the Pool

Massive parallel processing is extremely simple to understand and is vastly different from traditional mainframe processing. In traditional mainframe processing, all information must line up in serial fashion in order to pass through from one to a half-dozen processors for any computing task to be accomplished.

MPP, on the other hand, employs a mainframe with hundreds or thousands of processors that all work in unison to essentially break a computing job into small pieces. Each piece can get processed in parallel with every other piece instead of "waiting in line" to go through one or two central processors.

I like to use a swimming pool analogy as a further explanation of MPP. Suppose you have an Olympic-sized pool that needs repair work and must be drained of its millions of gallons. The normal method is to hook up a pump to a hose in the pool and pump all the water out through it (serial pumping). If you wanted to dramatically improve on the pumping time, the solution would be to hook up 10 pumps or even 20, with a hose attached to each, and turn them all on together (parallel pumping).

MPP is nothing more than parallel pumping of data through a software program to derive a solution to a mathematical problem. The big difference between MPP and traditional processing, therefore, is that there are a lot more pumps assigned to any single task.

Speed Changes Everything

Think about wagon trains 150 years ago taking eight months to a year to travel the 800 miles of the Santa Fe Trail from Missouri to New Mexico. The family car can do 800 miles in two days of easy driving. The Concorde travels 800 miles in 30 minutes. A business person in London can make the 11:00 a.m. Concorde to Kennedy in New York, arrive in downtown Manhattan for a 9:30 a.m. meeting, and catch the mid-afternoon Concorde back to London in time for a nightcap.

MPP has created a Concorde-type approach to traveling the computer equivalent of 800 miles. The largest serial processor mainframes currently process information at 50 to 100 million instructions per second. That's wagon train speed compared to MPP machines, which routinely do 6 billion instructions per second.

This change in speed has simply made the impossible, possible. It made smart weapons technology possible for the U.S. Defense Department. As we approach the mid-1990s, it is making Right Time Marketing possible for the commercial world. As I stated early in this chapter, the key to successfully using the hardware technology we have before us is one word: software.

MPP has been slow to make the transition from advanced military and other scientific computing uses because of one simple fact: as of 1992, there is virtually no software written for MPP to do commercial database applications.

Put another way, in the United States and throughout the world, most mainframe processing is based on IBM software and operating systems that have been developed for serial processing over the past 30 years. With MPP, none of that legacy software works. Totally new software needs to be developed that not only makes multiple processors parallel process a computing job, but also allows the MPP machines to "talk" to conventional mainframes so data can be moved back and forth between the two systems.

American Express has been the first company to invest in the development of marketing database software to dramatically improve customer service in ways just not possible before. AMEX has used its marketing systems subsidiary, Epsilon, to develop commercially viable marketing database software for a large MPP machine it purchased in 1991.

Over the next few years, Epsilon, which I manage, is expecting to provide marketing solutions to other firms with massive customer data management needs.

Memory: The Fundamental Use Of Any Marketing System

The real purpose behind investing in and maintaining a marketing database is not well understood by the technology community that builds systems for marketers and is not well articulated by the marketing community for whom these systems are built. My assessment of the confusion is that technologists are used to building systems for a specific, predetermined function with predetermined outputs or reports and well-defined data parameters, i.e., a limited amount of data elements attached to thousands or millions of customers.

This sounds reasonable. Yet more than ever before, marketers are slugging it out over fickle consumers with ever-changing needs and wants who expect personal attention, are willing to pay for it, and should get it whether they are 1 out of 100 or 1 out of 10 million customers.

To manage these customer expectations, marketers need a system that has no predetermined pathways that lock them into one way of storing customer data or certain types of reports or well-defined queries to well-defined marketing problems—there are no well-defined marketing problems.

What marketers need is what MPP can finally give them. They need all customer data, of any type, stored in its most basic form all in one place (the database), where it can be easily accessed over short periods of time (seconds, minutes, or a few hours) in a total ad hoc environment. In other words, they need a *central memory repository* that allows quick, random access to certain data, such as a specific customer record, and at the same time solves queries that may involve processing many millions or billions or, yes, trillions of bytes of information.

Oh, and for good measure, the system must cost the same or even less than the systems of old in which so much money and time have already been invested.

Yes, MPP can do all the above. It can do the impossible—give marketing people what they want.

Right Time Marketing will occur because using MPP, billions or trillions of bytes of data can be processed in minutes to determine which customers among thousands or millions should get which messages or services or promotions or endless unique sequences of all three, over days or weeks or years. This definition is the future of marketing that MPP has enabled us to create.

Here's just one concrete example of what was impossible before. In this case, Epsilon harnessed MPP for the early stages of Right Time Marketing. A financial services client (not American Express) wanted to create a model that would determine, across 70 million households, the absolute best prospects for a particular financial product. In the past, the client ran a predictive model using only a fraction of the data available because of time and cost constraints. But by using Epsilon's MPP computer (made by Thinking Machines Corporation, the leader in MPP machines), the client could use all available data—750 billion bytes of it—to look at each household on a truly stand-alone basis.

Yes, this 750-billion byte job could have run on a conventional mainframe if the client were willing to wait three months for an answer, hope the job did not hiccup during three months of round-the-clock processing, and pay a small fortune to tie up an expensive mainframe for one job for three months. Clearly, this path was not an option.

Instead, on Epsilon's MPP machine using Epsilon-developed software, this 750-billion byte modeling job ran between midnight and 6:00 a.m. on the third shift on a Saturday night in Epsilon's computer room. It was no big deal for an MPP machine with the right software. And the results for the client were as impressive as the speed with which this job was executed.

Okay, But Can Little Guys Use Supercomputers, Too?

Absolutely. You do not need to have millions of customers or prospects to take advantage of MPP. Epsilon has developed software tools already in use for companies of all sizes, including non-profit organizations. Other companies are sure to follow Epsilon's lead. As of early 1993, Neodata's subsidiary, Wiland Associates, has announced a partnership with Kendall Square Research, a manufacturer of MPP hardware. Kendall Square is literally down the road in Cambridge, Massachusetts, from Thinking Machines Corporation, which has partnered with Epsilon.

While the main target of these alliances is the Fortune 100, the modeling, analytical query, and promotional execution tools developed for the "big guys" can be used on a stand-alone basis by smaller organizations. As mentioned above, Epsilon is already providing many clients with access to its supercomputer's awesome processing power to create and run data-intensive advanced models.

We're Talking the Big Bang Theory in Reverse

If you remember junior high school science, you learned that around 20 billion years ago, give or take a few eons, all matter in the universe consisted of one minuscule, extremely dense particle, which blew up (the Big Bang), spreading forth gases and matter that formed galaxies, stars, planets, comets, and other heavenly bodies. This matter is still spreading "outward," so the theory goes, and at some point will begin to rush back together in one mass, as it began.

A similar kind of "big bang" happened in the computer world, but only during the past 30 years. From the late 1950s through the early '70s, most firms had one mainframe that provided all their data-related functions and stored all the firm's data in one place. The "big bang" didn't occur until the '70s and '80s, when one mainframe and one operating system could no longer handle the dramatically increased data collection and processing required for most medium to large firms to just stay in business.

What happened was inevitable. Lots of little independent "data galaxies" popped up within a single company. These multiple systems sometimes passed data back and forth and sometimes did not, but even when they did, the data transfer was rarely pure.

Throw into this mix four or five major operating systems that don't communicate well with each other, often with each being used by different departments or divisions within the same company. Add to this mix mini-systems, PCs, and then workstations, and you have a lot of data spread out farther and farther from where it all began, with no hope of getting it back together.

Then the '90s came along with major restructuring by corporate America, in large part, to focus all available resources on the customer. Unfortunately, getting a total view of each customer relationship, past, present, and going forward, was next to impossible because the necessary data was spread over many systems, often summarized within systems, and never totally brought back together.

Part of this predicament was the fault of information processing folks not allowing others in the company to participate in managing and understanding how data should and could be used. Part of it was the fault of hardware and software manufacturers. Part of it was probably no one's fault

There just was no practical and cost-effective solution to ultimately storing all customer data in one place, what I referred to earlier as a company's memory, until MPP came to be. MPP allows us to bring all the data back together from all those "data galaxies" and to store it and analyze it to our heart's content for the good of the individual customer— and the company. MPP will allow Right Time Marketing—getting the right offer to the right person at the right time—to become the way all effective marketing is done in the future.

Can Your Internal Technical People Build a Right Time Marketing System?

By themselves, chances are slim to none. The MPP field is too new, and those with proven commercial software experience are few. Plus, connecting all the pieces, both hardware and software, from MPP supercomputer to traditional mainframes to robotic data towers to workstations and client servers, is just too complex a task without getting outside experts to assist in a significant way. In fact, outsourcing the building of your company data memory and Right Time Marketing functions will be significantly cheaper and faster if you leave it to the experts.

With MPP, for the foreseeable future, you do not want to be the pioneer, especially when it comes to building software. Proven MPP software, which you can lease or purchase, is the one single most important element for your future marketing success. There are no shortcuts or hardware miracles that will change this fact.

Parting Shot

Three things in life are a sure bet: taxes, death, and buying Microsoft, on the cheap, right after the next stock market crash. What is not sure at all is whether the American business community will come to realize how *vitally* important marketing-oriented software utilizing Massive Parallel Processing will become. Having access to MPP software, and using it wisely, will determine the ultimate success of every 21st century company. How your company manages its investment in marketing software today, and over the rest of the 1990s, will largely determine whether it will be around to do business in the year 2000 and beyond.

It is that simple.

7

New Heights for the List Broker

The Top Ten Challenges

Linda McAleer

Linda McAleer is Executive Vice President, Millard Group. Circulation planning and list universe analysis are Linda's areas of specialty, and she brings more than 12 years' prior experience in the publishing industry to her job. She has also served as Circulation Manager for the *Harvard Business Review,* and Circulation Promotion Director for the *Atlantic Monthly*.

When looking forward, it frequently pays to look to the past and present in order to justify suppositions made about the future. So it is with the past and the present I would like to begin.

When I began in this industry, circa 1979, the list industry was in the awkward teenage years. Mailing lists were no longer being maintained in shoe boxes, but on big mainframe computers. None were available on diskette. Many list owners still released their names only on Cheshire labels. Selections on lists were rare and included mostly active or 12-month buyers. Many list owners simply did not rent their lists at all. Later on, the list broker/manager role became researching lists independently and bringing them to the market, and much time was spent simply in getting lists onto the list rental market.

Since that time, selections on lists have increased (to include RFM, product, original source of names, demographics, psychographics, you name it). As a result of this increased marketing information, list brokers have become smarter in their recommendations. Recommending lists just isn't enough; now we need to know selections within lists (and what they mean). . . and how to fine tune files and make them work better for our clients. Simply finding that magic list was no longer the headache, it became a matter of understanding the lists better than your competitor that got you the orders.

Meanwhile, merge/purge became far more sophisticated. Many mailers now rely on merges, and information culled from merge output to drive their marketing efforts. Now brokers had to understand the merge process, data manipulation, and how to effectively mail names as they came out of the merge. Buzzwords such as "universal merge," "mega-merge," "mastermail file," megafile," "intra dupes," "super dupes," and "inter dupes" started working into our language. What are they and what should we do with them?

As a result of more efficient merges, mailers are mailing less (more efficiently, of course) and this has affected the prices of lists. Response rates have fallen, and all related in the mail costs are higher than ever. Thus enters the world of "serious" list negotiations. Negotiations between list owners (through the brokers and managers) based on volume, reduced net names, reduced base, and selection charges became commonplace. Like Avis, we vowed to "work harder"—and for less.

So where this leaves us as a springboard is that today's list brokers are now responsible for knowing vitually all they can about lists and markets, should be counted on to consult in the merge/purge process, are frequently called upon to provide analytical services (more about this later), and at the same time must negotiate reduced rates for our clients.

This is a long way from the days of pushing data cards across our clients' desks!

Computers and technology and the impact of tighter margins faced by all mailers have had a lot to do with this change, but equally so has client expectation levels. List brokers should be part of the "marketing team," much as the creative people, statisticians, and circulation professionals are. Bad advice on lists, poor counsel on merge/purge, inaccurate circulation plans, and unprofitable pricing terms will all spell disaster for a client, and ultimately the list professional as well.

But what hasn't (or shouldn't have) changed is service. We are first and foremost a service business and in spite of all the changes in our responsibilities and where we go in the future, service levels must remain as good as, if not better than, in the past. In order to do this, we need better education of the newcomers in our field (and, believe me, possibly of some of the old-timers, too) to ensure that staff members at all levels can help our clients and each other avoid making mistakes, suggest innovative solutions to problems, and continue to deserve the title of list professional. We need to trust our competition and work with each other.

So, with that said and done, where are we going in the year 2000 and beyond? Here are my "top 10" thoughts with apologies to David Letterman.

#10. We will all abide by ethical standards to protect the consumer's privacy (and the consumer wins in the long run).

#9. Public and private databases will continue to be created and thrive.

#8. Selections on lists will multiply like rabbits in spring.

#7. We will be masters of the machines to increase efficiencies.

#6. Modeling and regression analyses will continue to thrive.

#5. List brokers will become consultants.

#4. Compensation for the brokerage community will change.

#3. Strategic alliances will go back to being called partnerships and continue to thrive!

#2. The interactive electronic revolution will spill into the list community.

#1. Service will be paramount.

#10. We will all abide by ethical standards to protect the consumer's privacy (and the consumer wins in the long run.

Above all else, the issue of privacy continues to linger in the background as a dark cloud. How much can we share about our customers and with whom? List professionals are caught right in the middle of the controversy. Frequently, to increase list rental we will recommend that "enhanced" selections on the file be made available. But if we add too much sensitive data (credit or life-style information, perhaps) and this information is misused, then the walls of Jericho in list land could come tumbling down. Moving forward, we need to be extra careful with what we recommend that clients do with data and how they use it. Target marketing is smart, but if we cross the line and target too specifically, we run the risk of "trespassing." By the year 2000, we will use information wisely, counsel all customers to do the same, and the consumer will benefit.

#9. Public and private databases will continue to be created and thrive.

Currently there are only a handful of public databases that are "true" databases: interactive and multilevel relational. This will become a thing of the past. Lists will be available more commonly as segments of larger files. The hurdle of cost (by passing so many names and pulling off only certain subsegments) will become far less as data processing costs continue to become reduced. As a result, merge/purge will become far more effective, because names you receive going into the merge process will be clean and netted out.

Private databases are on the rise but will have to overcome some obstacles to become omnipresent. Secrecy about who is in the database, where the information is culled from, and what exactly is being pulled out of the database will be wiped out. Secrecy implies that there is something to hide and in this age of privacy awareness, most smart mailers want to know exactly what they're mailing when they mail. Black boxes may work (usually they don't over the long term), but at what cost?

Consortium databases, in which like list owners create monthly, quarterly, or biannual mega-merges among themselves, will also continue to be more commonplace. After all, many mailers are already commingling at the printer. Commingling from the onset at merge/purge will make all our lives easier!

It is commonplace today in the business to business environment to find consortium databases of this sort. In the future, for example, similar gardening offers (Breck's, Rodale Press, *Horticulture,* and *Garden Way*) that reach much the same market but sell noncompetitive product lines will perform massive intelligent merge/purges together, pool their names together, and maximize mailing efficiencies. But for this to work, the list suppliers will need to spearhead the effort, and today these competitive forces just aren't working together well enough. But if the end result is that the mailers will benefit, the list industry will move toward creating these databases. After all, without happy customers we're all out of business!

#8. Selections on lists will multiply like rabbits in spring.

As has happened over the past 10 years, selections on lists will become that much more fine tuned. It is now the exception rather than the norm to be able to combine demographics with RFM, product type with recency. The smart list owners are changing this. Product purchase history is a powerful selection tool, yet few list owners offer this selection. As mailers move into the year 2000, they will have to offer more selections on their lists or be doomed. "Smart" databases or list files will become a prerequisite. With rising postal, paper and even list costs, mailers will need to fine tune their selection criteria even more in order to continue to mail.

In the future, offers will be so highly targeted, benefit-oriented, and precise in reaching the appropriate audience that direct mail will be unobtrusive and welcomed. By being able to precisely target exactly (or as nearly as possible) the potential customer's needs based on life-style, demographic, and recent purchase information—so long as we use the information wisely—our response rates will rise, and we'll have more satisfied customers and a healthy business.

As an example let's say that you're selling books for children ages 5–7. In today's environment, we can find people with children in the appropriate age group and lists of people who have purchased children's books by mail, but rarely a large pool of names combining the two data elements. By the year 2000, it will be commonplace to merge this information—couple it with other important buyer information and reach more targeted prospects and fewer suspects. We're on the way already, we'll just refine the way we target.

#7. We will be masters of the machines to increase efficiencies.

Automation will create more efficient flow of orders and information among brokers, managers, list owners, and mailers alike. Common machinery and computer language will begin to be adopted by the major list rental fulfillment houses, and automated online order entry will flow from list order at brokerage houses, to managers (with copies to clients), to fulfillment houses, and back to managers and brokers. As a result, dual data entry errors will be avoided, list order turnaround will become a nit, and clients won't drown in paperwork, saving trees to boot!

Today's list companies are bogged down in unnecessary data entry and paperwork. Today in my company (and from what I understand, we're typical of the industry), we revise over 40% of every order we enter (creating one more piece of paper), and subsequently bill, thus creating a three-time transaction via paper for virtually every single order. Subsequent paper trails are simultaneously created at our manager counterpart company, and if any part of the billing process is wrong, subsequent documents are created.

Imagine an electronic world where orders are transmitted online from a client to a broker to a manager to the fulfillment house. Tapes are created with no paperwork. The merge/purge is run, information is electronically transferred back to the broker, and the bills are created and sent electronically to the client. This is the wave of the future and the way we must go.

The only way this can happen is if list professionals work together to create systems that work with each other. Standardization is critical. List professionals who refuse to standardize will become (and are) dinosaurs. (I'm sure that the list owners who held out on offering their lists on mag tape in 1960 lost list rental incomes, after all.) By the year 2000, the companies who work together to create systems that manage this information flow will still be around, and the others will not. It's that plain and simple.

#6. Modeling and regression analyses will continue to thrive.

The current force that's uncovering new opportunities on both house and outside lists is regression. For years, few but the smartest, largest mailers could afford regression analysis and make it work. Most of the smaller companies started testing with zip (or state) select models. They didn't work and they then were turned off on modeling systems in general. Solid regressions are being built in-house by mailers as well as by list owners who are smart and want to increase their list rentals. By the year 2000, I doubt any of the mid- to large-sized mailers will be mailing without any sort of regression model. List brokers who want to stay alive will have to understand these models so they can effectively recommend and analyze information for their clients. By the year 2000, the way current models are being created, there will most likely be a better mousetrap. Not being a statistician, it boggles my mind!

#5. List brokers will become consultants.

List brokers will be consultants specializing in lists, but consultants nonetheless. We will no longer be allowed to just peddle lists, push data cards, and reap the rewards. (Few do this now, but for the handful who still do, beware the way of the dinosaur). We will be participating in new product development and introduction; analytical circulation work; and consulting on database development, use, and refinements. Many clients are working this way with their list contacts, yet many are not. The smart mailers will continue to involve their brokers in more of their marketing efforts as part of their team.

In the future, as clients begin their budget process, list professionals will be brought in to help determine how many names they can truly afford to mail and at what cost. Rather than have to refine mail plans based on eleventh-hour advice, we will become a part of the process at the planning stage.

Because we will know how to reach audiences (using all of the above-mentioned techniques), we will be able to guide expectation levels for product introduction. In today's environment, it is not uncommon for mailers to find a product with a natural audience, misdirect their marketing expectation levels (by not understanding audience size and composition) and end up being disappointed. By using the list broker's knowledge of universe size and potential and his or her ability to reach this audience, expectation levels regarding return and audience size will be set realistically from the onset. In short, we will play an integral role in building and enhancing relationships between clients and their customer base.

#4. Compensation for the brokerage community will change.

As a result of what has been outlined above, much of our services will no longer be related to ordering lists of names for our clients, but rather to improving mailings, working with in-house databases, etc. The issue of compensation will need to be adjusted. Brokers are moving toward charging on a fee basis. As brokers become less list brokers and more consultants, the types of arrangements they have with their clients will change. But some mailers will continue to want their brokers to remain only their brokers in regular commission rate structures. "Chinese menu" pricing will become more commonplace, and clients will be paying for what they're getting. Like advertising agency clients, one size doesn't fit all, and it's high time the list industry recognizes this! By the year 2000, all but the most naive direct marketers will rely on their list broker for just list information. Because our business is currently only a 14–15% margin business at best, ancillary services will need to be compensated for. Clients will pay for what they need, not for what they don't. Brokers will provide information the clients want, not what their archaic list and data card systems simply spit out. Customization of services will result in customization of pricing and compensation.

#3. Strategic alliances will go back to being called partnerships—and continue to thrive!

So much of what happens to a list after a broker orders it is determined by merge/purge houses with little input from the brokers. This will cease to exist. Data processing companies will work together with brokerage houses in the future to maximize the output of merge. Data processing folks know how to sort data, brokers know what the data means—the marriage is inevitable! Brokers will comment on how to handle input, output, and names into the mail. A small fraction of "smart" mailers are doing this today. This will become a prerequisite to survival in the future. Frequently mailers are eliminating the most productive prospects from their merge, simply because they don't understand that these names are valuable and their merge house enters the lists as just that—lists of names. As an example, if a cataloger has three separate and different catalogs, the buyers between these lists are multis, not interfile dupes. In the near future, this kind of costly mistake (of eliminating these names) will not happen!

#2. The interactive electronic revolution will spill into the list community.

As consumers continue to purchase more products via interactive PC networks and cable TV, the need (and benefit) of direct mail products will become less important. Once this new technology becomes more cost-effective and as more and more direct marketers can offer their products at a reasonable CPO in their living rooms using electronic media, many current direct mail marketers will switch how they order (via catalog, direct mail offers) to this new media.

As alternative sales opportunities arise, fewer lists for direct mail offers will be ordered. We will have to learn how to capitalize on this new medium. As list brokers, we currenlly sell names of people who have a desire to purchase certain products via direct mail or the telephone. We will learn to sell names of people who purchase certain interactive media and who have a desire to buy our clients' products. We know how to find markets; we must learn how to use new media for these market opportunities. If we don't sell this, someone else will. Guaranteed.

#1. Service will be paramount.

First and foremost, we will maintain and improve our current client service levels. As we move forward and automate so much of our business, the potential to allow human service to fall to the wayside is all too great. Automation will free up more of our time, allowing us the freedom to become more of a marketing partner with our clients. Perhaps the nature of the service that we provide our clients will change, but not the necessity.

We will still need to know good information from bad, be able to consolidate what our clients need from the myriad of data available, and complement the marketing efforts of our clients. Our job still remains to find cost-effective markets for our clients to market to (perhaps via direct mail and perhaps not!) and make sure that the information resource and brokerage resource that we provide is a true benefit to the customer, in this case, the mailer or the marketer. The year 2000 is not very far away, but there seems to be so much opportunity to improve how we're doing what we're doing and expand all horizons. It'll be a wild ride for sure.

8

A Media Planner's Guide to the Future

More Choices, More Tools

Jack M. Klues
& Jayne Zenaty Spittler

Jack M. Klues joined Leo Burnett's media department in 1977 and rose to become a media supervisor in 1979. He was promoted to media director in 1985 and became a vice president of the company the same year. Currently a senior vice president, he oversees media for the Amurol, Nintendo, Samsonite, and Tropicana accounts.

Jayne Zenaty Spittler is Vice President and Director of Media Research at the Leo Burnett Company in Chicago. She supervises a staff of 15 people, with responsibilities for tracking and projecting the performance of all media vehicles; producing major agency guidance documents and points of view; developing procedures and systems for better media planning and buying; and monitoring and evaluating media research studies and sources.

Traditional media planners define their primary objective as delivering the right message to the right people at the right time in the right place often enough to be effective. These advertising professionals address this task armed with an understanding of the overall marketing goals and a charge to spend their clients' budgets as cost-effectively as possible.

The media options available to the planner at any given time often are referred to as the media planner's toolbox: helpful implements to build the successful media plan. The size and inventory of the toolbox have depended on the transmission technologies of the day, the economics of creating and supporting particular media vehicles, and the sociological trends of the times. For example, it was the Industrial Revolution, driven by steam power and an urbanized consumer population, that gave birth to the mass marketing and mass communications possibilities with which we are all so familiar today.

But technology is never finished. The industrial and post-industrial societies stand to be transformed into the information society by the promise of the computer, digital technology, and fiber optic connections. Futurists speak of an electronic superhighway of 500 or 5,000 fiber optic, digitally switched channels, on which large, fairly undifferentiated audiences can be segmented into small, homogeneous groups to receive customized marketing messages rapidly and cost effectively. And the one-to-many phenomenon of radio telephony recycles again as the "point-to-point" transmission of Morse's telegraph, only this time on glass wires with sophisticated switching networks and megabytes of digitally stored full-motion video signals.

At the same time, a few non-electronic transformations have been occurring in the media world. Direct response techniques have been fused with mass media delivery. Television has expanded beyond the home to an array of different locations, from schools to airports to supermarkets. Consumers are hard-pressed to differentiate the promotional offer or the product mention in a newscast or the sponsorship of an event from any other advertising message. Because "it's all advertising" to the consumer, even more tools enter the media planning toolbox.

With the haze of electronic promise on the horizon and the reality of an ever-widening definition of advertising at the door, the media planner's basic task still does not change. In a contrary sort of way, the complexity of additional options highlights a single-minded purpose: find the right people, find the right places, send the right messages. One-to-many broadcasting, with a single message, eventually could be replaced by custom-tailored point-to-point communications, depending on the marketing objective. In the interim, media planners are discovering that they can make old media do new tricks (like direct response print or television) and teach new media vehicles old tricks (like building brand equity in an FSI). It's a world of one-to-some.

Making Sense of the Possibilities: Why Is This Happening?

To prepare to deal with the 500- to 5,000-channel "communicopia" of consumer- controlled viewing options and more and different definitions of a "medium", a media planner needs to understand why this revolution is taking place. He or she also needs to identify key media developments that may impact the effectiveness of current tools and offer some new ones along the way in order to plot a course for the future. This chapter does those three things.

A confluence of three factors is leading the movement toward demassification and increased choice in U.S. media today. These are: demographic and life-style shifts, technology, and economics. Together they set the stage for a transformation in consumer communications that existed before only in science fiction stories.

Demassifying the Masses

Significant shifts in the demographic composition and life-styles of Americans have led to a demassification of the mass market. Today's mindset is one of being an individual, rather than one of the group. America's melting pot, so important to the immigrants of the 1930s and '40s, today has become a smorgasbord of ethnicities and life-styles. Some defining trends: the polarization of America into a country of economic "haves" and "have-nots"; fewer traditional households with two parents, one income and several children; more women in the work force; growing Hispanic, black, and Asian populations; an aging American population; and consumers' "time poverty"—busier lives with less free time.

Databases filled with electronic transactions that differentiate these myriad consumers have made segmentation and targeting possible and necessary. Manufacturers, released from the economies of mass production by better technology, have responded to the different needs and characteristics of their consumers. One standard product (or three broadcast networks) has been replaced by a dizzying array of sizes, flavors, forms, and options. It's not coincidental that two well-known advertising campaigns tell the consumer "Your way, right away" and "What you want is what you get."

Upgrading the Technology

During the 1970s and '80s, more choice and control was added to the consumers' media world by the development of alternative distribution systems and better hardware. Specifically, the transmission of television signals via coaxial cable brought more viewing options into the home. At the same time, the use of satellites to distribute all types of media signals—television, radio, and print—speeded delivery, added variety, and brought specialized television to new venues. New hardware, like cable converters, remote controls and videocassette recorders, gave couch potatoes easy ways to explore their choices.

Four Key Technological Developments

Cable, satellites, and VCRs brought a significant change to the electronic environment. However, they pale in comparison to the quantum leap the next technological advances may provide. These combine the strengths of television, computers, and telephones. More distribution channels will be available to programmers, editors, retailers, and marketers because of four key developments:

1. The digitization and compression of signals

2. The development of massive digital storage facilities

3. Digital switching

4. Fiber optic distribution networks

These four technologies are important for three reasons: they increase the amount of information and entertainment that can be sent or accessed by the consumer, they allow information and entertainment to be customized and delivered on demand; and they have the potential to integrate and enhance cable, computer, and telephone capabilities. Here's a brief description of each.

Digitization/Compression

For the most part, electronic signals transmitted today are *analog*. This means they travel as waves, which need to have both their amplitudes (height) and frequency (length) included in the signal. As such, they take a lot of room in the electronic pipeline. *Digitization* is the process of translating analog signals into the zeroes and ones of computers. These digitized signals still are quite large, but compression techniques enable them to be condensed and packaged as smaller versions of their former selves.

For example, several cable networks (such as HBO, the Disney Channel, and MTV) currently send several different channels of programming via satellite to cable systems. Using digitization and compression, the cable systems are able to offer two or three channels to their subscribers using the same amount of "signal space" that an old analog signal required.

Digital Storage

Developments in electronic storage, both in technology and economics, allow the digitized electronic signals to be stored in great numbers at low cost. This opens the possibilities of programming on demand: calling up magazines, encyclopedias, or television programming at the consumer's whim. It eventually may make the VCR obsolete. More significantly, it allows for the integration of computer and video capabilities. Imagine looking up information about a vacation getaway on your online computer service, and being able to walk through the streets of Hong Kong with a tour guide as well. Televisions will begin to act more like computers, while computers will take on more video characteristics.

Digital Switching

Digitization, compression, and storage by themselves provide enormous choice and flexibility to consumers. But it is the ability to direct those signals with the precision of a telephone to a specific location that digital switching offers. This phenomenon is called *addressability*. This technology will make more targeted programming and advertising possible in both television and video print. It will allow this programming to be available on demand, which could be thought of as a one-way interaction. It also will allow responses from the home to make their way back to a programming or information supplier, opening up sophisticated two-way interactions. This is the development, now being tested and engineered by telephone experts like AT&T and the Regional Bell Operating Companies (RBOCs) and various computer concerns, that will bring true two-way messaging to the 21st century. It currently is causing some seemingly strange strategic alliances as the concept is translated into reality.

Fiber Optics

A wired network links information providers and receivers together. Currently, much of the United States relies on copper twisted-pair wires and copper coaxial cable to carry telephone and television signals. However, there is a limit to the amount of information these wires can carry, the number that can be pulled through underground conduits, and the distance a signal can be transmitted without losing its quality. The network of the future will be made up of glass fibers, hairlike strands that will replace their copper ancestors and carry enormous amounts of information. Signals carry farther and with greater quality along fiber, and the maintenance and repair of fiber are significantly easier and longer-lasting.

How soon the fiber optic network is in place nationwide will depend on other groups of strange alliances. At the present time, both the RBOCs and major cable companies are switching their distribution plant to fiber or fiber and coaxial cable combinations.

Paying the Bill

It is critical to remember, however, that technology will not be the sole, and perhaps not the primary, determinant of a new order in the communications environment. Government regulation; the cost of programming; the movement of ad dollars across various media outlets; the availability of investment capital; the spirit of cooperation or competition among disparate, but vital parties; the spreading of our society's creative talents; and finally, consumer acceptance will all play a role in shaping the communications industry in the future.

From a technological standpoint, the communications superhighway could be built tomorrow. How the construction will be financed offers some potential hurdles. First of all, the economic picture is not bright, tightening money for any type of research and development. Time-Warner Inc., with substantial debt remaining from the merger of the two communications giants, has sold $25 billion of its stock to U.S. West, an RBOC with which it will build a "Full Service Network," beginning in Orlando in 1994. Second, the geographic scope of partnerings of this type remains mired in regulation; telephone companies cannot own cable systems and vice-versa. Third, recent cable regulation has forced cable operators to reduce their subscription prices, at a time when consumer-based revenue streams are critical for media success. Fourth, marketers have been faced with hard economic times and are not certain whether to invest limited funds in start-up projects.

Clearly there are opportunities for risk-takers in technology, programming, and marketing. It is this regulatory/economic gate that requires the vigilance of the smart media planner, to be able to weigh the costs and benefits of new media and communications opportunities.

This chapter looks at some specific developments in media and communications from that viewpoint, knowing that media professionals will need to be less reliant on traditional marketing and media tactics as we approach the 21st century. The hope is that in understanding the possibilities of a new generation of tools and techniques, more personalized, relevant, and actionable media plans can be developed to help our clients' businesses succeed.

Specific Developments to Watch: Better Targeting with Existing Media

We now finally appear to be in the position to satisfy the long-standing advertiser demand for greater planning precision beyond general demographic characteristics, by using new tools that will allow communication with consumers on an individual basis and in a way compatible with their life-styles. While media planning practitioners no longer will be slaves to "largest potential audience" and "lowest cost per thousand" as primary evaluative criteria, our existing knowledge and experience will prove invaluable as we attempt to identify some specific developments worth hands-on exploration.

We see existing media options—magazines, television, radio, outdoor, etc.—improving their ability to target advertising messages toward selective segments of their total audiences.

Customized Print Opportunities

In early 1991, *Newsweek* magazine was one of the first large-circulation consumer periodicals to introduce a sophisticated printing technology known as *selective binding*. The service, fueled by computerized printing techniques and databases, allows advertisers to reach only the subscribers they want based on a combination of demographics and purchasing behaviors. *Newsweek* now uses the technique to customize its issues for readers, adding pages to the magazine based on the recipient's interests, age, work, and leisure activities.

As more and more publishers and advertisers build databases on their subscribers and customers, the use of the selective binding technology is expected to grow. According to Deborah Cray, R.R. Donnelley's Selectronic/ Distribution Product Manager, the biggest indicator of how many publishers and advertisers are interested in selective binding is Metromail, a Donnelley subsidiary. The number of databases it is building for the explicit purpose of selective print advertising has increased tremendously.

(Debora Toth, "Selective Binding: A New Era in Personalization," *Graphic Arts Monthly* 65 [January 1993], p.54.)

Beyond Demographic TV Targets

In television, dayparts and programs increasingly are being chosen on the basis of reported or actual purchaser preferences rather than broad demographic profiles. In the absence of true electronic "single source" data linking purchases to television viewing, new media research tools like the Donnelley Marketing Information Services (DMIS) National TV Conquest allow media planners to link data sources that provide purchase information (scanner products, manufacturer information, or syndicated sources like MRI or SMRB) to television ratings from A.C. Nielsen. This process enables the media planner to determine what consumers with various product usage behaviors are most likely to view.

Certain products and targets lend themselves to this kind of geodemographic segmentation better than others, depending on the characteristics of the users and the brand/category and the marketing environment. Geodemographic analysis of existing databases also opens the door to better regional and micro-marketing opportunities, determining the best prospects for brand sales all the way to the grocery store level. These analyses, once in the realm of the promotion planner, can be integrated with the media planner's efforts for a synergistic effect.

Addressable TV Possibilities

As cable and telephone companies develop and install sophisticated digital switching technology, we will gain the ability to divide the signals of television programs and/or their commercials into distinct packets for various target groups. This will allow us to send unique, relevant versions of our brand message to consumers on a household-by-household basis, with a precision far beyond the currently available geographic regional copy splits of broadcast network television. For example, a viewer tuned to a certain program may see an ad for a luxury car, while another person watching the same program would see an ad for an economy car, mini-van, or off-road vehicle. These decisions could he made on the demographics of the household, present car ownership, or a stated preference for particular brands or categories.

Addressable television programming experiments that try to satisfy viewers' appetites for choices in programming are underway around the world via satellite and cable. These systems enhance an advertiser's ability to reach the best consumer prospects. The Pan-Asian satellite network known as Star TV brings Western music, sports, "unfiltered" news, and advertising into 38 different countries, including Hong Kong, India, Indonesia, Thailand, Singapore, South Korea, Malaysia, and the Philippines. Its developers have capitalized on the combined technology of satellite transmission and digital compression to accommodate the needs of the disparate cultures in the region, overcoming language barriers by speaking to each in their native tongue.

In Montreal, a cable television service allows its subscribers to build a personalized newscast, select different camera angles for sporting events, and select customized exercise programs. Digitally compressed signals containing all viewer options are transmitted over four cable channels. Hardware in the consumer's home selects the signal chosen by the viewer, accommodating more individualized interests without the need for sophisticated switching and true two-way interaction with the viewer.

The major benefit of these addressable efforts is targetability. It will give advertisers and their media planners the ability to send relevant brand messages to specific households. In a sense, the technology reverses the "mass" of broadcast television.

Radio's Local Edge

Radio stations continue their 40-year evolution toward even greater personalization with their listeners and become important local tactical partners with advertisers. New consumer formats that can meet the needs of listeners and advertisers among any geodemographic or psychographic group in any number of markets have been developed. Among the latest formats to gain popularity are all news, all sports, and all drama/mystery programming. Some stations are moving away from one exclusive format to two or even three formats, depending upon the time of day and demographic appeal.

Radio also has placed renewed emphasis on being a "citizen" of the community. It can help advertisers strengthen retail business alliances with specially designed promotions and events that capitalize on the medium's local knowledge/expertise. Because radio is among the most portable of media, it can be used to deliver important brand reminder messages exceptionally close to the point of purchase.

New Options with Interactive Media

The development of two-way interactive electronic communication with the consumer is the hottest topic in the media industry today.

As noted earlier in this chapter, technological change is ushering in a new age for television. Companies now are competing with each other over the "pipeline," sometimes called the electronic "superhighway," that will bring vast increases in programming services to America's living room. This new communications network will bring personalized news, films on demand, groceries, and classes from the local university; screen phone calls; buy gifts for relatives; and play games.

"The most important thing about the next generation of televisions is that they will be digital," says V. Michael Bove, Jr., a professor of media technology at MIT. Digitization will allow information to flow into households just like electricity does today. "Rather than having 500 channels and still nothing to watch," says Bove, "my TV will be a personal agent that looks for things that interest me based on what it knows about my viewing habits."

The impact of this new age of television sets and delivery networks will be felt in two ways. Television schedules and channels most likely will become obsolete as fully empowered consumers use menu-driven screens to decide both what and when they want to watch. The immediacy of a television commercials placed in scheduled programming will disappear; brand messages will occur at the viewer's convenience. A major rearrangement in the roles of program producers, distributors, and television "channels" will occur. Moreover, of even greater consequence, the television viewing experience will become an active, two-way adventure, rather than a passive experience.

A number of companies are experimenting with interactive programming, at various levels of sophistication. While some currently look like "regular" television with a telephone response, the concept and experience of developing a dialog with the consumer is one that media planners must begin to explore. Experimenting with current "crude" interactive systems now will prepare media practitioners for the full power delivered by the sophisticated electronic superhighway, when and if it is built. Some companies offering (or soon to offer) interactive TV programming systems include the following:

ICTV

TV Answer

TVI (Montreal)

Interactive Network

NTN Entertainment Network

ICTV, on the more sophisticated end of the interactive spectrum in the United States plans to offer limited movies-on-demand, classified advertising and home shopping, electronic TV listings, game playing, and other options designed to personalize the TV for each user.

TV Answer will offer a similar system that also will have the capability to prompt the viewer for more information as a particular brand's commercial airs. TV Answer is working with Hewlett-Packard to develop its set-top converter box and expects to begin testing in the fall of 1993, pending FCC licensing.

TV Answer currently is licensing a version of its product to Montreal's TVI, but this system goes one step further in its commercial targeting capabilities. Dubbed "viewer selected targeting," the TVI system prompts viewers to select one of up to four different creative executions, based on the answers to one or two simple questions. TVI also offers interactive advertising, which has been used by Coca-Cola and Volkswagen.

Interactive Network and NTN Entertainment Network offer a more limited version of interactive TV compared to the previous services. These systems allow viewers to play along with programs such as "Jeopardy!" or a football game, or to compete against other interactive players. They do not offer viewer-prompted advertising copy, or any of the other convenience services already mentioned. Interactive Network (with strategic partners NBC, Cablevision Systems Corp., and A.C. Nielsen Co.) currently is testing in Southern California and anticipates national roll-out by year-end 1993. NTN Entertainment, the longest-running interactive service, is available in 450 hotels and bars nationwide, via GTE's fiber optic network and General Electric's Genie online service. It plans to enter home cable systems in the fall of 1993, pending FCC approval.

The general advertising industry is looking at these interactive TV developments very closely, because they can offer the opportunity for demand-based advertisements, as well as new forms of advertising not currently available. Sponsorship of interactive menu screens, personal news and features, electronic shopping malls filled with long-form commercials and interactive sessions, electronic couponing, two-way video conversations between home shoppers and retailers, and options waiting to be developed will offer new challenges to the media planner always attempting to deliver relevant messages to a target prospect. The records of viewers' interactions will be fertile fields for targeting efforts, and may replace more traditional audience measurement services entirely.

More Direct Marketing

In an environment exploding with new media choices, direct marketers will continue to lead the way as direct contact and response are possible in all forms of media. To them, the promises of interactive television are a logical extension of the interactive strategies and tactics they employ today. They know, maybe better than anyone in the business, how television and print can be adapted as a means of interesting only the best prospects for what is being sold.

Direct marketing consultants Stan Rapp and Tom Collins try to explain the change in marketing/media planning emphasis, by advising readers that now is the time to rethink their use of mass media and capitalize on its fragmentation for the purposes of more direct selling:

> Increasingly fragmented product lines, markets, and media have made it steadily less efficient to reach your targeted prospects by spending all of your ad dollars blanketing the entire market with a saturation advertising campaign.
>
> In Direct Mass Marketing, you use mass marketing to catch the eye and learn the identity of your true prospects, and then direct additional communications to them alone. The means of accomplishing this, of course, is to make an offer and invite a response by any appropriate means—mail, phone, fax, computer, video game machine, or interactive cable TV. Then the advertiser uses this response to build a bridge between the advertising and the sale by naming the nearest dealer, sending out information, or a free sample . . . or any other advisable means. (*The Great Marketing Turnaround* [New York: Plume, 1992].)

A growing number of marketers are taking such advice to heart, experimenting with new direct applications that eventually will be able to exploit recent electronic technological developments.

Long-Form TV Ads: The Infomercial

One promising television opportunity has been around for a while, but it makes even more sense today. It is the Infomercial, a long-form television ad or program-length commercial. What was once the near-exclusive domain of pocket fishing poles and super-sharp knives now is being explored by several Fortune 500 companies and a recent candidate for President of the United States. The number of infomercials increased by 119 percent over the last four years, according to the National Infomercial Marketing Association (NIMA). This group projects that there will be over 170 infomercials on the air by the end of this year, driving approximately $1 billion in direct sales.

Long-form transactional programming delivered to the home represents a tremendous opportunity to build a database of interested customers for current and/or future marketing activities. By virtually ignoring the traditional 30-second commercial boundaries, advertising messages can bring marketers closer to the sale and be more conversational in providing viewers with detailed information, advice, and discounts on products and services. While today's response to the infomercial is done by telephone, tomorrow's long-form ad will exist in the realm of the 500-channel environment, with opportunities for more interactivity, selectivity, and measurement of its effectiveness.

Home Shopping Services

Home shopping is another "veteran" direct media option that stands to grow and develop in the new technological environment. The two premier carriers—QVC and the Home Shopping Network (HSN)—are about to be merged under the leadership of media mogul Barry Diller. Together, these broadcast and cable-delivered channels are available in two-thirds of U.S. television households. A broad variety of quality goods and services at reasonable prices are showcased 24 hours a day, seven days a week.

For participating manufacturers, home shopping shows represent a less expensive alternative to other direct selling methods. They save the production and media expense of a long-form infomercial. As a planning tool, a presence on dedicated home shopping programs/networks can provide a platform for quick and easy testing of new product concepts, different pricing points, and key copy points within an advertising message.

QVC/HSN also could become viable cable networks for standard 30-second commercial messages, should Barry Diller elect to accept them. The merged entity would be one of the five largest cable networks in the country in terms of potential coverage and would reach a viewing audience already predisposed to buy.

More Entertainment/Events

Over the last few years, the number of entertainment and community events subsidized by enthusiastic advertisers has increased. They apparently recognize this as a new media form, if you will, possessing the unique ability to break through the clutter of thousands of commercial messages that bombard consumers daily. An event can enhance and link other elements of a marketing mix—advertising, public relations, sales promotion, and direct marketing—to create a singular, high-visibility experience for the consumer.

Events literally bring products to participants in an innovative and personally involving manner. For example, Samsonite luggage was interested in introducing active, college-aged adults to its new product line of duffels, daypacks, and casual bags. In addition to advertising in the expected magazines and television options, Samsonite co-sponsored snowboarding competitions at ski resorts; migrated to Florida with the annual MTV Spring Break, offering product giveaways and contests; and demonstrated the product's features and benefits through a network TV college campus tour. These events also included promotional outdoor and radio media that otherwise would not have been part of the standard media plan.

Events also can subtly, yet effectively, reinforce the brand image of the product or service in the mind of the consumer through an event association using celebrities, locations, and/or acknowledged industry leaders. Video game manufacturer Sega of America is acting as the title sponsor of this summer's *Sports Illustrated* Sportsfest. The Sportsfest is an elaborate traveling exhibit that will visit the seven Six Flags amusement parks, a cousin of *SI* in the Time-Warner family, across the country. Park visitors, mostly kids and teens, will get the chance to meet famous professional athletes, participate in clinics, and see related sports memorabilia. There also will be a designated Sega video game play area where kids can get hands-on experience with the company's latest sports software.

Because many events like the ones mentioned are either media-owned or media-designed, it seems obvious that this new tool should be part of the media planner's repertoire. It is he or she who will be in the position to identify event opportunities that meet their client's communication goals, and who has the relationship with the media vendors to negotiate the best deal.

Place-Based Media

The opportunities to advertise in places other than in-home media vehicles continue to grow. Place-based options, many video-based and some interactive, are available in about every venue that attracts people. Like events, these "media places" attract consumers of particular mindsets, which can work to make brand messages more effective. The following are a few examples.

The Airport Channel is a private television network transmitted by satellite to monitors in airport gate areas.

ActMedia is the largest of over 20 different companies offering in-store advertising opportunities. These range from shopping cart and aisle directory signage to limited-capacity personal computers on VideoCarts.

Channel One is a 12-minute commercial "newscast" beamed into schools via satellite 194 days per year by Whittle Communications. As Channel One begins its fourth full season, 13,000 middle and high schools are enrolled.

AdTime NBC arena signage network currently is used in 11 markets, including Atlanta, Chicago, Boston, Detroit, Los Angeles, and Philadelphia. The signage system is a 70-foot-long billboard across the scorer's table, with panels that rotate advertisers' messages throughout the game.

Six Flags Promotion Network is a multimedia program of promotion vehicles, designed to capture the attention of, and then sell through products/services to, 18 million people who visit the Six Flags theme parks across the country. The audience is held captive waiting in line for various rides.

These place-based media vehicles help marketers get their advertising messages and/or products noticed at the most relevant time and the most relevant place. In some cases, they reach a target audience that does not use "traditional" media vehicles. They also give suppliers an additional way to amortize escalating program costs, by using product in two places (e.g., Turner's Airport Channel relies on news stories from CNN).

Media Consolidation/Unusual Partnerships

One of the most significant developments to watch as technology begins to change the media landscape is the reconfiguration and redefinition of the media companies themselves. A stagnant economy, audience fragmentation, more advertising options, and overextended investments in the '80s have all had their impact on media companies. The trend is one of consolidation and multimedia ownership, which should improve overall cost efficiencies for both supplier and advertiser.

However, changes in media corporations offer different opportunities for securing vehicles to carry brand messages. Cash-strapped television networks are open to advertiser-developed programming ideas again. Programmers and publishers will look for partners to share the rapidly escalating costs of entertainment and information production. Integrated communications planning directs advertisers to approach the source of their interest, such as the Olympics or the NFL, instead of negotiating in pieces with the networks for television rights and the League office for promotions. Evaluating the portfolio of options offered by a company becomes more of a tie-breaker in negotiations than CPMs or audience guarantees.

How media will be bought in the coming years and decades will evolve. It is safe to say that it will be based more on transactions than total audience; that investments will have a better grounding in measured effectiveness than they do today; and that all types of partnerships and alliances will develop to find the competitive edge in the media world of tomorrow.

How Do We Get Ready for the Future?

This gaze in the crystal ball suggests that there are a lot of uncertainties lurking in the media environment of the future. How technology, the government, the economy, and the interest of the consumer will play out remains to be seen. However, there are several action steps that seem a certainty, if media planners are to be ready for the future.

Embrace Change and Learn Quickly

Media planners need to embrace change and quickly !earn new media tools, those mentioned in this chapter and those to come. Structures and organizations must adapt so that we can capitalize on new opportunities to deliver relevant messages to consumers with whom we strive to establish ongoing relationships with our advertisers' brands. Marketers must recognize media planners as essential participants in the communications planning process.

Encourage Media Experimentation

We will learn by doing. Media professionals must not be afraid of "smart failures," as long as they learn from them. Early learning in many of the options mentioned in this chapter will avoid higher out-of-pocket cost risks later on. In addition, experimenting with options will serve to simplify our vision of our role and responsibilities. We need to encourage our clients, our agencies, and our media suppliers to develop options that don't exist yet, so that we can meet the future halfway.

Talk to Everyone

This brief discussion of media futures illustrates that new ideas and successes can come from anywhere. Media planners should initiate contact and dialog with prospective new media partners outside traditional business boundaries. Operating on the principle that anything can be media will keep all options open.

Develop New Measurement Techniques

We're a fair way away from having perfect measurement of the effectiveness of every brand contact. However, there is room for the current traditional system of vehicle audience measurement to blend and evolve with the different measurement scales of the direct marketer. In order to make sense of many of these options, we need to articulate our research needs. Media professionals should be working toward a structure that facilitates communication among media and marketing researchers to make best use of all research efforts.

Final Thoughts

Today's media planner continues the task of finding the best media vehicles to deliver brand messages to consumers at the right time, in the right places, and with the best cost/value relationship. Up until now, in many cases, the less than perfect targeting ability of mass audience vehicles has made reach, frequency, and cost-per-thousand audience the evaluation criteria of the day. Media planners have been a last stop on the marketing communications flow chart.

The future, from a technological standpoint, says that anything is possible. A look at media availabilities from a consumer standpoint says that everything is media. Media professionals who are successful in the future will be those who do not become tangled up in the intricacies of fiber optics or turf wars as to who does what. Rather, the successful media planner will be the person who continues to think about communicating brand messages to individuals in a variety of places in order to build enduring relationships.

The New Media Company

What Magazine Companies Need to Offer Direct Marketers

Hershel Sarbin, William Duch, & Toni Apgar

Hershel Sarbin is President and CEO of Cowles Business Media.

Bill Duch is Senior Vice President of Cowles Media Services & Consulting and Executive Director of the National Center for Database Marketing.

Toni Apgar is Editorial Director of *Direct: The Magazine of Direct Marketing Management.*

Magazine companies must redefine themselves in a way that frees them to look at a much broader range of opportunities than the old model of publishing. In the 20 years leading up to about 1990, the magazine business was fed on ad revenue and circulation revenue. Certainly there were some companies that understood they had great asset value in their quality editorial products and in a quality subscriber list that could be used to generate profit. Those companies looked on themselves as having a family of opportunities, rather than thinking of everything other than ad revenue or subscription revenue as "ancillary." Thus, companies that were able to develop conferences with strong exhibitor revenue, directories, newsletters, books, records, or other revenue streams by trading on the reputations they created with their core product were not as vulnerable as we entered the '90s. They are truly positioned for the decades ahead. To them, it is automatic to be media-neutral. Media-neutral is a mindset that encourages development of strong magazine franchises into much broader information service companies. It means you're neutral on what form the medium takes: It could be a magazine, a newspaper, a fax service, a newsletter, a trade or consumer conference, and so on. The culture of a media-neutral company allows, indeed *commands,* that a product or revenue stream not be thought of as ancillary, but as part of the whole.

Bill Ziff heads up one of those media companies, and he has often mentioned media neutrality as a vital concept for strategic planning at Ziff Communications. Back in September 1991, he outlined an excellent plan for any company to move into the next decade and beyond in an article in *FOLIO* magazine:

> We want to offer a whole portfolio of media services rather than try to sell something we happen to own. . . . It's not okay to have a self-interested, ignorant bias toward a medium simply because you have it to offer. We want to deliver to our customers not only information but also opportunities to connect vendor and customer in whatever media form best serves. ("Ziff and the Art of Magazine Maintenance," *Folio* 20 [September 1991], p. 66.)

For those companies over the past five-plus years that refused to think "ancillary" and thought instead of a family of opportunities, their timing was perfect. We were just entering a time during which advertising revenue was eroding and the value of advertising was being challenged. Subscription and newsstand revenues were dropping, too, and building a subscription base itself was more costly and difficult than it had ever been. Conventional wisdom was not good enough, and conventional magazine economics did not work.

By and large, the magazine industry ignored some extraordinary, successful models during the recent past, like the *Reader's Digest.* Take their foray into condensed books. They did not keep secret the significance of condensed books, although maybe it wasn't known how many condensed book readers there were. Creating that revenue stream was simple. They found out that one of the most popular features in the magazine was the book condensation at the back of the magazine, and some smart person said, "Maybe we ought to do a longer condensation of the book and actually put it into book form. And maybe we'll put in two or three of these condensations, bind it, and see if we can sell it." It wasn't earth-shattering. But it ended up 20 years later accounting for the majority of the worldwide revenues and profits of the *Reader's Digest* company.

The other model that was ignored was the relative ease with which *Reader's Digest* entered the European market. All they did was take magazine condensations and translate them into other languages. They also put a staff of magazine people together in those countries and started publishing the same magazine internationally. Condensed books followed a few years later, along with original magazine articles of local interest.

On Being Competitive in the New Era

The companies that structured their businesses to seek opportunities for major profit centers, and not just adding ancillary revenues, are positioned today to take advantage of new technology in a way that others may not be. They've had a head start, because they are organized to think in the right way. Marketing databases permit you to access very detailed information about your customer, to profile your customer, and to track your customer. Those who know how to do this are way ahead of the game. All they need to do is apply current technology to the basics of their business. This is important because it is going to take an enormous effort for companies that have not thought that way to get up to speed and to put in place the kinds of people and systems that will make them competitive in the new era.

Delivering quality editorial and quality service is, of course, a critical ingredient of competitiveness. The traditional vocabulary of "we deliver news and information" or "we deliver customers to advertisers" represents a barrier to action within a company that wishes to seize the new opportunities and recognizes the enormity of the change that is taking place. Building brand equity and building long-term value of the customer base is the winning combination in today's competitive environment.

A better way to think of media neutrality is, "I deliver information to people who will pay for it, and I want the capacity to deliver it through varied media channels." To fail to see it in such a light is a guarantee that you will not succeed.

Advertising—Down But Not Out

In order to entice readers, publishers have devalued their product. We devalue our brand by offering readers clock radios and answering machines and three free issues. When we do that we don't really bring in a very good subscriber. You can't renew these people, but publishers keep doing it because of the pink sheet—the magazine publisher's statement on average paid circulation. The pink sheet supports the advertising establishment's outdated rules. Most advertisers are still looking for tonnage, not quality of the circulation. Most of them believe that the more people that see their message, the better off they'll be.

All of this aside, advertising revenues will remain the core revenue for most magazine companies. It creates the capital needed to do the other things that you want to do. All these new things take investment. What you want is not to be as dependent on advertisers as we once were and also to be exploiting the other opportunities we have that really go beyond advertising and create a larger pool of dollars—a kind of diversification within the media company.

If a media company becomes too dependent on its advertising revenue, then it isn't exploiting its other assets. It was Ziff who said, "A media company's most valuable assets are off its balance sheet: Its employees, its active name pool and its ability and reputation to create satisfied customers." None of those three things is directly related to advertising.

Look at it this way. Take a fresh look at your corporate folder. Look at *all* of your assets. Here you have this wonderful editorial product that goes to a quality audience and delivers ad revenue. But you know you have a problem in terms of eroding advertising revenue or an inability to count on advertising revenue to sustain growth at this time, or even circulation revenues to sustain growth. Then the question becomes: What do you have within your company that you have not yet recognized as assets? It's very simple: Quality products attract quality readers and quality readers attract advertisers. Once that is established, the question becomes: Now what else can we do?

The Next Step

As you become more media-neutral and find that you can derive significant revenue for a new product or service, the next logical step is to ask: Can you incorporate advertising as a component of the new service? Can you deliver your product through some online medium like Dialog or Prodigy, and how do you tie in the advertiser?

The fact is, maybe you can and maybe you can't. You won't know for sure until you've developed the new product. By having alternatives, you have other opportunities to develop. When companies adopt media neutrality as their game plan and start offering different products, advertisers won't necessarily ride along. The point is to develop what the market wants, not just what advertisers want.

Never forget two things. First, keep your eye on the quality of the core product and the advertising that you can sell in the core product. Second, remember that other opportunities that emerge from these assets may be just as rewarding as the core opportunities. And if companies don't think of them in that neutral sense, then they may not develop the newsletter, or the directories, or the conference, or the electronic products that the market needs.

Fighting City Hall

Media neutrality is not easy. You'll be fighting city hall. As you want to develop a newsletter or some other property, your ad sales director will say, "Hey, why not spend the money on another sales rep? That way I can guarantee you more revenue. Pour the money into the core product."

But you must go out and *do it.* Invest some money in the testing process to find out if in fact you have something. Then estimate the profitability of it. Everybody faces the challenge of alternative places to put their investments. You should go for the highest return over the long term. Both projects may have up-sides and down-sides. The up-side on advertising is that you may have a product that if you just throw more people at it, you will sell more advertising. The down-side is that we all know that lots of advertisers are putting more money into promotion than ever and that the trend is downhill. The up-side of developing new products is they have much higher margins than the magazine ever will. The down-side is investing in media channels customers don't want.

Easy, It Isn't

This is not a no-brainer. The only place where the analogy of a magazine and its relationship to an advertiser is obvious is in conferences. A conference delivers the information and the trade show delivers the advertising, very similar to the magazine model. What we as an industry have to do is find ways to do that in other media, which may not be so clear.

Take the seminar companies. If they didn't sell books, videotapes, and cassettes from a table in the back of the room, even the biggest and best might not be in business today. There is an advertising message in the seminar, and it usually comes just before the lunch break. The seminar leader says, "We are talking about this subject and I can't cover everything. So l want to draw your attention to some very carefully selected products that I have chosen for you to look at and to make available to you that enhance all the things I am talking about." It's not unusual for the revenues from the sales of the product to equal the revenue generated from enrollments at the seminars.

Redefining Media Companies

We in media cannot just think about what our traditional competitors do. We are forced to think about how other people in the same broad marketplace are redefining themselves and taking the kind of action that could affect us, in some cases adversely. The only way to get really focused on your business is to think broadly.

The evidence that all of this is true is the number of strategic alliances that media companies are putting together. Companies that are totally unrelated to each other are forming alliances to create new products. They're going into the marketplace with a unique selling proposition to a customer who either they couldn't have counted or haven't counted on their list recently. In a way, a magazine and its advertisers were the first strategic alliance. The magazine says, "I'm lending you my audience and you are giving me money. But it only pays to speak to my audience with a product that is consistent with what my audience is seeking. You need to pay me X dollars for that, because my audience is valuable to you."

Some advertisers are going it alone. Take the case of a doll manufacturer. In addition to creating commemorative dolls, it decided to produce a magazine for that audience. It's an audience that is easily defined and enumerated, so there was no trick to assembling the audience, or knowing what their interest was.

There are nontraditional ways for advertisers to communicate and to build their brands and market share. And to that end, some media companies are helping them do it, like the *New York Times* magazines, Meredith, and Times Mirror. Both trade and consumer publishers have created custom magazine operations as a significant revenue stream.

No Cookie-Cutter Solutions

Not every magazine or magazine company is in a position, on its own, or with its present resources, to develop these kinds of opportunities. Not every pool of customers is large enough to build other product lines, to do newsletters or books. Not every marketplace lends itself to new conferences or new trade shows. In some cases, the traditional way of doing things will have to do. If, however, you are a niche publisher, you should be searching for alliances with other companies that will allow both of you to collectively leverage the franchise.

The Database Is Key

All of this expansion is only possible if you have a database and know how to use it. The database is a media company's transportation to media neutrality. You know who your readers are, you know who your customers are. You know who some of your ex-customers are, and sometimes you're able to enumerate every last one of your prospects, as well. It's not possible in every consumer case, of course, but in some cases, where you're looking for lawyers, CPAs, doctors, and so on, you can actually get the names and other data for every single one.

Take your customers first. You have their names and addresses, and you know what they subscribe to. You know how long they've subscribed, and, in the case of consumers, you know their "demographic topology," because you know where they live, and you can make inferences about them from that. In the business-to-business environment, you might know, or you can generate, some information on their title and function. Then you can survey these readers and find out what other kinds of things they might be interested in. Granted, if you ask busy business people if they want another book to read or another seminar to attend, they'll probably say no. You have to come up with a compelling product so that people say, "Oh, l have to have this."

Ask your customers: "Here's a list of seminar topics that we're considering producing. Tell us, for each one of these, if you would attend, have some interest, or would not attend." There is a huge amount of data-gathering you can do once you know who your customers are and whether they are good customers or average customers or poor customers. Any company wants to focus on its best customers first, because they're the ones who are going to buy most of your new products via your new media.

Your customer database is your key to getting your advertisers interested in something besides the printed page. You can repackage your consumers in a way that fits the needs of the advertiser, or in a vehicle that fits better. If one of your advertisers wants to reach children with a new product introduction, you can identify your customers who have children at home. Then you can package a special insert or ride-along with the magazine, or even come up with a custom, one-shot magazine sponsored entirely by the advertiser. The point is: Figure out what you can offer your advertiser based on what you know about your readers.

Other Media

We started this chapter talking about exploring other media, such as books, maybe CD-ROM, and so on. To know if your customers are interested, all you have to do is ask. Do you have a VCR? a PC? a Mac? a CD-ROM player? Would you like every recipe we ever published on a CD-ROM? Would you like it on Prodigy, CompuServe or America Online? Are you interested in learning more about fitness or vacations via the computer?

Say you get some interesting answers to those questions. Ask yourself if you should go to your advertisers and make them your partners. Maybe your advertiser has thousands of recipes sitting in a shoe box somewhere that uses its products. Partner with the advertiser.

What the advertiser will be interested in is *target markets*. Do you have target markets no one else has? Information the advertiser wants? You have names of people who are interested in your advertisers' products, and that is extremely valuable to them. Is there some kind of directory or bibliography or historical data you have that your advertiser needs? By the way, worry about price later. Don't let those kinds of obstacles mar your vertical thinking.

The Year 2000

Database sophistication is resident in only a very small number of media companies right now. But there are a lot of companies that are deciding that they need a database and need to know how to use it and market it. You don't have to have a database to get on with this broader thinking, but the transportation is easier if you do. A circulation fulfillment file is a rudimentary database and can provide a certain amount of transportation to the new media.

Media companies are incredibly well positioned for the future. They are better positioned than packaged goods companies or car manufacturers, because they communicate constantly with the end user. Buick spends a lot of money wondering how and when to communicate with its customers and its prospects. Media companies do that automatically. *That's what we do.*

By the year 2000, everybody will have a database. The question is, what will they be doing with it? If they are going to make money with that database, they better have something to sell other than their magazine.

PART III

Messages for All Media

▼
10

Looking Back
Is Looking Ahead

Every Syllable Counts
in Making Creative
Messages Stand Out

Herschell Gordon Lewis

Herschell Gordon Lewis heads Communicomp, a Plantation, Florida, direct marketing creative source. He is a direct response writer and consultant, with clients throughout the world. With Ian Kennedy and Jerry Reitman, Lewis is producer of the recently issued "100 Greatest Direct Response Television Commercials."

The communicator of the 21st century would do well to look back, not just to the 1990s, but to a golden time before the era of instant communication, one in which direct marketers gave greater homage to the craft of communication than to mechanical tricks.

Omens for the 21st century aren't universally favorable. We show no signs of emerging from public cynicism generated by advertisers' corruption of the Golden Rule: "Do unto others before they do unto you." The 1980s gave us a decade of sharpshooting, led by collectibles and health-related products and, yes, fund-raising. Claims were based on speculation as much as fact; and some marketers got rich, which spread the infection of cynicism from the patients to the doctors.

Next came the 1990s, and during this decade we see the thin line dividing puffery from fact shimmering into nothingness. Catalogs advertise "the best nose-hair trimmer"; television infomercials tell viewers (how many naive ones can be left?) they'll get rich by buying and selling houses or by borrowing money and not paying it back.

Will our legacy for the next generation be consumer disenchantment and mistrust? Could be. Our targets just don't believe us. That's as ghastly a legacy as the national debt.

Have you noticed how many practitioners of the 1990s still blithely and blindly hoist two deadlier caution-flags?

1. Greater attention to form than to substance, to production than to message, to winning art directors' awards than to getting the phone to ring

2. Apathy toward the direct response copywriter's most significant and most powerful competitive edge: *information optimizing*

Those marketers have a philosophy more allied to P.T. Barnum than to John Caples. They're like cars running without oil, burning out and in constant need of engine replacement. They don't know what we know or have the weapons we so carefully hone—well-oiled weapons of word use rather than deception.

The Crucial Difference

Understand, please, the difference between information optimizing and information distortion. The copywriter who distorts (and that's a euphemism for "falsifies") information is lying; the copywriter who optimizes is a true *force communicator:* He or she generates a receptive reader/viewer/listener attitude without changing the facts.

Will the copywriter of the years 2000 and beyond know or care about little copywriting tweakings? Will they yawn and ignore the logic of "Save as much as $200" being light-years more powerful than "Save up to $200"? Will they know *why* "Buy one, get one free" consistently outpulls "Two for the price of one"?

Those who do know and care will be masters of the communications universe, because the laws of economics (if no other factor) have to overcome ego sooner or later. By the second decade of the 21st century, record-keeping will unmask the phony rationale behind so many "creative" awards. Our time will come!

The Difference between "Journeyman" and "Wordsmith"

I have no quarrel with writers who simply regurgitate facts into their word-processors. They're journeymen . . . they do no damage. . . belatedly, they parrot innovations (usually when those innovations are burning out) . . . and like so many stolid laborers, they earn an honest living.

No, I have no quarrel with them; I simply hope they're my competitors. The writer who doesn't recognize the difference between "when" and "if" will use those words interchangeably; and those of us who *do* recognize the difference pounce, destroying the pretender.

In the 21st century, our victories will be better-noted because record-keeping will be automated. So assuming somebody is testing direct response packages written by the two of us, and you use "if" and I use "when," and mine pulls .01% better, the profundity of the difference between journeyman writer and wordsmith will be far clearer than it is in the waning decade of the 20th century.

Just in case you're reading this and asking, "If *when* and *if* aren't interchangeable, what *is* that blasted difference?": Use *when* when you want to suggest something will happen; use *if* when you want to suggest something won't happen.

So if I'm selling you insurance, I'd never write, "If you have a claim . . . "; I'd write, "When you have a claim . . . ," because I want you to believe you *will* have a claim.

Selling you some equipment, I'd never write, "When something goes wrong . . . "; I'd write, "If something ever goes wrong . . . ," because I want you to believe it's unlikely anything will go wrong. (I threw in *ever* for the same reason writers embellish *leather:* It's *genuine leather,* not just *leather.*)

Am I suggesting the writer scrutinize every word for potential increase or reduction of impact? You bet I am! That's what professional wordsmiths do. Correction: That's what professional wordsmiths *are supposed* to do.

Punctuation: Copywriter's Friend or Foe

A quick self-explanatory thought:

Can you believe how much emphasis punctuation adds? Or, if you prefer, removes?

Take a look at that sentence. Then re-cast it, changing only the punctuation:

- Can you believe how much emphasis punctuation adds . . . or, if you prefer, removes?

- Can you believe how much emphasis punctuation adds—or, if you prefer, removes?

- Can you believe how much emphasis punctuation adds? (Or, if you prefer, removes?)

Same words. Different types of impact. Even this simple example indicates the power lying in wait at the copywriter's fingertips. And, believe me, this is the copywriter's decision. The creative team can blame the boss or the client for vetoing a creative concept; they seldom can level that charge about punctuation.

Five quick rules:

1. Forget asterisks. Your reader automatically thinks an asterisk will lead to an *exception* to your promise.

2. Use parentheses to downplay a thought.

3. For the first use of a term some of your readers may not recognize, use quotation marks so the reader won't think you're showing off how much you know and he or she doesn't.

4. Use a dash for a strong break and an ellipsis (three dots) for a soft break.

5. A colon draws hard attention to what follows, which should be an explanation or expansion of what you just said.

I, for one, am terrified of the next generation of writers. Why? Because from samples I've seen, so many have such modest command over spelling and grammar. They expect salvation from their word-processor's spelling-checker—not as we do, to be sure our fingers haven't slipped onto the wrong key, but because they've never learned how to spell. Punctuation? Ugh: Sentences joined by commas; no idea whatever of how or when to use colons and semicolons; periods after partial sentences; dependence on two or three exclamation points instead of salesworthy ideas. They come into the arena needing editors, and their editors have the same deficiencies.

Is this a plea for literacy as a requirement for a job in communications? You bet it is!

Look at All the Help We're Going to Have!

With all these problems, will the 21st-century chore of cleaning up loose communication be impossible? Nope. It'll be easier and easier, paralleling the ease with which people who never learned how to multiply or divide can beat the best pencil-and-paper experts by using their pocket calculators. By the year 2020, electronics will cover almost every creative deficiency—a mixed blessing, with overdependence leading to sameness.

If anybody (notice, please: for additional impact I'm using *somebody* and *anybody* instead of the more genteel *someone* and *anyone*) had told a writer of the 1970s that soon he or she would have spelling- and grammar-checkers and a thesaurus built into the keyboard, such a prophet of what we now accept as commonplace would have been regarded as a dreamer. As the 21st century dawns, we already are seeing primitive versions of force communication programs.

The 21st-century communicator will, before starting a message, key in the psycho-demographics of the individuals he or she wants to influence, plus information about what's being offered. Wrong word choices? A red flag goes up: "Don't use that terminology to that target."

So the creative team and the slide-rule team will, at last, live in non-adversarial harmony. The database will dictate the message "thrust"; creativity (we hope) will make the message palatable.

In the pre-electronic age, the neighborhood grocer knew, as he spotted his customer entering the store, that she wanted center-cut lambchops . . . she shelled her own peas and wouldn't consider canned peas . . . she regarded "table wine" as a lower-class insult . . . she wanted her bread unsliced. The grocer's memory was, in every facet except electronics, a database. Not just his creative salesmanship but his competitive survival was based on an implicit brain-powered database.

In the post–World War II period, supermarkets replaced the friendly neighborhood grocer, joining manufacturers and distributors at a distance from the ultimate buyer. A self-serve society recognized the check-out cashier as the only contact with the store, and that cashier was nameless and faceless. The gulf between seller and buyer rested on the tenuous bridge of universal product codes.

Missing from the marketing mix, *except for direct marketing:* rapport.

For conventional marketers, expensive focus groups and multiple analyses have become (undependable) latter-day techniques for predicting consumer behavior. Will this sell? If so, to whom? And are we in a competitive marketing position?

A Look Back Becomes a Look Ahead

Thus we look backward in order to go forward. Marketing has come full circle. The difference between all the terminology and obfuscation of computerized dissection and the old-fashioned "Good morning, Mrs. Jones" of the neighborhood grocer is one of methodology and quantity, not intent or accuracy.

The direct marketer, in the 21st century, will enjoy the best of all possible worlds: the happy combination of *rapport,* which only a one-on-one message can generate . . . and *targeting,* which increasingly accurate and useful databases will provide.

Golden times? That depends on three bases:

1. *Professionalism:* The result of literacy resulting from the fusing of formal education, an ongoing study of motivators, and personal writing discipline

2. *Market awareness:* The result of saturating one's senses with information, reading publications and watching television programs aimed far outside the writer's own sphere of interest, wandering the shopping malls, and avoiding the isolation so many "creatives" seem to prefer

3. *Salesmanship:* A too-rare trait among writers and artists who regard "selling" as a nasty word

I'm not worried about 21st-century writers having those three traits every neighborhood grocer had half a century ago. If they don't, their companies will fold soon enough.

Is There a Future for Direct Mail?

Problems and Prognosis

Alan Rosenspan

Alan Rosenspan and his teams have won over 100 international, national, and regional awards for advertising results, including 18 DMA Echo Awards, a Gold "Effie," and several Best of Show Awards from NEDMA. He is an instructor at Bentley College and the Boston Ad Club; the author of the chapter "Psychological Appeals" in the 1991 edition of the *Direct Marketing Handbook* (McGraw-Hill); and the creator of the "Direct Marketing Shoestring Awards." Rosenspan is a Creative Director of Bronner, Slosberg, Humphrey, Inc. in Boston.

In the early 1990s, I caused a bit of a stir by proclaiming that Direct Mail will wither and perish by 1999. It wasn't a difficult conclusion to reach.

Direct mail is under so much pressure, from so many different directions. From consumer privacy advocates, to government regulatory issues, to environmental concerns, it seems you can't find anyone who *isn't* against direct mail. Even mighty Sears got out in 1992.

But I've also tried to see the other side, to look at all the positive factors that favor direct mail and try to foresee all the ways in which it might survive, and even prosper, in the coming decades. Not surprisingly, the first place to look is here and now. We can ask ourselves, what are the changes that are happening in direct mail right now, an how will they be shaped in the years and decades to come? I'll address five major areas of change, some of which we are already seeing, and I'll offer my own prediction.

The End of Database Marketing?

You don't need a crystal ball to see that privacy issues are shaking the very underpinnings of our industry. It is more than a little ironic that, as we've become more adept at targeting appropriate prospects for our direct mail, people are becoming more sensitive to this issue. And they will become even more attuned to it in the years to come.

Eric Larson, in his recent book *The Naked Consumer,* writes about the innovative ways direct marketers obtain and use information about consumers. But what is most interesting about it is his point of view and his choice of language. He speaks of people betraying facts about themselves, which marketers can then capitalize on. Not volunteering, not revealing, but betraying. And other experts have pointed out that there is more consumer resistance to direct mail than ever before. That may be why so many direct marketers report ever-decreasing response rates.

So where is this going to lead us? In all the excitement about database marketing, it is easy to forget that it is a relatively new and even fragile idea. In fact, Bob Stone never even *mentioned* it in the first edition of his 1975 book *Successful Direct Marketing Methods,* which was considered the bible of direct marketing.

It was the advent of the computer that made it possible to look at consumers as individuals, rather than groups or even clusters. That was a great leap forward, but perhaps it's time to take a step back. Perhaps we'll discover that database marketing is an idea whose time has come and gone.

People increasingly feel that direct marketers know "more than we have a right to" about their life-styles, income, credit history, personal hobbies, and interests. And in the late 1980s, we saw a number of products fail because of this.

Lotus Marketplace was one of them. This was a CD-ROM disk that contained 80 million U.S. household records, including marital status, gender, and average neighborhood income. On the surface, it was an excellent marketing tool. Lotus received over 35,000 protest calls and letters within the first three months of the launch. The product was hastily dropped from the Lotus line.

And if you think your fellow Americans are concerned about protecting their privacy, you need only look to Europe. You won't like what you see. A number of measures have been introduced by the Commission of European Communities that are due to be ratified soon. They address the issue of what they've called "informed consent," and there are two interesting articles. Article 8 states that the private sector (that's us) can collect and process data *only with the consent of the data subject,* unless a contractual relationship exists between both parties. This would require a company to notify everyone on their list whenever they sell or rent that list and get everyone's consent. In other words, they'll have to send out mail to get permission to send out mail. Article 24 states that "the transfer of personal data may take place only if a country ensures an adequate level of protection." When governments concern themselves with protecting consumers from direct mail, we have to be a little concerned.

And so the question you may be asking is, can it happen here? Of course not! We'd never let that happen. To which I can only ask, "What do you mean *we?*" Who will stand up for direct mail? Do you know anyone, outside our business, who is in favor of it? Can you imagine any politician coming out in favor of direct mail? Can you imagine the public demanding it? When you think about it, direct mail can be compared with plea-bargaining. People are unhappy with both, but they generally tolerate it. There's one major difference; only one of them is a necessary evil.

But before we declare that database marketing is dead, it is important to note that one of the most dramatic and effective database marketing programs was introduced and has grown dramatically during the last few years.

We Know Who Your Friends Are

Now, you may consider frequent flyer programs to be a good example of database marketing, but there's an even better example. The airlines may know where I travel, the hotel chains may know where I stay, but nobody knows who I talk to. Unless I'm on the MCI Friends & Family plan.

The way it works is that MCI will give you a 20% discount when you call someone else who *also* has the Friends & Family Plan. And that person also saves money on calls to you. It sounds like a simple friend referral program, but it can have the ripple effect of a chain letter, with millions of interlocking "friends & family" circles. And every so often, you get a printout of what they call your MCI Friends & Family Tree. It includes people you call who don't have the plan; people who've dropped out of the plan; and any new people you may have called that month.

There's been some backlash, and their rival AT&T has gone to great pains to point them out. Many people are appalled at the idea of giving up lists of their friends and family to anyone, particularly a phone company. But, in a sense, it doesn't matter. MCI won't attract everyone. But they have attracted what I call the "players," people who are willing to take an extra step or give up additional information about themselves to gain a promised discount. How may "players" are there? Well, you may want to keep in mind that the coupon was once considered an unusual marketing device, certainly not something with any widespread appeal.

Database marketing is being used by MCI as a competitive weapon. But what happens when AT&T and Sprint start developing similar programs? What happens when the consumer gets two, three, or more direct mail pieces a month, each of them listing exactly to whom, when, and where long-distance calls were made? And what happens when the weapons get even more advanced? It took less than 10 years to go from "We know where you live" to "We know who your family and friends are." How long will it take to go to "We know what you think"?

Privacy concerns aren't the only reason that database marketing may become an endangered species. It is the very success of database marketing that may ultimately lead to its downfall. At some point, it will theoretically be possible to know everything there is to know about everybody.

Mike Slosberg, Executive Creative Director of Bronner, Slosberg, Humphrey, has an interesting way of looking at database marketing. He says that early efforts were focused on finding the right people, almost as if they were the little specks of gold in a prospector's pan. But now, it's all gold. It will soon be possible to buy or create lists on which virtually everyone is a legitimate prospect for your product or service.

This may represent a shift in the fundamental equations of direct mail. It used to be that the list was many times more important then the creative, or even the offer. But soon, what you say and how you say it might be the most important competitive weapon at your disposal. And that is why we will see the following developments: a return to creativity, mail as the relationship medium, and cooperative mailings.

A Return to Creativity

This is the second big trend that I think will affect direct mail in the next century. In fact, I believe it will be the single deciding factor on whether or not direct mail has any future whatsoever. Even a quick glance at the other chapters of this book reveals that other media will make major strides in the next decade. Interactive television, virtual reality, and on-line shopping are all available or being tested right now.

Advertisers have never had so many ways to "reach out and touch" customers, and, more importantly, the reverse is also true. The customer can now reach out and touch us at will, almost anywhere and any time they wish. This isn't just a question of ubiquitous access, this is pure economics. Direct mail is getting so expensive that online communications may very well wipe it out altogether.

It is an absolute fact that these new technologies will drive down the cost of reaching customers and prospects, accepting orders, processing them, and fulfilling them. And let me point out that one of the original intentions for interactive technology was to allow processing of more orders per second than could be handled with ordinary fulfillment systems. Today, interactive technologies can handle 600,000 transactions per second. That may not seem very useful, because it would only take about two and a half minutes for every household in America to respond. But that's not the point.

The advantage is that they can capture everybody who responds in the same two or three seconds. Nobody will postpone their decision or change their mind. It will all happen too fast.

So what will happen to poor little direct mail? Well, the direct mail medium will still have a number of important advantages that transcend even the most advanced interactive media.

Take "virtual reality." As I understand it, virtual reality will attempt to create an experience—such as shopping—by making it seem like you are actually doing it. It is all based on sensory input. In a sense, it is like fooling your eyes and ears (and perhaps even your nose) to perceive something that just isn't there.

But direct mail is "real reality." Consider this: direct mail is almost like sending a sample of your company to a potential customer. How it looks, how it feels, its very presence, all communicate a certain image in a tangible and involving way. In fact, it may be the only part of your company that people will ever hold in their hands.

Direct mail has another important advantage over interactive media, and that can best be illustrated by the following example. Picture yourself in Paris. It's a bright spring morning, and you are walking down the streets, listening to the happy people sitting in sidewalk cafes. Now imagine you are passing a bakery. The smells of the fresh-baked bread and pastries surround you . . . got the picture? Chances are that your picture of Paris is very different from my picture of Paris. We've each brought our own memories, impressions, perceptions, and imagination to bear.

Direct mail can encourage you to paint images in your head that are more vivid than any photograph or anything you can see on a television or computer screen. What's more, the images are unique to us and are therefore as personal (rather than simply personalized) as possible. But there's another benefit working here. By allowing the prospect to "complete the picture," rather than presenting the entire picture to them, you involve them in a very powerful way. You can make them think. You can even make them feel.

Thus, direct mail is still an active medium, rather than the primarily passive one of simply watching or pressing a few buttons. It is the ultimate "involvement device." So let's get back to creativity.

The times of greatest struggle for the human race have produced dazzling bursts of creativity. For direct mail to survive in the future, it must regain the creative momentum it seems to have lost. As I see it, the first problem with most direct mail is that it fails to recognize the pervasive power of the medium.

The "Miracle" of Direct Mail

Do we take direct mail for granted? Absolutely, and that's why it is important to step back and examine it from a recipient's point of view. It will improve our vision.

Direct mail allows you to send something to someone. (Just like sending flowers or candy.) It can be a gift. It can be an invitation. It can be almost anything you can imagine. And it can come from thousands of miles away.

It gets delivered to their homes, or the place in which they work. They don't have to do a thing. It just arrives there. And although you may not believe in Santa Claus, direct mail arrives just like Christmas presents, except it happens almost every morning of the year. And unlike Christmas presents, direct mail doesn't have to wait to be opened.

It is personal, just for them. In fact, it even has their name on it. It will probably include the only form of advertising copy they'll ever read that will begin with "Dear."

It's relevant, provided it's done right. Unlike television. Why should I have to sit through dozens of beer commercials if I don't drink? But nobody ever talks about "junk TV."

And unlike other advertising, which may be too coy or clever, direct mail copy is usually sincere and simple. They don't have to worry about not getting the joke, or missing the point.

Direct mail is also under their control. (After all, it's literally in their hands.) Miss that 30-second commercial? Better hope it runs again. What did the announcer say? I'm not sure. Direct mail can be read and re-read. It can be shared with another person. It can be filed away for future reference. It can include everything the recipient will ever need to ask about a product or service.

And unlike online or even interactive media, people can access it wherever and whenever they want and easily skip to the parts they are most interested in.

By now, you are either misty-eyed about direct mail, or you're asking "Is this guy kidding?" I assure you that I am absolutely serious. It is only because we have forgotten the power of direct mail and regard it as "just another way of reaching people" that we have ignored its immense potential. And as other media become even faster, cheaper, and more exciting, direct mail must return to its strengths in order to survive.

Consider this: In an age of instantaneous telephone contact, fax, and e-mail, why do people still write letters? Why do people still need to "see it in writing"? Why are people still surprised and delighted when they receive a surprise package in the mail? These are fundamental human characteristics that will not change, even in the next century. And so the real question becomes: what are we doing right now to take advantage of them?

There is a phenomenon in retailing that goes like this: a store can be either high-tech or high-touch. It can seldom succeed in being both. High-tech stores are superstores. They're huge warehouses full of almost every kind of merchandise, but with a limited selection of brands. They're low priced, but there are no sales representatives to assist you in making your selections. They deal in volume, volume, volume. High-touch stores are usually much smaller. They have a deeper selection of products within a sharply defined area (for example, gourmet foods). They are higher priced, but they have very knowledgeable salespeople. This store will do things like grind your coffee for you, give you crackers to snack on while you shop, and treat you more like a guest than a customer.

Now here's the comparison. For the most part, direct mail has become a high-tech business. We talk in cost per thousands. We mail in the millions, hoping to get at least 2% or 3% to respond. We look for the short-term response, rather than creating a customer over the long term. We also deal in volume, volume, volume.

To survive, I believe we must return to being a high-touch medium. We must become more targeted in our mailings. We must stop regarding everyone as a prospect. We must treat legitimate potential customers with dignity, intelligence, care, and even warmth. And we must go even further than that with existing customers. We must recognize that every time we are allowed in a person's home or their place of business, we are guests. And we have to act like guests. But that doesn't mean we have to be boring. In fact, we can't survive if we fail to capture the enthusiastic interest of our audience. And that's why, now and in the future, we will have to continually push ourselves to go (perhaps even literally) outside the envelope. And that means we need big ideas.

Let me give you an example. I've been a judge of several Echo Award competitions, and I have written the Echo Award show. In this capacity, I had access to many winning entries and a lot of the thinking and marketing background behind them. One recent one stands out in my mind. It came from a financial company that lends money to Fortune 500 companies. Its challenge was to reach senior executives who could say yes to a multimillion-dollar deal and who hadn't responded to letters, telephone calls, or sales calls.

So they sent out baseballs. The first one was autographed by Mickey Mantle. When you responded to that, you received another baseball, autographed by Stan Musial. Now here's the "catch." They also sent you an elegant display unit designed for three balls, and not just one or two. But the only way you could get that third ball, autographed by Willie Mays, was when you met their representative. Was that a big idea? Absolutely, in fact, it was a $120 million idea, because that's how much it created in new loans. It also passed a crucial test; it cut through the clutter. And that's the first hurdle that any direct mail package has to leap.

What about Clutter?

Clutter will be a much bigger problem in the future, but for a paradoxical reason: There's going to be less of it.

Why is that a problem? Think about your own mail for a moment. If you're like me, you probably separate your mail into an "A" pile and a "B" pile. The "A" pile represents mail that I have to open, such as bills, greeting cards, and personal letters. The "B" pile is advertising. And if I weren't in the business, I'm not sure if I'd open any of it.

But things have changed over the years. To begin with, many people have started paying their bills electronically. It's faster and more convenient than going through the mail. And that means they don't get as many bills delivered to their door. They also don't get as many personal letters. People tend to call more often than they write, and even with the vicissitudes of answering machines, they somehow manage to connect. So the good news is, we'll have a lot less clutter. But, unfortunately, that's the bad news.

Here's the problem. Once the non-advertising messages have been taken away from my daily pile of mail, *I don't have to look at any of the other mailings.* And, best of all, I don't even feel a bit guilty about it. Once the clutter goes away, direct mail stands naked at our door, without the illusion of being important to our lives. And we don't have to let it in.

Our challenge will be to turn direct mail into something that people look forward to receiving and enjoy when they do. But that's not as hard as you may think. Just as mass marketers sponsor television shows, direct marketers may have to "sponsor" something else of value to the consumer. It can be education. It can be relevant news. It can even be entertainment. But if we don't add value, there will be no reason for our existence.

There's one further aspect of creativity that we need to address. In the future, we will all have access to the same lists, the same media, the same printing, and the same production techniques. Creativity will become the only real point of difference between your direct mail and anyone else's.

Mail as the Relationship Medium

In an age of multimedia, can direct mail do it alone? Perhaps the future of direct mail may be influenced by how well it works in tandem with other media or even other events. It has long been proven that direct mail in conjunction with telemarketing can result in a huge lift in response. But that's about as far as it goes. What will be the new relationships between direct mail and electronic media?

One possible future for direct mail is as the "fulfillment medium." In other words, prospects can be reached and customers created through other, faster, more cost-effective ways. But once the "fish" is caught, it is direct mail that reels it in. If direct mail takes this more limited role, it is possible to imagine a day when the only direct mail you will receive will be at your request. And you may not receive it every day. This means that you will look forward to your direct mail. You asked for it, and now it's coming. The arrival of certain pieces may even be heralded like a new movie:

"Coming Soon. To a Post Office Near You. The Latest Catalog from L.L. Bean!"

I believe the role of direct mail will be much greater than that. I believe we have the opportunity to re-create it as the relationship medium, the main channel for all communications to existing customers. You see, there's a problem with interactive media. It can cut both ways. On one hand, it enables the consumer to access the marketer on demand. And that's good. On the other hand, it may also enable the marketer to access the consumer on demand. And that can be very dangerous.

Consider how telemarketing has evolved. When Joe Sugarman put the first 800 number in his advertisements in the *Wall Street Journal,* people said, "How convenient!" But what did most people say when the technology turned around on them and allowed telemarketers to call them? It is a paradox that most people want instant access to things, but they don't want others to have instant access to them. So interactive technology might not be the best place to build a relationship with your customers.

And there are even privacy issues. You can't talk on a public telephone these days without worrying that someone is copying down your calling card numbers. You can't talk on a mobile phone without worrying about security. It would be ironic, but perfectly appropriate, if direct mail became the only medium that respected your privacy.

Obviously, direct mail will have to evolve a great deal in order to become a medium that people trust. The reason is that we've been burned too many times. The only mail we receive from most of the companies we do business with are bills and solicitations. Or self-serving "announcements" that so-and-so has been promoted. And just as bad art drives out good art, bad direct mail makes it virtually impossible for good direct mail to get through. The medium is stronger than any one company that uses it. And that's why companies may soon have to stick together.

United We Stand

For a long time now, people have been talking about "strategic alliances" between two companies. And often it is very large companies: Disney and AT&T, Delta and Disney, Microsoft and IBM. There's going to be a lot more of it, and we're going to start seeing it affect direct mail.

How many companies will be able to afford maintaining their own database, doing their own lead generation, and absorbing all the costs of doing direct mail? But cooperative mailings have more advantages than just cost savings. Because the interests of individual companies are often served by helping other companies.

We see a lot of it in the software business, where large hardware vendors often co-promote and pay for mailings from software companies. So one thing that may begin to happen is that companies will pay even more to be part of a cooperative mailing then they'd pay for an individual mailing. The reason is that they want to capitalize on the image or brand equity of another company.

There are other strategic advantages, and they involve taking a customer focus. Many supermarkets have changed from a product orientation to a customer segment orientation. And their buyers had to develop a different point of view. Previously, their focus was to buy from manufacturers or distributors. Now their focus is to buy for a specific market segment, for example, the Hispanic family customer. And their main interest is to have all the brands and types of food preferred by their specific market segment. This concept of being customer- or prospect-focused can easily translate into direct mail. Let's imagine a company that "owns" the highly affluent, entrepreneurial, adult segment. Let's call them Riches 'R' Us. They have the best list, regularly updated and maintained. They are a known and acceptable medium to this market. (Meaning that the people on their list are happy to accept direct mail from them. People who "accept" direct mail? More about this later.) They work hard to ensure that they are always credible and relevant to the people on their list. And, by the way, they don't rent or sell or trade their list. In fact, that's why they are always credible and relevant.

Now what happens if you want to market to the segment that this company owns? You could develop your own list, but that would be expensive and time-consuming. You could reach these folks in other media, and there will be some exciting alternatives. But if you want to mail them something, an offer, an introduction to your company, or even a sample, you may find it faster and easier (and more cost-effective) to "partner" with Riches 'R' Us.

And that's only if they let you. Just as you jealously guard your corporate secrets and your most valuable company assets, so do they. And their main asset is credibility with their customers. By customers, I mean people who may have signed up for, or even been paid to be on, their lists. Another advantage of cooperative mailings is that they may create companies that are large enough to assume all the risks of direct mail. In fact, the "powerhouse aggregators" of the future may even be in a position to guarantee success.

Donnelley Marketing "owns" one of the most famous women in history. She's been a guest in over 16 billion homes over the course of the last 40 years. Her name is Carol Wright. The Carol Wright promotional program distributes billions of coupons every year. And it's done in a very smart and strategic way. Donnelley is able to customize the coupons that each house-hold receives, based on their database.

For example, I own a dog, and my neighbor does not. I enjoy oatmeal every morning, and my neighbor hardly ever buys it. What Donnelley can do is this: I'll get coupons for dog food, and my neighbor will not. But even more importantly, we'll both get coupons for oatmeal—except that his will be of a higher value, because he needs a bigger incentive to buy. Their thinking is that I'll probably buy oatmeal anyway. They may give me a higher value coupon if they want me to switch brands, but otherwise, they'll give me just enough to keep chugging along.

Carol Wright does more than just distribute coupons. She is known, liked, and trusted to provide product news and information. It is estimated that about 90% of Carol Wright envelopes are opened and that an average of 5% of the coupons inside are redeemed. So here's my question. If you had to decide whether to use Carol Wright and get your product or offer inside that envelope or try to get into as many millions of homes on your own, without Carol's blessings, which would you choose?

Paid to Be a Prospect

Did he say *paid to be a prospect?* Now that's a wild thought, but let's consider it. List brokers already charge more for some groups of customer names than others. And some lists are already "paid for" by controlled circulation magazines.

Let's take *DM News*, which I have always admired. The fact is that *DM News* pays me, and lots of other people, for the use of our names. The currency they use is excellent articles and news about things of interest to me. In return, I have agreed to be exposed to the advertisements they place, and I also accept (for the moment, but this may change) the direct mail from their advertisers and purchasers of their list.

It sounds like a good deal for everyone concerned, right? But suppose the value of my name and address and various demographic and psychographic factors goes up? For example, suppose I became the chair-man of a huge advertising conglomerate. My demographics will decidedly change. More importantly, I am now responsible for making far more decisions, and far more important and expensive decisions, about which companies we will do business with.

My vendors will recognize this by treating me very differently. They may "assign" me to someone higher up in their organization. They'll schedule appointments, rather than just drop by. Why? Because my time has sud-denly become more important. And so has my name on a list. An up-to-date mailing list of new presidents of large companies is more valuable to some people than a list of copywriters or even creative directors. And chances are that the money spent on each mailing to me will also increase. Let me give you an example.

The mailing was from a large company that was selling the most advanced and possibly one of the most expensive color copying machines in the world. They wanted to attract the attention of the presidents of leading advertising agencies. Presumably these people would be hard to impress, right? The copier company sent out enormous books filled with some of the world's most famous paintings (many were actual size), all of them beautifully reproduced using their copier. You can bet that direct mail package got the attention it deserved, and it won a well-deserved Gold Echo. But here's the kicker. They only sent out six of them.

Was this direct mail campaign expensive? It all depends on whether you look at it from an absolute cost point of view or as a return on investment. They spent a small fortune on each name on their list, but it was worth it, based on their results.

So what happens if people begin to wake up to the growing value of their names? Suppose I am a 39-year-old male who owns his own home and even a vacation home. I invest in stocks and real estate. I play golf and tennis and take lots of exotic vacations. Now Publishers Clearing House may not be interested in me. And I might not be worth a lot to the folks at Fingerhut. But how about Mercedes-Benz? What am I worth to them, particularly if there's a good chance I'll be in the market for a new luxury car? And how about Charles Schwab? Wouldn't it be worth a lot to get me to do my investing with them?

Now, I'm an investor, and I know the value of things. So starting tomorrow, I'm going to start selling my name and address. And perhaps even my good reputation, my credit history, and other information that you'd never know unless I told you. How much would that be worth to Mercedes-Benz, Charles Schwab, or any of the companies whose customer profile I fit?

While I am not predicting that people will start selling their names (or, at least, not soon), it is obvious that the inherent value of a name, which differs wildly from consumer to consumer, will become something that will require more attention. And the transactional equation that exists in lead generation, "What will you give me for filling in this coupon?", may become "What will you give me for allowing you to mail to my name?"

Two Final Factors

So far, we've dealt mainly with the internal pressures on direct mail. What should we be? How should we change? How can we add value? These introspective questions are important, but there are two other pivotal factors that will have a great influence on the future of direct mail.

The first, of course, is the environment. We've abused it big-time. And people are starting to notice. In fact, one of the first best-selling books of the 90s was entitled *50 Simple Things You Can Do to Save the Earth.* It was the ultimate self-help book. The first item on the list? Stop junk mail.

In 1990, a total of 63.7 billion pieces of unsolicited direct mail arrived in homes and offices throughout the country. (As much as 25% was never opened or read.) And the average adult receives 41 pounds of direct mail every year.

It's more than a little ironic that most environmental causes couldn't exist without the funds they raise through direct mail, but that's another subject. Yes, we use more recycled papers. Yes, we are starting to experiment with soy and even banana-based inks. Yes, there are exceptions. But direct mailers on the whole have been painfully neglectful of environmental issues. It all adds up to 150 million trees every year. Television, which was once called "the vast wasteland," has given way to the real wasteland created by direct mail.

Yet environmental issues can be turned around in our favor. For example, consider the Smith & Hawkins company. They are one of the large catalog companies who have taken a proactive stance on the environment. Their catalogs have nine guidelines for "socially responsible, environmentally sustainable mailings." They give customers a choice of which catalogs they wish to receive. They clean their list continually and offer a $5.00 gift certificate to customers who receive duplicates of any catalog. They also encourage their readers to keep their catalog as a reference book. In return, they've committed to keeping their products in stock for a longer period of time.

All that said, it seems like even the most conscientious direct marketers have taken a tack similar to the physicians' oath, "Above all, do no harm." But what can we do, if anything, to benefit the environment? Can we proactively start direct mail recycling centers and offer a bounty, like the people who make aluminum cans? Can we take the "junk" out of junk mail and perhaps suggest other uses of our packages? For example, as plant food or as part of a compost heap?

I recommend that we take our own initiatives, because another group exists that would like to decide for us. And that's the government. Government is the second major external factor that will have a great influence on direct mail. We've seen how government is dealing with direct mail in Europe. How far in the future do you think we will see a candidate whose campaign promise is to "Stop Junk Mail"? Somehow I can't envision a debate where another politician takes an opposing position.

Government, despite being a vast user of direct mail (the U.S. Congress sends out almost a billion pieces every year), has begun to look closely at direct mail. In 1990, George Bush signed the Deceptive Mailings Prevention Act. This banned mailings that masquerade as government notices. You may notice that it hasn't been rigorously enforced. But what will the Deceptive Mailings Prevention Act of 1995 ban? And how about the Consumer Privacy Act? When do you think that will be passed?

It is a fact that government could wipe out unsolicited mailings or even database marketing itself in a matter of weeks. Or they could begin taxing companies to receive it. Don Libey, the direct marketing futurist, sees a time when the government might charge you for your third-class direct mail in order to pay for its disposal and recycling. Now that's something most companies won't agree to. But it's happening right now. Motorola and General Motors are just two of the many companies that routinely screen and throw away promotional mailings. It's called "corporate dumping." How can we reach decision makers, when we can't even get out of the mailroom?

There's another issue as well. As Shakespeare wrote, "Those who the gods will destroy, they first make mad." In America, it can be updated to "they first make legally liable." What do I mean by that? Well, as far as I know, no company has been sued for failing to deliver on a stated benefit. But that may change.

When I work with clients, I am astonished that they apply much stricter standards for their direct mail than they do for advertising. "We can't say that," they say, and then I point out that they've already said it in their television commercials. "That's different. This is written communication. It's more important to get it exactly right."

So what happens when consumers get fooled and then disappointed by a piece of "deceptive" mail? Mail that may even be judged illegal by the tougher standards to come? Just as the first medical malpractice suit changed the way doctors treat their patients and the entire economic model of the health-care industry, the first direct mail malpractice suit will cause profound reverberations in our business. And to paraphrase a famous outer envelope, we may have already lost.

My Prediction

While some people *talk* about change or even *write* about change (guilty as charged), others make change and respond to new realities in the marketplace. I do not believe that direct mail will perish as a medium, but I do believe in evolution. Only the strong and the most adaptable will survive. And I hope you're one of them.

▼
12

The Future of Catalogs

New Technology, New Markets, New Horizons

Maxwell Sroge

Maxwell Sroge is founder and president of Maxwell Sroge Company, catalog creative development specialists. Mr. Sroge's books on catalog marketing include *How to Create Successful Catalogs* and *101 Tips for More Profitable Catalogs.*

Predicting the future in the world of marketing is about as accurate as long-range predictions of the weather. I recall reading, some twenty or so years ago, treatises by brilliant Harvard Business School professors predicting that electronic shopping would arrive in the 1980s and that the impact on retail stores would be devastating. I'm sure that these well-meaning professors were extrapolating from technology then in development and that they were anticipating a given rate of integration of that technology into our daily lives, as though it were some absolute linear expansion not affected by economics, organizations, and a feeling that what we have is good enough, so why go out and shake up our lives and risk our money?

What I think technology forecasters often miss is how busy we all are doing today's things today and how tough it is to make a dollar doing the things we all really know we have to do. Therefore, we are reluctant to stick our necks out into uncharted waters and risk the shark attacks that come with that kind of exposure. I don't know about you, but my feeling is that people and companies talk a lot more about technology because it seems to be the thing to do, rather than acting to implement the technology. College professors and other forecasters of the future (as I'm about to become) have much easier jobs. We don't have to do it—we can simply talk about it. Now, having displayed appropriate respect for you as a reader and proper humility for the task I've set for myself, I will predict where I think the catalog business is going. But before we set forth on the nearly uncharted waters of the future, let's appraise where we are today.

The catalog business in the United States today is a robust enterprise, albeit one that's highly fragmented. Nobody really knows how many catalog businesses there are; moreover, the catalog business is divided into two major segments: business to business catalogs and consumer catalogs. For our purposes today, let's agree that when we use the term *catalogs,* we mean consumer catalogs. The two categories are so different that they really shouldn't be talked about in the same breath.

There are about 10,000–12,000 catalogers in the United States today, of which only about 500–600 do over $10 million a year. There are roughly a half-dozen who do over $1 billion. The growth rate for the business as a whole is excellent. It's growing at about twice the rate of over-the-counter retailing. The factors behind its growth in the 1990s are the same factors that propelled growth in the 1980s: working women; totally employed households; and the conveniences of 800 numbers, credit cards, and overnight package delivery. For instance, few people realize that overnight delivery capabilities alone accounted for an additional 10–15% increase in total sales for catalogers. For a few, the figure is even bigger. Look at it this way. Many catalogers do 35–40% of their total business during the last quarter of each year. Before the advent of Federal Express and the like, catalogers had to advise their customers that they could not guarantee delivery on orders placed after December 12–15. Today they guarantee delivery of orders placed up to two days before Christmas.

There are other factors behind the growing acceptance of catalog shopping, and not the least of these is the response to opportunity of the catalogers themselves. While retailers were trying to economize by cutting down the number of salespeople and paying less to those who remained while reducing the amount of training they got, catalog people were doing just the opposite. Sensing the shift of the tide in their direction, catalogers early on started to focus on customer service. Their computers told them that they only made money with repeat customers. That the fastest way to rack up sales and profits was to raise the annual revenue generated from existing customers. Realizing that the only way to accomplish this was through value and service, they really went to town. As the costs of computers and telephone technology dropped, they made bigger and bigger investments. Many moved their warehouses to locations convenient to the major package delivery services, and to serve time-starved customers even better, they offered 24-hour order taking. Call one of their 800 numbers night or day and well-trained, polite salespeople will discuss the item with you, tell you whether it's in stock (if it's not, when it will be), and suggest related items in which you might be interested, then charge it to your credit card and it's delivered to your home or office within a couple of days. If you don't like it, call the package carrier and it will be picked up for return. Is it any wonder that catalogers have been the beneficiaries of such rapid growth?

Technology . . . technology. Necessity is the mother of invention. If you build it, they will come. It's as if some master hand is finding the answers to consumers' changing needs. No, the answer is that the technology has always (or maybe not always) been there in the wings, waiting for the cue to appear on the scene. That's where the Harvard professors missed the boat. They figured that if the technology was there, it would be used. Which comes first, the chicken or the egg? In this case, it's the need, and then the technology is fit into place to fill it. As we stand here peering into the future, the technological array we see is so mind-boggling that it defies the ability to forecast which need will be filled first. Let's look at some of the present barriers to catalog growth and see what clues we might find there that will lead us to predictions that have some reasonable foundation.

The first problem the catalog business has today is that it is not adept enough at sending the right offerings of merchandise to the right people at the right time. So it's a cinch to predict that with rising postage and printing costs and with people besieged with catalogs, there will have to be a major change in the way catalogs are produced and distributed.

Prediction: Catalogs will be more appropriately called PRISMS—Personalized Individualized Selections of Merchandise. Through a merger of computer technology and printing technology, catalogs specifically tailored to the lifestyle and buying history of the individual customer will be produced economically. It's possible that no two catalogs in a mailing of millions will be exactly alike.

While the portability of catalogs and the fact that no machine is necessary to use them are significant advantages, the fact that they are two-dimensional is a serious drawback. It's obvious that the best way to sell apparel, for example, is for a model to demonstrate the best features of the clothes or, if you're selling food, to show how it's prepared and served. Of course, the best thing of all in both of these situations is for the prospective buyer to try the clothes on and to taste the food. Well, maybe virtual reality will do it, but I'm not enough of futurist to make that prediction. But we're all aware of the imminent growth of interactive communications. Whether it's 500 channels of cable TV that you can respond to by using some kind of box or CD-ROM discs or one of the dozens of other technologies fighting for position today, there's little risk in making the following prediction.

Prediction: By the year 2000, consumers will be shopping from some kind of live-action color image to which they can respond immediately. They will be able to search for any product classification they wish at any time of the day and select one of several merchants, just as a shopper can walk down Fifth Avenue today and choose which store to walk into.

Now don't rush out and sell your Champion Paper stock or your R.R. Donnelley stock. If catalogs don't exist in the electronic world of the year 2000, we'll have to go out and invent them. In all of the tests that have been conducted to date of interactive electronic shopping, the presence of a printed catalog to support the electronic media has more than justified its cost. Go back again to the marvelous advantages of the common catalog: it's amazingly portable, you can read it anywhere at any time without any special equipment, and it's economical to produce.

The catalog business today is thought of as an American business. We Americans, although newcomers on the world scene, have a tendency to think in nationalistic terms.

There's no question as to the greatness and power of our nation, but when it comes to the catalog business, like a few other businesses, there are some surprises in store. First of all, some of the premiere American mail-order businesses are not owned by Americans. One example is Spiegel, which owns Eddie Bauer, but the whole shooting match is owned by Otto Versand of Hamburg, Germany. And then there's that most American of all American companies, Harry and David. It is owned by a Japanese pharmaceutical company. And the very essence of New England Americana, Talbots, is owned by a Japanese retailer. I'm not railing on about this because I don't think that foreigners should have the right to own fine American companies. I think foreigners should have the right to do in our land what we have the right to do in their land. Nothing more, nothing less.

The reason I raised this issue is that catalogers who have had the United States as their primary base of operations are waking up to the fact that there's a great big world out there for them to conquer. The interesting thing is that again technology is coming to the fore. International 800 numbers, satellite transmission, and super-fast delivery services are tearing down international borders. Many top U.S. manufacturers learned a long time ago that international operations were critical to their very survival in the marketplace. It's not beyond reason to speculate that in order to deal with worldwide competition, catalogers will have to become worldwide marketers whether they wish to or not.

Prediction: Of the 250 largest catalogers in the year 2000, 25% will have operations in England, Germany, France, and Japan, and another 25% will be operating in the United Kingdom. The rest will have plans to start operating overseas within five years, provided that they have not already been bought up by foreign investors.

Since predictions are the order of the day, permit me at this point to make some predictions first about what new kinds of businesses we will see in the catalog world and what will happen to some of today's leading catalog businesses. Please appreciate that here I am giving you some very valuable information. (It's the kind of help that corporations and investors have paid me up to $2,500 a day for.) I'm sharing it with you because of something I was told by one of the smartest marketing men who ever lived. His name was Sol Polk, and he was a pioneer in the discount revolution in America. Before Wal-Mart and Kmart, there was Polk Brothers. Sol was smart enough to own one-third of the major appliance business in Chicago. And who owned another third? Sears Roebuck. Sol used to say that he'd tell anybody about how he planned his promotions. Why? Because it isn't a matter of what we do, it's a matter of how we do it. To Sol, execution was everything. How true that is. What's the difference between a winning team and a losing team? Execution. So now, given that admonition, which at least makes me feel better about sharing these thoughts with you, here are my predictions of catalog businesses to come. Although I stated at the beginning of this chapter that I would restrict it to consumer catalogs, the subject of computer software is so pervasive that I'd like your permission to deal with it here.

Prediction: The number of catalogs devoted to computer software and peripherals will grow tremendously. The growth will not come by emulating the catalogs of today, but by taking advantage of sizable segmented markets that are now developing. Software for lawyers, for accountants, for engineers of different types, and so on ad infinitum. And in other areas you'll see catalogs for teens and any number of new catalogs appealing to the over-age-50 market and the over-age-70 market. Catalogs of financial services will be commonplace. And what a ball they'll have in the food business. You name the ethnic segment and there will be a catalog for it. And for another twist, watch for the bigger specialized catalogers to buy up magazines in their categories to benefit from the use of their circulation lists and space. *Reader's Digest* and Time-Life took publishing assets and turned them into catalog/mail order assets, so turnabout is fair play. And if you're so fortunate to work for or own a major communications medium of any sort, the catalog opportunities will be coming at you fast and furious.

Now I'm really going to stick my neck out. I mean no harm to anybody or any company by making these predictions. I'm sure you realize that larger companies are in the public's eye and people are curious about them, just as they are curious about any celebrity. These predictions are based on a lifetime of watching companies and their principals and key executives in action. For over forty years now I've been an observer of the corporate world, and I must say that there seems to be a certain predictability about it. So after all that hemming and hawing, here goes.

Prediction: Land's End, although a public company, will merge into a major retail chain like Dayton-Hudson or The Limited. Omaha Steaks will be bought up by a major food company that will use it as a base for expansion into other catalog food businesses. J. Crew and Tweeds will meet the same fate as Land's End. Time-Warner, because of its overriding interest in electronic communications, will float a public issue of Book-of-the-Month Club and Time-Life books, retaining the right to use their titles and publications in electronic form. Cabelas will merge into publicly owned Gander Mountain, and Cabelas will end up being the controlling interest. Sears and Montgomery Ward will again become dominant factors in the catalog business. But this time they'll do it right, with specialty books and great service. And, finally, a few well-known companies will cease to exist. However, I think it would be too hurtful to put those predictions into print.

The other question I believe many of you may have concerns your role in this new world. The year 2000 is not that far away. If you're 35 today, you'll be only 42 when the page turns. If I were in your shoes, I'd do the following. Learn everything you can about computers. Get with a company that's willing to invest a little money at least in such areas as television marketing and overseas markets. Get on the cutting edge of the technologies that will impact database segmentation and production techniques. Don't be afraid to experiment with some unique ways of using ink-jet printing and electronic binding techniques. Watch as the ships of opportunity sail down the river past you and jump aboard the one that looks good to you. Venture out and be an entrepreneur. We won't all be Bill Gates, but half a Gates or a quarter of a Gates is not too bad, either. Have fun and add a little adventure to your life. It's going to be a great world—may your efforts and energies be blessed. When you fall (and we all do), pick yourself up, dust yourself off, and start all over again—just the way it's sung in the song.

▼
13

Integrated Telemarketing

Sheathing Telemarketing's Double-Edged Sword

Ernan Roman

Ernan Roman is President of the New York–based Ernan Roman Direct Marketing Corporation, specialists in developing and implementing integrated direct marketing campaigns. Clients include many divisions of AT&T, Hewlett-Packard, Citibank, and IBM.

We have created a monster.

Marketing executives see telemarketing as a highly successful sales and marketing tool. But talk to people who get the calls, and you hear a different story.

Our company recently conducted several research studies focusing on business executives' perceptions of the sales and marketing process as well as the various media used to communicate with them. These executives reported receiving:

- one telemarketing call a day

- 20 to 60 pieces of mail per day

Yet the vast majority—75%—expressed an overwhelming preference for the mail, even though the volume of mail was considerably higher.

As further proof of a spreading resistance to telemarketing, business-to-business "Do not call" requests increased by 600% in 1993 over 1992—all from what is perceived as only one call a day. The conclusion is obvious: receiving one telemarketing call is seen as far more disruptive and annoying than 20 or 60 mailed messages.

Yet look at the other side of the telemarketing story. The use of 800 numbers is growing astronomically due to increasing acceptance among businesspeople and consumers alike. People are calling 800 numbers for everything from information to service to outright purchases. Just by including an 800 number in your mailing, you can increase response rate by 50% to 100%.

Why is inbound seen as a welcome convenience and outbound an annoying intrusion? The answer is intuitively clear and has to do with choice and the personal, one-to-one nature of telephone communications. With both mail and 800, customers get to choose *when* to respond and *how* to respond. Furthermore, since the customer initiates the call to do something that he or she wants, it has intrinsic value. An outbound telemarketing call that arrives "cold," however, has little perceived value and may, in fact, violate the recipient's sense of privacy.

Unfortunately, many telemarketers are using the telephone for mass communications, "broadcasting" the same message without any concern for whether the message has relevance or value to the person on the other end of the line. And, while still extremely effective, these calls are "strip mining" the market and creating a general, deeply held resistance to any unsolicited sales or marketing over the telephone.

So what's the solution? Do we simply wait until customers respond to us? And let our message get cold in the meantime? Of course not. The solution is to plan both the content and the timing of the outbound telemarketing call—as well as the inbound call—so that it is meaningful to the customer and productive for your organization.

Ten years of experience with our clients has clearly demonstrated that when telemarketing is properly integrated as part of a total, customer-oriented strategy, it can, in fact, increase customer satisfaction and strengthen business partnerships. Integrated Telemarketing (ITM) is part of our Integrated Direct Marketing (IDM^{sm})* process and incorporates the telephone as a powerful marketing channel.

Telemarketing, better than any other medium, reinforces the message and establishes an interactive dialogue with customers and prospects. That dialogue is your pathway to customer satisfaction and long-term customer service. But unless we face up to the growing consumer annoyance, and do it soon, we'll have to eliminate the telephone from our direct response repertoire. And we'll have no one to blame but ourselves.

A Short History of Telemarketing

To determine where telemarketing is headed, we need to take a quick look at where it has been. In its past lie the seeds of some of the problems that are plaguing the industry today.

Personally, I've been watching the ups and downs of telemarketing for most of my life. I literally grew up in telemarketing. It doesn't seem long ago that my father, Murray Roman, founded the telemarketing industry in 1962 while working with a young Lee Iacocca to introduce an innovative little car—the Ford Mustang.

Using a network of 13,000 homemakers working from their homes, that telemarketing campaign called over 20 million people and generated at least two leads a day for Ford salespeople. As an outgrowth of his work with Ford, Murray founded a telemarketing firm called CCI. Throughout the 1970s and the 1980s, CCI was instrumental in making telemarketing a successful, professional marketing tool.

Those early days of telemarketing were exhilarating. I can remember driving around New York City in a station wagon with folding tables, some single-line phone sets and folding chairs to set up phone banks in storefronts or rented offices to "get out the vote" for political campaigns. Even after WATS lines were introduced in 1968, telemarketing was a fairly ad hoc proposition. I still remember the day the phone company ran WATS cable 10 stories up the outside of a building and over our terrace to supply the lines for our telemarketing center.

*IDM is a service mark of Ernan Roman Direct Marketing Corporation.

Throughout its short history, telemarketing has been viewed as a boiler room operation: an unglamorous but useful part of the marketing picture. In those early days of proving the professionalism and establishing the value of telemarketing, all of us in the industry were concerned with the quality of the information that was shared with customers. We wanted to be sure that the call provided value to the customer. "Talk time" was not an issue. It was OK to take the time to talk to customers and let them talk to us.

Telemarketing came on like gangbusters through the 1970s and 1980s. It provided an economical and effective way to market directly to the customer. Technology added sophisticated tools: databases, automatic dialers, computer-based scripts, ACDs, least-cost call routing, and so on. Clients and agencies started looking at ways to improve the efficiency and reduce talk time. The idea was "more calls, more sales." Telemarketing was seen as the great electronic hope of the 1980s.

But something happened to telemarketing on its way to success. In all the excitement generated by its newness, telemarketing forgot who it was talking to. Instead of relating personally, the telemarketing call delivered a pitch. Instead of answering questions, the telemarketing call focused on making the sale. Instead of integrating with other media, telemarketing became the primary marketing tool. Quantity replaced quality. And people's response to the calls quickly deteriorated from mild interest to outright annoyance.

The Medium and the Message

An essential part of the Integrated Direct Marketing methodology is IDM Depth Research to determine how people feel about the various media that we, as marketers, use to reach them. IDM Depth Research goes directly to the source—the people receiving the message—to get below the surface and examine individual media preferences: How do people like to be contacted? What will make them most receptive to our message? How does timing of mail or calls affect customer receptivity? The results provide the information to tailor both the medium and the message for optimum impact.

The psychographics of media preference are remarkably clear and strongly stated, especially about telemarketing. Surprisingly, the negative attitudes people express toward telemarketing calls have little to do with the content. Telemarketing calls, per se, are often perceived as bad. This relates directly to the "strip mining" calls that people are receiving. The intrusive nature and poor timing of these calls has made blanket resistance to telemarketing the first line of defense.

Resistance to the medium translates into resistance to the message. Forget the notion that you have 12 or 15 seconds to make or break your pitch. The first *five* seconds signal that it's a telemarketing call, and the person on the other end often just tunes out. Your message is often seen as irrelevant because people are frequently unwilling to devote the time to find out what the call is about.

What makes the current situation so disturbing is that, for now, telemarketing continues to be profitable for the companies that are using it—in spite of the strong and vocal customer resistance. These companies don't recognize that their calls are becoming enormously annoying to customers. People are simply running out of patience.

Telemarketing is the classic double-edged sword. It cuts both ways. One edge is the direct, person-to-person connection with a customer that leads to sales. The other edge is the invasion by telephone of a person's time and space.

The growing resistance to telemarketing should raise a large red flag for all of us with an interest in the future of direct marketing. Unless we do something to reverse the trend, we will have to write off telemarketing as a viable marketing tool. And that would be a great loss.

The Power of the Telephone

Consider the ubiquitous telephone. It links virtually every household in America with every other household; every business with every other business; even our cars are plugged into the global network. The telephone is a primary tool for person-to-person communication. What makes the telephone unique is its highly interactive, highly personal nature. It is not passive. It is not remote. And it is precisely these "high touch" characteristics that are often ignored by today's telemarketers.

Consumer annoyance stems from their expectation that the messages reaching them via their telephone should be meaningful. It can easily be seen as a waste of time to answer the phone and deal with an unsolicited sales call that has little or no value.

Even though databases can provide a wealth of information on the customer, the information does not seem to be making the connection to the content of the telemarketing call. The focus is on simple data: demographics, purchases, and other "customer file" information. To be truly useful, the database needs to be built around long-term business information: buying cycle, decision-making process, goals, media preferences, frequency of contact, and the like. We need to remember that we are calling a person with individual preferences, attitudes, and needs. One size does not fit all.

Even those who use telemarketing most tend not to pay much attention to it. Most of the budget in corporate media plans is skewed toward print, television, and radio, as is most of the planning and creative energy.

The Right Message to the Right Person at the Right Time

It's well known that using multiple media, with the right mix of advertising, direct mail, telemarketing, and field sales will produce the greatest return on the sales and marketing investment. And many marketers are quick to point out that they already use a multimedia strategy, with telemarketing as a key player. But given the low patience threshold of most consumers and businesspeople, just adding some telemarketing to the mix won't do the job. Instead, we need to rethink our telemarketing strategies to keep the good points and control for the annoyance.

Integrated Telemarketing is a customer-focused approach to telemarketing that is oriented toward building customer relationships, not just short-term sales. The ITM approach uses the telephone as part of a tightly integrated, precisely timed, carefully researched process. This type of integration allows the customer to see the relevance and the value of your call. The purpose of the integrated call can be as varied as the objectives of your marketing campaign: reinforce a message, confirm an offer, or provide additional information. The important thing to remember is that the call has a context that links it to the other communications. The prospect knows what your call is about, is willing to spend the time with you, and is in a better position to make an informed decision.

There are two schools of thought about the value of tightly scripted telemarketing calls. A number of professionals will argue against scripting, claiming that it makes the conversation stilted and mechanical. Our research proves differently. Our work with a number of our clients has clearly demonstrated that good scripts—interactive, customer-oriented, well-structured scripts with appropriate exit points for the customer—not only have positive results, but also can turn around negative opinions about telemarketing.

In a survey of 400 customers who had received the client's highly structured, carefully scripted telemarketing call and 300 customers who had not, the results showed some interesting trends. The customers who had not received the telemarketing call retained a negative impression of telemarketing. The customers who had received the calls were positive about telemarketing and reported that the call was welcome and informative: 97% of the respondents rated the calls better than or equal to other telemarketing calls.

The primary reason for the positive response was that scripts focused outward, on the needs of the customer, not the company. When we divided the 400 telemarketed customers into groups of non-buyers (those who had not accepted the offer) and buyers (those who had), we saw an even more interesting result. Fully two-thirds of the customers who had no interest in the product and did not accept the offer reported a positive response to the telemarketing. The majority "agree completely" that the representatives were polite, courteous, and knowledgeable. That's the kind of telemarketing that's good for all of us.

Redeploying Your Media to Make the Most of Telemarketing

Precision deployment of your media to strategically include telemarketing allows optimum use of traditional marketing and sales channels. The needs of the market are the drivers, not the sales targets of the telemarketing channel. The mail/phone blitz is undermining the strength of telemarketing and has to become a thing of the past. For telemarketing to work well with today's customers, it needs to be used with laser-like precision. People just don't have the time or the patience to listen to anything less.

Using IDM, each medium has a unique role based on the customer's media preference and the nature of the message. Matching the medium to the message is key to reaching the market in the most persuasive way. For example: Television can appeal to emotions on a broad, general level. Radio, on the other hand, can localize the message, complementing television and bringing the message closer to home. Print advertising puts a compelling spin on the message and provides more information on a less emotional level than either television or radio. Telemarketing reinforces the other media and adds a dimension of its own. It is primarily an interactive communication channel that lets you answer prospects' questions immediately. It can identify individual customer needs. It can be a powerful qualifying tool to determine which leads are most promising for field sales follow-up. And, clearly, it can be a highly effective sales tool in its own right.

The telephone can increase the relevance of the message and enhance the sense of urgency. Compressing the cycle between receipt of the direct mail message and the outbound telemarketing call can reinforce the importance of the message and answer immediate questions. It's very easy to set aside a direct mail letter and get back to it "later." We have found, however, that the first outbound call needs to be made no later than 24 to 48 hours after mail receipt.

Back to the Future: Telemarketing's Next 20 Years

Through rampant misuse of telemarketing, we are killing the goose that lays the golden eggs. Ignoring customer resistance will not make it go away. We need to take a step back and rethink the basics.

More technology is not the answer. The next 20 years will see more electronic media in customers' homes and in businesses and more business being conducted through computers and telephones. The telephone will be an increasingly important tool connecting us to our customers and prospects. Witness the success of the home shopping channels, the proliferation of 800 customer service and information lines, and the integration of cable and telephone to bring new services into the home.

Exciting as all this is, we must never forget that the technology is simply the facilitator; it cannot form the relationship that business must establish with the customers. These relationships are the result of managing the entire customer life-cycle, not just a series of quick-hit sales calls. Life-cycle management has to come from a customer-based strategy that integrates all the channels into a single laser-focused approach that uses all the media with precision. With telemarketing, as with all your media, the objective is to reach the customer or the prospect with the right message at the right time. That is, essentially, the overarching vision of Integrated Direct Marketing.

True database marketing is still in its infancy, but it holds great promise of improving our knowledge of our customers and prospects. In fact, with the software tools we now have and the ones to come, we are in the enviable position of being able to individualize any message. Not as a gimmick ("You, Mr. Roman of New York, may already have won . . . "), but as an important way to understand the customer and provide a valuable service.

Telemarketing is an extremely useful tool to add information to your database as well, expanding your knowledge of the customers' needs and enabling an ever more personal telephone sales call. By learning more about the customers and prospects, telemarketing can provide an added bonus for your salespeople. Rather than pursuing unqualified leads, the sales force will be able to do more of what it does best—provide consultative, value-added service to their customers during face-to-face calls.

Earlier we mentioned that 75% of the business executives in our survey preferred to be contacted by mail. The good news is that there are 25% who prefer the telephone and they do so because it answers their questions and provides the specific information they need to make a decision. In other words, it talks to them about what the product or service can do for them.

This is not blue sky. We've seen it work with our clients and seen it work as a tool, not a weapon. Telemarketing has come a long way since those Mustang marketing days. Its adolescence is over. Telemarketing can no longer get away with being the brash newcomer to the media mix. It's time to decide what type of adult this precocious medium will be. Manage that close contact with your customer to *everyone's* benefit.

▼
14

Sales Promotion
and
Trade Incentives

New, Electronic Horizons

H. Robert Wientzen

H. Robert Wientzen joined Procter & Gamble's general advertising department in 1967. Since then, he has served on the boards of several organizations, including Talbert House, YMCA of Cincinnati, Advanced Promotion Technologies, and the Direct Marketing Association. In November 1991, *Target Marketing* magazine named him one of the 200 most influential people in direct marketing. In July 1993, he became President/CEO of Advanced Promotion Technologies, Inc.

For many decades, the ways companies have marketed their products have changed in concert with fundamental shifts in society. In fact, cultural and economic changes are often seen first in the way marketers present their propositions to the public. These changes have been most evident in the way consumer goods companies have marketed their products. Because they deal with the everyday products of life, their communication to the public is very visible and often studied. Although many fundamental principles have remained the same, both the look and the techniques used by many consumer goods marketers have shifted radically over the past four decades.

Consumer goods marketing seems to have been outpaced by the evolution of direct marketing, which accelerated during the 1970s and 1980s. Direct marketers, pushed by innovative catalogers who took advantage of change, seemed to mow down all the problems that got in the way of growth. Driven by significant shifts in societal practices, as well as major demographic and economic changes, consumer goods marketers have struggled to deal with some major problems. For the most part, the challenges were brought about by struggles to achieve efficiency in the way the traditional marketers presented advertising and promotional offers to consumers.

The rapid increase in the number of employed women, major changes in lifestyles, and the resulting increase in the number of segments into which consumers could be divided continued to present increased challenges. In addition, media formats proliferated, fueled by the advent of cable television. The advent of site-based media, the loss of customer loyalty caused by an increased focus on price reduction, and the widespread use of cents-off coupons and other price incentives presented constant challenges through the 1970s and 1980s. Most of these issues continue at the present time. In addition, the rapid increase in the number of stock keeping units (SKUs) and the increasing difficulty in finding product differentiation points that were able to sustain consumer loyalty presented major challenges to both traditional retailers and manufacturers.

During most of the time that consumer goods companies faced these hurdles, they saw direct marketers going the other way. In fact, direct marketers were getting better at targeting and thus more efficient. They were becoming more sophisticated at finding and reaching the customers who were likely to buy. In addition, database marketing was opening up opportunities to shift opinions over time, and catalogers were proving that virtually anything could be sold if you reached the right people with the right kind of format at the right time. In addition, during the 1970s and 1980s, direct marketers were discovering and successfully employing new technologies like relational databases, laser printing, and new statistical techniques, all designed to drive down costs by increasing targeting success.

While direct marketers were honing their trade, other fundamental changes were impacting traditional marketers. Beginning in the late 1970s, shopping was shifting from a pleasant, leisurely, planned activity to a harried, less organized chore. Consumers were less likely to use shopping lists, and more and more purchase decisions were being made in the retail outlet. The Point of Purchase Advertising Institute (POPAI) annual study on consumer purchase behavior began to reflect America's changing lifestyle as it showed that more and more purchase decisions were being made in the store. The marketing battlefield was expanding!

Merchants, sensing that they were losing influence over buying decisions, sought to create a sense of theater in the store. Rather than just depending on their old standby, the weekly newspaper ad or flyer, retailers (especially grocery stores) began seeking ways to communicate with consumers during their shopping experience. Packaging, point-of-purchase material, display, and shelf placement all became the focus of scientific studies and elaborate tests. Computer technology became a key tool in arranging shelves to maximum profit by presenting the right category image to the consumer. Consumer goods companies began to pay more attention to the in-store appearance of their products, much as direct marketers were paying attention to the "look" of their offers.

Soon, the grocery store and other retail outlets were no longer simply a fancy warehouse where randomly stored goods were held for captive consumers who came by to pick them up. Retailers recognized that they could significantly increase their profits by scientifically assessing the way they presented goods to consumers, and manufacturers became intensely focused on ways to increase their store presence.

Meanwhile, the convergence of technology and the growing interest in finding new marketing techniques was fostering the growth of systems based on the newly implemented universal product code (UPC). Originally designed as a tool to increase store efficiency by speeding up the checkout process, the UPC code began to be used as a source of marketing information. Nielsen Market Research and eventually IRI, Inc., developed systems and consumer research panels that allowed consumer goods companies and retailers to precisely measure the impact of various in-store marketing concepts. Because of the UPC code, it was now possible to conduct limited tests much as direct marketers had performed in the past.

All of these developments, along with a continued decrease in media efficiency, led to a gradual shifting of marketing focus and a reallocation of some of the money spent on mass advertising vehicles like television and magazines to newly emerging in-store concepts. The battle for the consumer mind, once conducted principally in the home, was now being waged aggressively in the store.

The first transformation of traditional marketing concepts into the in-store environment was accomplished by ActMedia, Inc. Bruce Failing, Sr., successfully transformed traditional print concepts into the idea of shopping cart advertising. This concept eventually became a passive advertising format with no opportunity for consumer involvement, but it did open up the store as a new marketing venue. In a short time, ActMedia had a major presence in the store, with signage on the store shelf and above the aisle, as well as its cart advertising program.

Encouraged by its success, ActMedia soon offered in-store demonstrators, who became more directly involved in material distribution at the store entrance. In effect, they became direct marketers for consumer goods companies, who until then had seen the retailer as a passive distribution point for their goods. ActMedia also began to offer basic targeting, for example, providing certain items only to women over age forty. It also offered co-op opportunities to reduce distribution costs. Soon manufacturers were using ActMedia and other in-store demonstrators to distribute samples and to hand out mail-in offers and other traditional marketing tools normally distributed through the mail or other traditional means. The success of ActMedia quickly generated competitive interest, and a whole range of entrepreneurs soon attempted to develop other in-store ideas.

The success of ActMedia also encouraged a wide variety of consumer goods marketers and would-be marketing service companies to increase their focus on the retail store as a distribution point for traditional direct-to-consumer efforts. Although the use of product packages as a distribution vehicle for consumer materials was very common, most in-store marketing efforts had been decidedly low-tech. By the late 1970s the personal computer (PC) was a common business tool, and marketers were looking for ways to expand its use. Now, for the first time, the advent of the PC and low-cost peripheral devices made it possible to bring technology into the in-store marketing arena. Soon, various companies were testing the use of kiosks containing PCs as a way of conducting in-store direct marketing efforts.

Most of the early computerized kiosks simply incorporated a low-level PC, a screen, and a simplified keyboard allowing the consumer to indicate various choices. Through the use of computer graphics, the consumer was encouraged to select various promotional offers via the keyboard and would then receive printed material. Early efforts of this type were successful at attracting a great deal of attention as well as financial support. However, most simply failed to hold the consumer appeal beyond the introductory stages. As time went on, the kiosk became more friendly. Later versions involved color screens that allowed the consumer to touch the screen to receive information, coupons, or mail-in offers on selected products. However, beyond the selection of offers by the consumer, there was no targeting and little or no ability to track individual responses.

The computer kiosks marked the beginning of electronic direct marketing in-store, but they were never able to capture any significant segment of the marketplace. Consumers simply did not want to be bothered to seek out the kiosks, and they often found them intimidating in spite of the significant amount of creative innovation in the latter tests. Although some recent tests incorporated consumer identification numbers, they have not provided adequate targeting ability. The real value of the kiosks in the development of electronic marketing was to alert marketers to the potential of incorporating technology within the retail store environment.

Meanwhile, a host of other companies were looking at other creative ways to integrate direct marketing concepts and new technological developments into the in-store marketing arena. The pace of innovation has increased since the mid-1980s, and many new ideas have undergone significant tests.

Among a host of creative development efforts, Mike O'Brien and a group of former IRI employees began experimenting with the concept of printing cents-off coupons in conjunction with cash register scanning activities. This led to the formation of Catalina Marketing, which allows marketers to print out coupons in response to individual items as they are scanned at the front of the store. In effect, the Catalina program moved the kiosk to the checkout counter and allowed marketers to specify various UPC codes as targeting triggers. Thus, the program became more convenient for consumers and more effective for marketers who were looking for ways to reach a broader cross-section of the audience with a targeted vehicle.

In effect, the Catalina concept can be seen as a mini-direct marketing effort. A company selects a target in the form of purchasers of a specific product and then is able to deliver a printed coupon on the spot. Thus, the element of basic targeting was added to the delivery of in-store marketing efforts. The ability to deliver a targeted message without the postal expense achieved significant economies for the consumer goods marketers.

A major advance in the electronic direct marketing world occurred when Citicorp decided to enter the then-growing world of electronic marketing. Citicorp's motivation was to obtain access to a significant source of information regarding consumer behavior that could be sold to consumer goods companies and, at the same time, position themselves as a major player in the developing world of automated financial services.

The Citicorp idea involved its accumulating a significant amount of scanner data on individual consumers. The data would then be processed and made available to consumer goods companies interested in conducting various direct marketing activities via traditional mailings. In addition, Citicorp envisioned that its data would provide a rich source of market research information for manufacturers hungry for more individual household data. Finally, Citicorp saw the opportunity to enter the direct marketing supplier field by providing analysis, turnkey letter shop, and cooperative mailing opportunities to reach households identified via its database.

While the Citicorp concept was intriguing, it soon ran into significant impediments. First, privacy advocates and the press soon began to criticize the huge data accumulation plan envisioned by the Citicorp concept. Citicorp's inability to silence those who believed its system represented a new level of Big Brother snooping led to continued attacks in the press and resulted in numerous legislative and public relations battles. At the same time, while marketers were intrigued by the possibility of reaching known users of their products or competitive products, they soon recognized that Citicorp's system would be extremely expensive and not likely to pay off because of the low cost of the typical consumer goods sale. Citicorp's innovative efforts to combine numerous offers via co-op mailings were marginally effective but never reached a level that attracted major marketers. Again, however, the Citicorp effort alerted many companies to the potential of combining technology and the incredible sources of information available in the in-store environment.

Another creative electronic direct marketing effort was launched by VideOcart. This effort was built around the concept of incorporating a portable PC in a typical shopping cart. The fundamental idea was to communicate with consumers electronically as they moved about the store. By flashing messages to consumers at precisely the moment they were in the process of making category choices, it was hoped that VideOcart would increase product sales significantly. The exciting vision of being able to communicate with individuals in a targeted fashion without the use of printed materials and without the time and expenses of using the U.S. mail system was appealing to many marketers. However, like many early pioneering efforts, the VideOcart program soon ran into significant obstacles.

Plagued by a host of hardware and other technological difficulties, the VideOcart program soon stalled. The sophisticated screen on the VideOcart equipment was subject to pilferage and other vandalism. In addition, the inability of the system to print and its very limited targeting capabilities were seen as significant restrictions. While consumers liked receiving entertaining information as well as using the terminal to locate items in the store, they never seemed to receive enough value from the information and other offers provided to maintain their active involvement. In addition, the high costs of outfitting the stores limited VideOcart's ability to expand the system.

While Citicorp and VideOcart were attempting to establish turnkey third-party database electronic marketing systems, a number of other concepts were being developed as well. Food retailers, recognizing that Citicorp's concept had great merit, began to develop software designed to allow them to conduct their own database efforts. IBM and the Wegman Stores of Rochester, New York, were the first to develop viable software that enabled them to access individual household purchase data and issue targeted price reductions. Soon other companies, including Publix Markets of Lakeland, Florida, and Smiths of Salt Lake City, Utah, were experimenting with various electronic direct marketing concepts. For the most part, these ideas involved having consumers identify themselves through the use of check-cashing or other magnetic-strip cards that enabled retailers to associate purchases with an individual household. Thus, the retailer was able to utilize existing in-store technology (the UPC scanner and back-room controller) to develop a massive household database.

However, many soon discovered that using the data thus compiled required significant technical skills as well as sophisticated direct marketing knowledge. Also, virtually everyone who experimented with early electronic marketing recognized that the cost of implementing direct marketing programs via the mail carried a very heavy overhead burden and thus were not likely to pay off. In effect, they could collect the data, but they found that it was difficult and expensive to use it.

The most recent in-store direct marketing concept has been implemented by Advanced Promotion Technologies (APT), Inc., of Pompano Beach, Florida. The APT Vision Value Network™ integrates household database collection and in-store targeted delivery in a single device. In addition, by incorporating financial services into the program, the APT Network allows retailers to achieve store efficiencies at the same time they are developing and utilizing a sophisticated database marketing concept.

The APT Network is based on a terminal at the front end, which is linked to the front-end scanner and provides full-color video and sound with a touch screen. In addition, it incorporates a wide-body printer and a card reader that allows the consumer to be identified and then receive individually targeted printed messages. To a large degree, the APT concept represents the integration of state-of-the-art direct marketing techniques via sophisticated electronic equipment located in the retail environment.

Because the APT Network can print letters, coupons, recipes, or other material, expressly targeted to the consumer based on demographics as well as past purchases, it represents a way for consumer goods companies and other manufacturers to address the high cost of traditional direct marketing delivery techniques. At the same time, it offers even more targeting sophistication than the traditional management database systems, because it incorporates individual household purchase data as well as demographic and other traditional direct marketing information. Because of the high-quality, wide-body printer and the video screen that deliver both video and printed messages concurrently, it achieves a degree of awareness that prior systems were not capable of delivering.

Having learned about the perils of the privacy issue, APT allows consumers to opt out of the database. Because consumers voluntarily provide the initial demographics and involve themselves in the system by use of the card, the APT Vision Value Network avoids some of the privacy concerns that haunted the original Citicorp concept. Because consumers are in control and must choose to identify themselves via the card, the privacy issue seems to have been significantly eliminated.

Although the APT Vision Value Network represents the current state of the electronic direct marketing art, it is most likely only the beginning. As the cost of technology comes down, and as consumers become far more adapted to its use, we are quite likely to see other forms of electronic direct marketing both in the grocery store and in other locations as well.

PART IV

Special Applications

15

Direct Response TV

Keeping an Eye on the Prize

Ron Bliwas

Ron Bliwas, President and Chief Executive Officer of A. Eicoff & Company, has established himself as the country's leading authority on television direct response and trade support advertising. Under Bliwas's leadership, Eicoff has grown to become one of the top agencies in Chicago, with clients such as Sears, Beltone Electronics, Rodale Press, Time-Warner, Banc One, Meredith Corp., Campbell Soup, Duracell, and American Express.

Few marketing disciplines are changing as fast as television direct response. In recent years, the proliferation of cable stations and independents, the infomercial trend, and new telemarketing technology have transformed our industry. The traditional one-step direct response commercial for a relatively inexpensive product has become an anomaly. In its place are a wide range of two-step offers, many of them for high-ticket services.

Not only have the offers changed, but so have the media and creative approaches. Media buying strategies have become far more sophisticated than in the past. The traditional direct response ghetto of late nights and weekends has opened up; virtually every time period is a possibility. Buys are much more targeted than they have ever been, with cable providing buyers with scores of options.

The transformation in the creative approach is even more pronounced. Production values have soared. Fortune 500 clients have demanded high-quality creative, and agencies have dramatically upgraded the look and content of these spots. While the objective of this advertising remains results-oriented, it also maintains a desired corporate image.

Yet as much as our business has changed, it will change even more within the next ten years. Let's focus on some key areas where those changes will occur.

High-Ticket Offers

Boats, cars, computers, furniture, furs, financial services, homes, travel services—all of these high-ticket products and services will be part of the television direct response advertising future. It wasn't so long ago that direct marketers believed you couldn't sell anything priced over $19.99 through television direct response. In recent years, that price ceiling has been raised, and in the future there will be no ceiling.

We recently tested a spot with a low-four-figure price tag. What surprised us wasn't that the spot worked—it was a terrific spot and a terrific product, and we were convinced that people would respond. What surprised us was that people called and didn't require additional information from a salesperson, a brochure, or any of the other typical and lead-generation steps; they simply watched the commercial and responded with their credit card number.

As surprising as that might seem now, it will be status quo in the future. Part of the key to this prediction is that these offers will come from companies with well-known and trusted names. As companies such as IBM, Ford, and Coldwell Banker make television direct response an integral part of their marketing efforts, they will eliminate the "trust" issue. Viewers won't question whether the offer is exactly what it seems to be, because they won't doubt IBM's word.

High-ticket items typically have used targeted advertising media. In the future, no medium will be able to target like television. Hundreds or even thousands of cable channels will be available. It will be possible to create an almost perfect match between the demographics of a Cadillac buyer and the demographics of viewers of a certain channel. If that isn't sufficient, advertisers will have another option: learning channels.

Learning Channels

The logical extension of infomercials, learning channels will be a higher-quality mix of information and selling. Each of these channels will focus on a specific area of interest: travel, computers, music, and so on. A channel may have a sole sponsor (Ford as the sponsor of the automobile channel) or a non-competitive mix of sponsors (a vitamin manufacturer and a health club chain as co-sponsors of an alternative health channel).

These channels will present high-ticket direct marketers with opportunities to tell their product stories with greater depth and more dramatically than ever before. Unlike most infomercials, these channels will have large budgets for programming and talented production people capable of turning out highly sophisticated shows. Those shows may include documentary-like features, demonstrations, and interactive question-and-answer vehicles.

The premise behind all these learning channels will be that given sufficient information, viewers can make educated buying decisions about products and services regardless of their cost. The direct marketer's goal will be to make that learning process as easy and as credible as possible.

Changing Roles of Agency, Client, and Station

As of this writing, NBC is talking about starting its own shopping channel. It is not inconceivable that other networks will also get into the act, recognizing the inherent advantages they have over other, non-media-owned shopping channels. Given the possibility of client-sponsored learning channels, the big question about the future is: what roles will agencies play?

It is possible that agencies will take on more of a consultant role. Their clients may be both advertisers and stations that require strategic direction.

Television direct response agencies will probably retain their creative responsibilities, and those responsibilities may even be expanded. They could have a creative department that is expert not only in standard-length, two-minute commercials, but in longer-form documentaries, home shopping shows, and interactive programming. In some instances, agencies will be coordinators, helping facilitate partnerships between stations and advertisers.

Given the rapidly expanding number of media options for television direct response advertisers, agencies that become intimately familiar with the hundreds or even thousands of options will have a leg up on the competition. Any agency that can help clients choose the strategically perfect 10 stations out of 1,000 for their offer will have a secure place in the future.

Technology

Telemarketing technological advances are already giving us a taste of the future. The new systems are now capable of taking 10,000 calls per minute, bringing the future goal of network television direct response into the present. For a long time, the technical barrier of handling a massive number of calls simultaneously stood in the way of a network spot. Now that this barrier has been cleared, we've begun testing these network commercials, and the initial results are promising. In the past, networks weren't overly receptive to direct marketers—network rates were too high, and they preferred the more profitable, non–direct response, 30-second spot. But as ad dollars shift away from the networks to syndication and cable, networks will become more receptive to direct marketers and more flexible.

In the past few years, 900 numbers have created a stir, but they have lost some of their luster recently. Part of the problem has been unsavory advertisers that have soured mainstream direct marketers on the concept. My theory is that 900 numbers are going through the same evolution as television direct response advertising. In the early days of direct response television, the advertising was dominated by the same type of marginal advertisers: pitchmen hawking slicers-and-dicers, miracle hair cures, and the like. I would bet that the psychics, phone sex purveyors, and personal injury lawyers will eventually give way to more legitimate advertisers. The 900 number concept of automatic billing to the caller's phone number is enticing. Mainstream advertisers will find a way to adapt that concept to their needs.

Interactive direct response, a concept that has excited people in the industry for years, won't become a widespread reality until the costs come down on the interactive "box" installed in viewers' homes. As of this writing, the lowest price I've heard quoted on these devices is $500, and that is too much for most people. When the interactive devices are affordable, however, and when all the bugs have been worked out of the technology, this two-way communication will be a boon for the direct response industry. Not only will it allow viewers to obtain more information faster about products and services than ever before, but it will also enable direct response advertisers to learn a great deal about their customers and prospective customers.

But even without this interactive capability, television direct response advertisers will increasingly use their advertising to develop customer databases. Telemarketing services have become adept at securing information from callers, and companies have translated this information into computerized databases that increase the creative and media buying effectiveness of future offers.

In the future, it is likely that telemarketers will be able to access a startling amount of information about every caller in those critical seconds or minutes when the call comes in. They will be able to determine a respondent's salary, assets and liabilities, credit history, job title and place of employment, related purchases (related to the offer), and so on. Using this information, telemarketers can determine whether the caller is a credit risk, whether Incentive A or Incentive B will work best, and if the caller might be more likely to buy another type of product or service. Armed with this information, telemarketers will be in a much better position to qualify respondents and close sales.

An Integrated Element

Ten or so years from now, television direct response advertising will be even more an integrated part of a company's larger marketing program than it is today. Organizations will no longer treat television direct response as a segregated tactic. We're seeing a trend among our Fortune 500 clients to coordinate our work with that of their general agencies. The objective is for television direct response advertising to communicate the same image and message as their other advertising. That means not only that the words dovetail, but that the images also go together. Many organizations can't conceive of airing a direct response commercial that has significantly lower production values than their other advertising.

Some Things Will Remain the Same

If we were able to peer into the year 2000 and see a direct response commercial, we would find that a few elements have not changed. Television direct response is always going to sell harder and more straightforwardly than general advertising. Future spots will still be geared toward catalyzing viewers to pick up the phone and dial a number. Product demonstrations will continue to be part of the package, as will presentations of product and service benefits. The present staples of television direct response advertising—insurance, book and music series, magazine subscriptions, innovative products, exercise-related offers—will continue to be in the mainstream.

Despite all the changes that are bound to occur, we're not likely to see 15-second direct response spots, ones that are deliberately esoteric and arty for art's sake or commercials for pure commodity products (where there are no demonstrable differentiating traits or benefits).

Then, as now, the best television direct response advertising will produce immediate, measurable results.

CHAPTER

16

Business to Business Direct Marketing

*The Fundamental Forces of Change**

Donald R. Libey

Donald R. Libey is President of the Libey Consultancy Incorporated, a marketing and strategic planning consultancy and seminar production firm; Publisher, President, and CEO of Libey Publishing Incorporated; President of Regnery Gateway, Inc.; and founder and Chairman of the North American Society for Strategic Marketing, direct marketing's first futurist think tank.

A rational futurist view of business direct marketing is much like watching waves breaking on the shore: massive amounts of water in motion crashes, splashes, recedes, and repeats in many different patterns; over time, small, logical, structural changes occur to the landscape, and, over longer periods of time, permanent alterations to the land mass can be predicted with reasonable certainty. The chief elements of cause and effect are water, wind, tide, and time. Each element has its momentary dominion over the process of change, but each is moving in an ineludible extrophy that must chafe and collide with the static of *now*. Nothing will be again as it is now—not in a second, and hour, a year, or a century.

The forces altering business to business direct marketing are, like those altering the land mass, fundamental forces: economics, technology, social and cultural forces. Although each element has its periodic dominion, the confluence of forces is destined to produce an accelerated period of change unprecedented in the relatively short history of business to business direct marketing.

Economics

The economics driving the future of business to business direct marketing are increasingly complex and hostile. Marketers once concerned primarily with inflation, interest rates, availability of capital, and relatively stable manufacturing and labor costs will be forced to manage a diverse new series of economic influences and the economic implications of social and cultural costs. Mastering economics will require adaptation to the long-wave business cycle, global competition, protectionist hemispheric markets, continental consolidation and discounting, and the inevitability of national and continental monetization of debt and hyperinflation.

The basis of economic concern for the future is the astounding fact that the level of U.S. debt by 1996 will reach the level of the value of all U.S. assets. The economy is approaching technical bankruptcy. The budgetary reforms of the Clinton administration and the Congress are, in all probability, too little, too late and are likely to be economically regressive.

The Business Cycle

If, at the brink of the 21st century, North American economic history is examined carefully and with an open mind, a pattern of economic advance and retreat is found occurring with regular periodicity. Since the Revolutionary War in the United States, the economy has peaked with absolute regularity every 55 or 60 years. The same phenomenon can be seen outside the United States, extending back in time. A natural cycle of economic boom and bust is not uncommon, nor does it come randomly. For some (the majority) the business cycle is recognized but not given credence; for others (contrarians) it is not only recognized but relied upon for strategic planning.

Fulfilling the 60-year pattern, the business cycle peaked in 1989. The next economic peak projects to the years between 2044 and 2049. Averaging the economic bottom, the economy projects downward to the years 2016 to 2019. The bottoms do not adhere to the fixed 55 and 60-year patterns, however, and can be precipitous as in 1929 or extended closer to the average. One thing is clear: Economic recovery is generally a gradual, upward move; economic decline and depression is often a fast, steep drop.

Global Competition

The nature of 21st-century global competitiveness is protectionist. Given the escalating economic, cultural, religious, racial, and ideologic tensions throughout the world, it is illogical to project some ideal, parallel, global trade utopia. Early exportation of direct marketing from the United States to Europe and Asia have reproduced questionable results. The expansion of business to business direct marketing on a global basis à la "Europe '92' is, simply, not that simple. Here, the economic futurist and the direct marketing strategist must confront the reality of the inherent biases of cultures, societies, and nations. No evidence exists, nor is it likely that any evidence will be forthcoming in the first half of the 21st century, for furtherance of an economically or ideologically viable commercial "League of Nations."

Global competition is most likely to evolve as competition for labor, raw materials, money, and technological intelligence. As such, global competitiveness is of a higher level than the pan-national marketing of widgets. Over the first half of the next century, competitive infrastructure will be ordered; successful competitive marketing of products and services will, necessarily, emerge only after the infrastructural foundations have been built through political and economic alliances between nations and the evolving hemispheric common markets.

Multinational corporations will continue to operate on a global basis, albeit under increasingly stringent margins and increasingly thin profitability. But multinational corporations are not at the center of business to business direct marketing. Consult any directory, and it is readily apparent that this is an industry of "small shopkeepers." Few business to business direct marketers have the resources, management expertise, or energy to plunge into the miasmic uncertainty of multinational operations. At best,

North American business to business direct marketers will have been successful if, as an industry, they can control the North–South American Common Market by the middle of the 21st century. That alone will be a significant and costly achievement; the individual or aggregate industry vision of global dominance in a protectionist period of economic evolution is grandiose at the minimum.

Protectionist Hemispheric Markets

The Asian market is defined. The European market is defined. The North–South American market is defined. There isn't a great deal more. These three "common markets" are the marketing "malls" of the next century.

While it is illogical to project one trading bloc's dominance over all three, it is logical to project that each trading bloc will attempt specific industry competitive inroads to the others. It is a fair assumption to recognize that competition abhors a vacuum and that Europe may make competitive raids on North–South America and Asia for specific industry advantage. Or, conversely, Asia may make competitive raids on North–South America and Europe in a different advantageous industry. Business to business direct marketing will follow these waves of competitive egress but will not initially attempt global dominance in that advantageous industry. The conclusion is simple: Hemispheric markets will consolidate for competitive and economic protection; *ergo,* protectionist strategies will dominate the next half-century.

The North American Free Trade Agreement (NAFTA), while fraught with short-term controversy, is inevitable in the long term. In one form or another, the United States, Canada, and Mexico must achieve agreement if South America is to be secured against Asian and European incursion and the North–South American trading bloc is to be secured as a competitive strength in the protectionist hemispheric contest looming on the economic horizon of the coming century.

Increasingly, visionary CEOs and boards of directors of progressive U.S. and Canadian business to business direct marketing corporations are recognizing the wisdom of securing their Canadian, U.S., and Mexican potential over the next 10–20 years in order to amass the strength for developing and capturing the South American markets between 2015 and 2050. As a result, early strategic alliances are being explored and evaluated in the 1990s with an eye to the competitive advantages to be garnered in the next 25 years. In the short term, it may be politically incorrect or ideologically unpopular to favor the progression to a North–South American trading bloc, but in the long term there is no other economically viable alternative. At the tap root of commerce is the prime commandment: Control your market.

Continental Consolidation

Under the logical projection of a strengthening North–South American trading bloc, there follows almost by definition the necessity for consolidation among U.S., Canadian, and Mexican corporations. Again, economics requires an infrastructural advantage; raw materials, capital, and labor must be served. Each of the North American nations has its advantage in these components of economics; together, greater strength is achieved. Clearly, Mexico has a labor advantage. Clearly, Canada has a raw materials advantage. Clearly, the United States, Canada, and, increasingly, Mexico have a capital advantage particularly when consolidated.

Over the past five years, from 1989 to 1994, U.S. business to business direct marketing companies have begun to recognize the potential of Canada. In the same manner of epiphany, Canadian companies have begun to see competitive advantage of expanding to the United States. During the same period, both the United States and Canada have awakened to the fact that there is a huge country located to the south, Mexico, and it represents a gateway to South America, economically, strategically, and culturally. As a result, a "simmering" of North American consolidation is underway in business to business direct marketing. With the fires of margin erosion and market expansion burning higher, that simmering is destined to reach the boiling point over the next 10 years, and the steamy bubbles of consolidation will form at the surface of the continental direct marketing industry. The implications are clear: (1) a larger theater of operations; (2) a larger capital requirement; (3) a higher pla-teau of corporate size; and (4) the disappearance of small, undercapitalized direct marketing companies either through competitive attrition or acquisition.

Discounting

An insidious force has crept into marketing that is straining our lifeline to profit. Take a focused walk through the retail world of today and you can only come away shocked at the recognition that North America is on sale at deeper discounts right now than at any time in our commercial history.

Forget the hysteria over NAFTA; forget the runaway cancer of our budget deficit and national debt; forget the specter of a widening import imbalance; forget the massive external forces exerting relentless pressure on our businesses. We are putting ourselves out of business through a short-sighted mania for discounting.

Everywhere you look, merchandise is being discounted as a norm. These are not the 5% or 10% discounts that were once offered as a periodic incentive. These are *routine* 40%, 50%, 60%, or even 70% discounts driven by the suicidal obsession with next quarter's operating profits and an abdication of the basics of marketing.

What is frightening for business to business marketers is that retail experiences trickle down into the business experience. A buyer is first a person. When that person is conditioned in the retail crucible to expect 50% discounts on personal purchases, that learned response ultimately finds its way into business buying.

Regardless of the industry—and today's business media is full of the evidence—a *prime tenet* of free-market capitalism is being savaged on the altar of discounting: margin. No matter how one dresses up the rationale to satisfy the short-term-focused shareholders, when margin erodes businesses die. You can get away with it for a season, or a year, but ultimately someone has to face the fact that discounting is simply another word for starvation; the body of the business is doomed to wasting.

In the new century, enlightened marketers will recognize that the "junk food" of discounting will only result in consolidation, homogenization of product, increased financial stress, and unavoidable and disastrous shortcutting of customer service. Enlightened marketers will find their way around this pervasive insanity and will ascribe to the only constant of commercial history: *a fair profit for a good product and a good service.* Recapturing that eroding paradigm is the key to survival for marketers hoping for continued, profitable growth—indeed, survival—in the new century.

The Rebirth of the Whole Price

If we don't stop soon, we may never see a whole price again. If we elect to carry into the new century the ragged and scrofulous garments of the discount mentality, then our collective national future is perilous. On every CEO's desk there should be a sign with the daily reminder, "Stop me before I discount again."

The rebirth of the whole price demands a competent selling force, particularly at the retail store level. When we turn over our retail businesses to minimum-wage, part-time, unenthused, uncaring cash register ringers, there isn't much that will motivate a customer except a deep discount. What happened to professional retail selling? As a commercial nation of shopkeepers, we may have to come to grips with the reality that well-paid employees with high levels of sales training are worth their weight in gold over the long haul. At some point along the discounting trail, we have to ask, "What is the lifetime value of a customer and what has to be done to assure that lifetime value is fully obtained?" If you expect a whole price—

and a whole profit—you must have a whole employee. To earn profits at the expense of competency only assures the erosion of customer loyalty.

The rebirth of the whole price in business to business direct marketing demands uncompromising customer-focused service. Find ways to provide service as the customer defines service, and you will find the common ground of rational pricing. Customers all over this nation are willing to pay for superior service. They are willing to pledge their undying devotion and loyalty if they could find competence. We have experienced the Quality Revolution; unfortunately, we did not first experience the Compentence Revolution.

Savvy Marketers are discovering the imperative of information and fulfillment technology as a hedge against margin erosion. Information technology, such as highly integrated relational databases, can be used to spotlight the needs and wants of individual customers. It's not the information that preserves the margin and the whole price, it's the relationship with the customer. Technology is at its zenith of value when it is used to form a relationship; those bonds preserve loyalty and lifetime value. All too often, technology is driven by the need to invoice, by accounting, by non-customer-focused demands. That is lunacy. The cost of technology is only justified when it produces new sales, and new sales come from strengthened, one-to-one relationships with customers. Deal the technological cards any way you want—people still buy from people they like.

Futurist marketers are already deep into the *interconnectedness* of new century marketing. They are creating new portals that customers will access in order to service the varied and time-denominated needs of those customers. Interactive communications portals include TV, telecommunications hybrids, cable, satellite, CompuServe, EON (TV Answer), virtual reality marketing, and a plethora of new marketing portals developing exponentially. Access superiority may be integral to recapturing the whole price.

Outside the intimacy of the customer relationship, margin erosion will be battled through increasing strategic alliances with other North American markets and service-delivery entities. Consortium marketing in the new century—groups of marketing organizations providing a totality of need and service—will offer a roundedness and wholeness that will justify whole pricing. When the customer joins a network of merchants, the shared efficiencies and conveniences are a compelling force on the collective acts of purchasing. Business to business marketers who learn to create strategic malls of linked suppliers will service the customer with a totality that resists the simplistic and short-sighted discount.

Recombinant Marketing

Perhaps the greatest value in strategic futurist marketing lies in the recombinant process of history. Go back to the earliest markets and you find that the price of the commodity is relatively equal; the price of the service that attends the commodity, however, accounts for the true margin. Merchants who undervalued good, competent service were left only with the price of the commodity itself.

Logic, arrived at from an understanding of the constants of history and tempered with the visionary's understanding of the future, tells us a few, simple things: you can't make money by giving away your margin; you can't survive if there is an inadequate contribution to overhead driven by an inadequate margin. If massive discounting is allowed to feed on itself, it will quickly establish irrevocable norms in the expectations of the customers that only the largest organizations controlling the means of production and the raw materials will be able to survive.

Inflation and Debt

For the first time since World War II, the United States and Canada stand at an economic watershed. Time and reserves are depleted; the margin for error has disappeared; the luxury of poorly conceived, stop-gap policy is no longer viable. The economic and societal momentum created by any legislative action will be felt for several generations, and the resultant economic legislation will determine the future of North American business for a very long time.

North America must have a growing economy to build employment and incomes in order to create excess revenues to pay off the debt. That reality is simple common sense and a foundation principle of sound business, be it government or private.

A primary concern of North American direct marketing CEOs is margin erosion. The restructuring and down-sizing of North American business over the past decade have been a direct result of margin erosion. Further relentless margin erosion will be devastating to the future growth and competitive strength of North America in a rapidly expanding, competitive, and global marketplace.

A massive tax increase will serve to empty the economy of incentives, disposable income, business cash flow, aggregate demand, and employment. Consider mid-1990s reality: Our economies are not growing in any meaningful way; business and consumer confidence is low; commercial and industrial loans have collapsed; jobs are virtually nonexistent; the dollar is at historic lows against the Japanese yen even in the face of a Japanese business crisis; gold has begun a move that represents a worldwide lack of confidence in the U.S. economy; the trade deficit is growing. Couple these facts with the most astounding fact of all: The U.S. debt will soon reach $5 trillion, an amount greater than the total asset value of the entire United States.

New tax legislation includes large increases on the marginal tax rates on personal and Social Security income, an increase in the corporate tax rate, an increase in the marriage penalty, increases on excise taxes on alcohol and tobacco products, an energy tax to be paid every time we use energy, travel, or purchase a good or a service. Special provisions will curtail deductibility of business meals and wreak havoc on the entertainment and restaurant industry. These new taxes may pale, however, when compared to the massive increases in payroll and employment tax that are inevitable over the next ten years in order to pay for national health-care reform and universal health insurance coverage.

The potential outcome of this decade-long barrage of taxation: a $500 billion (and growing) federal deficit, 10% unemployment (or higher), acute inflation, and a monetary crisis. Why? Consider the progression: Taxes kill the anemic growth in the economy. The deficit increases. Confidence erodes and investment money dries up. Foreign investors move out of the dollar and dollar-denominated assets. The prices of gold and foreign currencies rise. The bottom falls out of Treasury bonds. Interest rates move up sharply. Foreign economic powers will no longer buy U.S. bonds or accept dollars for oil payments. The Federal Reserve will be unable to support the eroding monetary situation with cheap money. Inflation surges, fueled by energy taxes, payroll taxes, and climbing export prices due to the dollar's decline. Margins erode further. Employment levels decline. Unemployment rolls grow. The national health-care system (which has payroll taxes of 20% to 30% levied for its funding) slips into deficit. Unemployment spirals higher. Emergency sources of revenues must be found to fund health care and other entitlement programs approaching bankruptcy. The value added tax (VAT) is imposed, further devastating disposable income and business profitability.

This progression is but one potential; it is clear, however, that the alternatives are becoming more limited, more contracted, more deterministic. Perhaps business leaders in direct marketing should take a more forceful role in questioning what will be good for North America, the long-term economy, their industries, and—last—their businesses. History is rife with examples of similar economic progressions. History also would imply that little is learned from the past. As North American business leaders debate the relative merits of one or the other likely solutions to our imminent economic crisis, the logic of historical perspective becomes a valuable commodity for structuring the strategic direction of the business to business direct marketing corporate future.

Technology

The business to business direct marketer of the future will not compete only with peers at other companies. The marketer of the future will compete with massive, integrated cyber-systems that elevate the competitive arena far above the unsophisticated playing fields of the '90s. The new century marketer will be clad in cyber-armor and will wield a cyber-sword that will cut to the quick of a new commerce, a new marketing construct, a new tournament where the joust is won not by sheer strength, but by cyber-driven intelligence, cyber-dominion, artificial intelligence, and virtual reality marketing.

Cyber-Dominion

Now you stand on the threshold of yet another logical evolution in marketing. As your predecessors stood at the entry way of the computer and information age of marketing, you stand at the portal of the cyber-dominion of marketing. You may choose to deny its validity, its speed, its palpability. You may choose to excoriate its reach, its potential, its inevitability; you may choose to ignore its immediacy, but you cannot deny that it will soon be either your future strategic coup or the nemesis of your evolving obsolescence.

First, cyber-dominion, artificial intelligence, and virtual reality must be understood in the context of the all-too-painful reality of North American commerce over the past and future ten years. Productivity gains at the expense of human overhead lie at the core of the redefinition of commerce that has been and is taking place. The loss of jobs that confounds politicians and the working populace is, in the cold light of reality, a loss of inefficiency and a gain in productivity, albeit a devastating outcome for the hundreds of thousands of individuals caught in the decades-long restructuring of the North American businessphere. Cyber-technology has eliminated jobs and will continue to eliminate jobs; the fast companies have already recognized the competitive inevitability of this; the slow companies tenaciously cling to the misbegotten belief that a "no-pain" return to the fulsomeness of the '80s is just around the corner. There is no recovery in a cyber-driven evolution, only ineluctable evolution. The fast companies are moving to the next level of positioning dominion; the slow companies are simply standing still, innocently and unknowingly waiting for the *coup de grace*. Manufacturing will continue the present shedding of its half-century-old skin; direct marketing is about to enter the most profound era of efficiency focus since our emergence as a defined discipline of commerce in the 20th century.

Twenty-five years ago, a person entered the profession of direct marketing with a required knowledge quotient of, say, 100. This separated the well-educated from the less-educated. Today, that same entrant requires a comparable knowledge quotient of 200 to even enter the field. In the new century, the entry-level ceiling will be raised to 800 purely as a result of cyber-technology. Intellectual skills that used to add up to a 200 will be accomplished in a matter of nanoseconds through artificial intelligence; the job entrant of the new century will begin at a level several hundred points above today's best minds. The computer will eliminate mid-level thinking and, consequently, mid-level thinkers. A "cyber-ceiling" will form in direct proportion to the speed of cyber-development over the next 10 years. Business to business direct marketing "rainmakers" of the next decades will be in primary competition with the capacity of artificial systems of intelligence that presuppose a higher level of efficiency. Gone will be the legions of marketing assistants who pored over nonintegrated computer reports to discern possible trends and product life cycles; gone will be the endless hours of meetings and analyses to simply determine what is happening. The integration of cyber-capacity with the needs of a hyper-competitive marketing environment will elevate the playing field to a level of efficiency and productivity only remotely thought of in the '90s. And it will come fast, borne on the wings of global, economic competitive necessity.

In the lists, during the joust, at the tournament of champions of the next kingdom of marketing, will exist the database. The integrated database is to tomorrow's marketing royalty what the horse was to the knights of old. It shall matter not what the marketing channel of distribution is, or what the configuration of selling force is, or what the products or industries are; it shall only matter that the total and efficient heuristic integration of accurate marketing knowledge exists and that the corporate participants are capable of speed, predictive response, and multidimensional understanding of the individual customer extending three or four dimensions deeper than that of the '90s. And that facile, dominant marketing strength will be derived and driven from the integrated database.

Artificial Intelligence

Artificial intelligence—cyber-systems that learn, analyze, and conclude—are tomorrow's marketing engines driving strategic understanding and experiential, real-time decision making. For the fast companies, the relational database is already obsolete; for the slow companies, too many have ignored even the necessity for a relational platform of customer information, and they are fast falling irrevocably behind the competitive challenge. As an example, a slow marketing company will slog through the data over a six-month period and determine, ultimately, that a group of products are—for some unknown reason—dropping in sales volume. The artificial intelligence systems of the next marketing evolution will simply send a report to the managers saying, "The AI Marketing System has noted a serious drop in sales volume for product group #DD345 beginning on August 17 and extending to today, September 23. The drop is prevalent in companies having between 50 and 75 employees and who are almost exclusively first-time purchasers. Analyses of product purchases, returns, and bad debts indicate a quality problem in 12 of the products in this group. The cost to satisfy these customers is estimated to be $4,900 versus a lost lifetime potential purchase value of $64,700 over the next seven years. All of the affected products are manufactured by the Sunrise Promotional Industries corporation. Inventory stands at $17,600 as of this moment. The order entry department has been alerted to product problems and the product numbers have been blocked from the ordering system. Alternative product suggestions have been substituted for sales and telemarketing contacts and current orders in process are being re-directed to customer service for outbound telephone confirmation and notification."

This is not a futuristic, someday scenario. It can be done now with existing cyber-technology. Fast companies with a strategic dedication to marketing dominion are putting the integrated database systems in place; they are investing the necessary capital now to assure that they can compete in the artificial intelligence-driven new century. Fast companies have examined the speed of the evolution of computer technology over the past 20 years, extrapolated the potential halving of time for the next technological adoption, and have concluded that systems of artificial intelligence allowing cyber-dominion over the routine and mundane marketing and analytic functions of their businesses provide a singular competitive advantage that they cannot afford to ignore. The foundations are being built right now by the major competitors having the vision to see where marketing will be in 10 years given the clear evidence of evolutionary change that has occurred in the past 20 years. These companies understand the reality of productivity and the next level of demand for survival efficiencies. These are the prophetic commercial leaders who will attract the all-important and increasingly scarce investment capital necessary to remain champions.

And hard on the heels of an artificial intelligence–driven database technology comes, perhaps, the most significant marketing advance ever: virtual reality.

Virtual Reality Marketing

Virtual reality is customized physical and psychological experience on demand. Through the power of cyber-technology, you will have the ability to create and modify experience as desired. Inputs and outcomes will be selectable by the individual. A parallel, experiential world can exist as a program. To enter the parallel world, one requires the coordination of the cyber, visual aural, and tactile sensory portals. In other words, the cyber-world coordinates the vision, hearing, feeling, and, therefore, the psyche. Forget that it requires a massive computer storage system, helmets, and gloves; all of those technological trappings will be reduced to simplicity and access immediacy. Within 10 years, virtual reality will be as accessible to the individual as video/VCR technology has become in the past10 years. Why? Because it is possible and there is enormous wealth to be made.

The first steps to a virtual reality paradigm began with the massive acceptance of video games, followed by the equally massive acceptance of Nintendo. The computer had created and entered the fantasy of the individual. And make no mistake about this technology—it is the dominion of fantasy that we are talking about. Sad though it is, on a global basis, the inhabitants of Earth are, in the overwhelming majority, ignorant and impoverished. The day-to-day existence is a crass exercise in survival with little joy. In every societal paradigmatic change playing out at the close of the 20th century, *escapism* is central to the will of the individual. We, as members of the business society, must recognize that our experience is not that of the representative individual; ours is an experience of association with the upper levels of wealth; ours is an experience with privilege. Virtual reality is, in its most lethal form, escapism; in its most positive form, enlightenment. Which one do you think will win?

Turning from the near-certain choice of a techno-narcissism by society for the transient fantasy pleasures of virtual reality, are there potentially revolutionary marketing outcomes associated with the ultimate cyber-pseudoreality? We believe that the early decades of the new century will find marketing driven by customer-customized virtual reality. For the first time, a customer will be able to express his or her "dream" in virtual reality. As an example, a customer who wishes to furnish a home will be able to create the virtual reality of the finished decor and then survey available products digitally with which to make the virtual reality *reality in fact* through purchasing. Another customer, wishing to make a fashion statement, will create the outcome in virtual reality using his or her own virtual body and then apply instantaneous, custom-designed clothing to that construct in order to place an order. You don't like it in blue; instantly it is red. The paradigm is that the final outcome of the product will be visualized before the decision to buy is made. Bring it to an even simpler construct. A business wants to see its letterhead before it is printed. Virtual reality creates 20 finished product samples before the decision is made—instantly and digitally. Virtual reality means *no surprises.*

The entertainment world is already using a crude form of virtual reality to create the virtual play. Increasingly, audiences are choosing—in real time—how a play will end, how a mystery will be solved, who gets the happy ending. This is not ethereal, it's in production all across the United States right now. It's called *individual choice.* Marketing is destined to be the science of delivering the individual choice.

Look at the rise of infomercials on cable television. In effect, these are mini–virtual realities. Tune in, choose a celebrity, imagine that your skin will look like that in just 10 days, call and get the cosmetic product. Tune in, choose a career, imagine that you can make millions in no-down-payment real estate, call, and get the book and the tapes. Your reality has been changed instantly and it is all virtual. Infomercials are in the business of virtual dreams. These are new paradigms that we have not explored before . . . electric, instantaneous, personal, sensory . . . and the customer writes the script! Television has not yet evolved its ultimate destiny: the access portal for any reality the customer desires. This is vastly different from the mere output portal of what the producers thought the customer wanted. Harness the individual's vision of the outcome—the dream—and present it in virtual reality back to the individual. Therein lies the greatest marketing aphrodisiac ever conceived.

Most of us have learned to market better over the years by presenting our products in a better light. We have learned about photography, sampling, offers, appeals, styling, good layout, good copy, sales, and lead generation. These progressive elements of the art and science of marketing have stood us in good stead. We have become more responsive to the customers' demands, to the concept of service, to the benefits of excellence and quality. Is there anything so different from extending what we do now to a live, moving, sensorially accurate individualized format? Is that really so *outré*? These early stages of the virtual reality paradigm are establishing the process of individuation necessary to unlock the next logical advance of marketing technology. This is no different from the first television advertisements or the first radio advertisements. First the foundations are put in place (TVs and radios), and then the marketing feeding frenzy begins.

Consider the multiple-step linkage necessary to use marketing and virtual reality. First, you have to show the customer the products that you offer. Next, you have to allow the customer to show you how those products will fit into the vision of the final outcome (the dream). Then you have to allow the customer access to a "dream machine" that uses your products and their vision to consummate a customized purchase. Not a lot of magic there conceptually.

The cyber-neural pathways that will be evolved and hybridized in the next 20 years are, by definition, to be evolved and hybridized from databases. Interestingly, more and more large corporations are abandoning a portion of their traditional advertising and marketing efforts in favor of establishing integrated databases. This is the early foundation laying. From these "marketing banks" will emerge individual, participating consumers, borne on the wings of cyber-technology, driven by dream vision and virtual possibility (concepts of marketing entirely foreign to traditionalists), joining with marketing organizations in the consummation of a near-addictive virtual reality.

Imagine something as familiar as looking for a house. Today, you spend two to three days with the real estate sales associate, driving hundreds of square miles looking at house after house. Appointments have to be made, owners have to clean up the living room and the kitchen, everything has to be redundant for every looker. Using virtual reality, you can visit every house the real estate agent has listed in the virtual reality–equipped office. You can walk through the houses, see the back yards, the neighbors' houses, and the surrounding neighborhood as if you were actually there. Turn your head and look into the dining room; open a door and look inside the closet. It is real, only it is a representative reality. Finally, you settle on a house that meets your needs, only you don't like the way the stairway intrudes on the living room. The real estate agent says, "No problem." A virtual reality remodeling program is accessed and—instantly— there is your new house with the stairs relocated. The program not only shows you what it will look like after the remodeling, but how much it will cost, and it automatically calculates the costs into the financing of the home. And you never even had to leave the office except to make the first and last visit after you have decided this is the house for you. This is virtual reality marketing at its simplest, at its lowest level of efficiency, at its least sophisticated potential. Imagine how you would sell automobiles, vacations, clothing, college educations, and the entire panoply of North American free-market capitalistic consumer choices.

Marketing will utilize virtual reality in the new century to link the artificial intelligence–driven databases that catalog changing needs and statistics to create the product-stream purchases necessary to accomplishing the successful mission of the corporation. Just-in-time concepts will be modeled in virtual reality and governed by artificial intelligence that "learns" instantly of changes in demand and supply. The new century CEO will be able to tune in and watch the evolving and constantly changing dynamic of the business in full sensory virtual reality. The ideal model will be achievable in the real world, because the variables will be controlled in the virtual reality model.

We have observed a handful of very bright marketers who are beginning to explore the potentials of these technologies. In some cases, it is simply entering the world of virtual reality as an experiential phenomenon. Many CEOs have donned the helmet and glove and have wandered through the digital landscape of tomorrow. They have emerged changed and with a profound vision of things to come. At least consider this technology. To deny it and excoriate it out of hand is to deny and excoriate the march of technology in the last 20 years. The technological applications for business to business direct marketing will, in all probability, follow those emerging for consumer direct marketing. As with 800 numbers, overnight delivery, discounting, and the menu of direct marketing delicacies, business to business tends to follow what works in the consumer milieu. Key to this recognition is the ability to remain open to the technological march forward. As technologies emerge, business to business direct marketers must be in the strategic position of adapting, discarding, or embracing those technologies. All else is but denial.

Social and Cultural Forces

On a societal, rather than a purely business level, socialcycles will cause enormous changes to the North American ethos in the new century. The degree, amplitude, and speed of change will be unprecedented in history. An individual maturing during the 1980s in North America and observing society in the year 2030 will not recognize the society that will have evolved in relation to the society from which it was born. While the same experience can be pointed to for almost every generation, the present generational passage is different. The society of North America, indeed of the world, is experiencing wrenching change and a necessary "cleansing." Not unlike the naturally occurring cycles of a lake, when every spring and fall the lake turns and brings up all of the impurities, detritus, and sediment of the bottom for exposure to the life-giving sun and the oxygenation of rebirth, the global society is dredging up its impurities and turning the waters for a normal, cyclical cleansing and return to positive, constructive values.

The evidence of this turning is ubiquitous and both positive and negative: the ending of the Cold War and the Communist philosophy; the self-determination of Eastern Europe with its attendant economic pain; the rise of the so-called Third World and the necessity for opportunity; the focus on family values and new standards of behavior; the specter of HIV/AIDS and its implications for the reevaluation of a standard of morality that was diminished in the last quarter of the 20th century; the confrontation of the politics of greed and special interest and the serious questioning of their effects on the fundamental principles of democracy; the diminution of the quality of life and the economic standards of exhausted, post-industrial nations; the increasing tensions of ethnicity, isolationism, and divisive ideological factions; the rise of welfare-driven poverty and homelessness among the world's underclasses; the impoverishment of spiritual, intellectual, and religious foundations; the massive increase in violent crime and the scourge of a global drug culture and economy; and the utter abandonment of any standards of decency by the global entertainment, television, and movie industries.

These are not the usual "generation gap" differences and concerns. These are monumental social problems testing society in ways that have not been required or experienced in our history. We stand on the brink of healing or inevitable decline; this is a moment of critical decision in the vast panoply of history. Albeit only another small decision point in the great stream of human and world events, it is the most important moment, perhaps, in the history of modern Western civilization and, certainly, in the history of North America. We, as a responsible, major world society, are commanding social and economic change that will define the very soul of our future existence and survival. These, then, are the socialcycles of our discontent. They describe negative as well as positive influences. Common to them all, however, and regardless of their positive or negative orientation, is the unalterable fact of their imminence and their inevitability.

Socialcycle I: Global Economic Stress

The nations of the world are entering upon a period of severe economic stress that extends decades into the future and will cause the revaluation of economic foundations. This is not calamitous; it has happened numerous times before. It is a naturally occurring economic cycle that exists in the hyperspan of history. Its time has simply come again. There exists an organic state of value; from time to time, it gets out of whack and must undergo correction. These periods are long, often extending 55 to 60 years. Having completed a post-1931 Great Depression period of sustained economic prosperity, essentially worldwide, it is now time to level that unrealistic, unsustainable, and artificial state of value and bring it back to the organic norm. Throughout modern history there have been periods of devaluation and the return to economic reality; that describes the immediate decades ahead in the new century.

Subcycle 1: Margin Erosion

The complexities and interdependencies of a lengthy period of global economic stress and devaluation must, inevitably, result in an erosion of margin. Periods of high prosperity have corresponding high margins; periods of low prosperity have corresponding low margins. It is not terribly complex, arcane, or mystical.

Microcycle A: Discount Pricing

During extended periods of economic stress and margin erosion, discount pricing is the normal economic response, a form of economic Darwinism. Again, this is not terribly complex or insightful. To conduct a reality check, consider the current, existing feeding frenzy of discounting in North America. There is no evidence to suggest that it will end or return to its previous closet. Cheap is chic.

Socialcycle II: Global Social and Political Stress

As the 20th century ends, the nations of the world are enjoying greater freedom and greater social unrest. As political tyranny is ending, economic tyranny is taking its place. The formation of three global markets—the European Common Market, the Asian Common Market, and the North–South American Common Market—provides the economic impetus driving the political and social stress; the world is positioning itself for the redistribution of wealth in the new century. As a consequence, an extended period of social and political stress is inevitable and, in fact, has commenced with the break-up of the Soviet Union and the reestablishment of sovereign Eastern European nations. Ideological supremacy has yielded to economic supremacy. At the same time, the political power of this socialcycle is causing massive polarizations in the social structures of the world's nations. In effect, nations are attempting to become "lean and mean," as did North American corporations in the 1990s; the result is disenfranchisement for vast portions of the world's unproductive poor. The natural consequence can only be an extended period of unrest, rebellion, and violence, which can be calmed only with economic opportunity. This, by definition, creates a self-fulfilling cycle of long-term political and economic-driven social stress.

Subcycle 1:   Fragmentation of Global Markets

Rather than three massed and interconnected global trading blocs, the world's nations will circle the wagons in the three major common markets, insulating themselves against global, economic tyranny by the economic superpowers. This will result in strong common markets but dysfunctional intercontinental common markets. The North American companies who are attempting to establish European and Asian dominion will, ultimately, be driven back to the economic, political, and social safety of the final North–South American Common Market.

Microcycle A: Share Wars, Mass Consolidation, and Protectionism

In a microcosm of the three world common markets, the three North American countries will, initially, compete for share of the North–South American Common market and ultimately be forced to a cooperative consolidation on a scale never before seen on this continent. The reason is clear: either an economically strong North America bands together, or it will have to battle the rising tide of a young, restless, and migrating South American population. The North–South American Common Market will, first, be in a consolidated fight for supremacy over the South American markets and, second—not until well into the new century—for a cohesive, cooperative North–South American Common Market. Protectionism will be turned inward upon the North American Common Market and then inward again upon the North–South American Common Market. At issue over the next 50 years is who will be the North–South American economic superpower and who will dictate and dominate the North–South American trade. It is a reasonable conclusion that it will be the alliance between Canada and the United States, with Mexico performing the role of the labor colony.

Socialcycle III: Negative Social Productivity

As the pressures exerted through socialcycles I and II mount in the first decade of the new century, the economic and social survival drive of the middle and upper classes will cause a harsh appraisal of the productivity of the social underclass and a self-deterministic realignment of scarce economic resources. Until that appraisal is quantified by legislation, the burden of paying for a growing number of poor, noncontributing members of society will fall upon the existing governmental taxing systems, which will inevitably deteriorate. This will result in an economic period of negative social productivity during the first decades of the new century, which will not be resolved without massive civil disorder. Historic North American compassion will, in all likelihood, continue to partially provide economically for a now permanently disabled social underclass; however, the continuing and escalating pressures of economic competitiveness and sheer competitive survival will result in sharply cleaved ideologic chasms and unrest. Ultimately, the economically fit will dominate, new social structures and class privilege will emerge, and the long period of negative social productivity will end in the last half of the 21st century. At that point, the concentrated quest for North–South American dominion will commence with Canada and the United States in control.

Subcycle 1:   Socialism by Default

To arrive at the goal, the economic dominion of the North and South American continents, it will be necessary to enter into compromises with the social and political consciences of North America. On one hand is the specter of civil war between the haves and have-nots, an alternative possibly acceptable to the fringes of both the conservative and the liberal wings. Such a solution would require, first, an ideologic war between the elitist and the populist factions. On the other hand is the palliative of partial social compassion, a palliative best described as a half-hearted socialism. Short-term socialism by default achieves the stability and time necessary for the larger goal: hemispheric economic dominion. The have-nots will continue to receive compassion through grudgingly legislated social programs and entitlements sufficient to maintain civil control, but not deep enough to bankrupt the drive to the ultimate objective. Of course, this places a further taxation burden on the socially productive classes, permanently condemns a large portion of society to poverty, and appreciably erodes return on investment. The alternative, however, is anarchy.

Microcycle A: Increased Tax Burden on Business

In order to secure and hold the mandate of the increasingly participatory, self-directed democracy, it will be necessary to establish an economic scapegoat to pay for the half-hearted and ideologically repugnant compromise of socialism by default. That scapegoat will be business. It certainly will not be the individual, who has the ever-increasing power and value of the vote. At least for the first half of the new century, margin erosion and increased taxation will feed at the depleted and anemic corporate trough; however, the carrot at the end of the stick is South America and the imagined riches first described by the 15th century explorers.

Socialcycle IV: Devaluation

Given what must be accomplished over the next three decades in light of the debtor nation status accomplished over the past three decades, the United States has two choices: default or monetize the debt. Controlling and reducing the debt is not an option, given the socioeconomic pressures of the first three socialcycles and the comparatively narrow window of time in which all of these positioning events must take place. Again, a compromise will be forthcoming in the first decade of the new century, or perhaps even in the last half of the 1990s: fiat money. Faced with crippling levels of debt, a need for compromise socialism fueled by taxes, and inflation, the North American power and legislative structure will choose inflation. The exact historical precedents are legion, and the behavior is predictable. The same circumstance is predictable for the European Common Market nations (particularly with a common currency) and the Asian Common Market nations, with the possible exception of Singapore, which desires to become a world financier and will, in all likelihood, act accordingly to attract ever-increasing levels of investment.

Subcycle 1: Monetary Reform

The natural outgrowth of a long period of hyperinflation is a strident and universal public demand for monetary stability and reform, most likely in the second decade of the new century. This time, the demand will come from every level of a beleaguered society and from every nation influenced by the stressed global economy; this time, reform will be serious, not the typical band-aid policies that have been forthcoming from special-interest dominated politicians over the past 30 years.

Monetary reform, for the first time, has a reasonable chance to be accomplished on a North American basis. By that time, the interconnectedness of trade, regulation, consolidation, and investment will not allow anything less. For the first time, meaningful monetary reform may be possible; the hemispheric dominion and world competitiveness will demand cooperative, overlapping, and real reform.

Microcycle A: Hyperinflation

The socialcycle of devaluation carries with it the guarantee of 10–20 years of increasing inflation resulting from the political compromise of economic and political expediency. We have had it before and we will have it again. Count on it.

Socialcycle V: Dispersal

North America is vast. The resources, size, and scope of the continent can scarcely be imagined. The pre- and post-industrial societies of the 19th and 20th centuries have congregated, essentially, wherever there are rivers and ports. There is no longer a compelling reason for that congregation. As a consequence of intensive urbanization during the industrial age, the cities have undergone positive and, now, negative changes; in short, they are bankrupt: monetarily, spiritually, and socially. The tax burden is increasing and the provision of services is decreasing. Businesses are leaving, the upper- and middle-income classes are leaving or have left, and the cities are becoming or have become armed enclaves of nonproductive hopelessness requiring massive infusions of money simply to keep them calm as they deteriorate further. The outcome: dispersal. Wealthy people first moved to the suburbs and, in the new century with the liberation of decentralization, the rise in telecommuting, and the deeper cleavage of class, will move farther and farther away from the festering and dangerous problems of the cities. Thus, a spiral of increasing taxation is inevitable and will hasten the movement away from the cities. Small as well as large corporations have relocated or are relocating to rural areas with stable societies and a quality of living necessary for future growth. The dispersal is not only physical but economic; investment and banking follows the movement of corporations, housing stock, and consumer purchases. Dispersal is also seen educationally; choice in school locations extends, first, physically outward and then away from the decayed and failed public system with its union labor and bloated bureaucratic death grip to the effective, for-profit, private academy having excellence of education and the preservation of values as its mission. The vacuum created by the dispersal of productive members of society and commercial organizations of all types is, predictably, filled by the dysfunctional, permanent and growing underclasses, and the cities are brought down under the weight of welfare and social entitlement programs. Whether these responses are positive or negative is not the issue. A compassionate and just nation answers those questions in the course of its history. The issue is that dispersal is a fact and that it constitutes a growing socialcycle that must be recognized, dealt with, and acted upon for the future, one way or another.

Subcycle 1: Tribal Exurbanization

In the socialcycle of dispersal, tribal thinking, identification, and association will evolve as people seek out and join groups with like values, standards, wealth, age, geographic preference, education, and race. With a primary objective of escaping from an increasingly dysfunctional urban and suburban social milieu, the growing numbers of exurbans will choose locations and group make-ups sharply delineated along racial, economic, and life-style boundaries. At base, this means the polarization of wealth will also polarize geographically and by class. Racial tensions and fear are beyond the idealistic hope of equality. Given the options of social equality, social dispersal, or social containment, the new century will see containment of the urban and suburban poor and dispersal of the exurban wealthy to havens of economic, social, and personal security.

Microcycle A: Services Exurbanization

When the wealth disperses, so do the productive and profitable services, goods, and investment. This microcycle, contained as it is in a massive upheaval of the structure of society, will require ever-greater decentralization, electronic access and remote consumer portals of entry, and far-flung fulfillment of goods and services. As more and more businesses disperse to meet the needs of wealth, size becomes an important principle. In the new century of dispersal, mega-size may mutate to mini-size; the structures of North American middle- and upper-class society may well be downsized and dispersed rather than upsized and consolidated as is true at the close of the 20th century.

Socialcycle VI: Colonization of Labor

Within the global consolidation creating three major trading blocs, namely North–South American, European, and Asian, is the *sub rosa* necessity within each bloc for the colonization of labor. In Europe, the East European nations will serve as the labor colonies for West Europe; in Asia, China will fulfill the labor colony role for the Asian Dragon Nations; in North America, Mexico will provide the labor for the United States and Canada, and ultimately South and Central American nations will be colonized as additional labor sources for an expansionist run at the Asian and European Common Markets by the United States, Canada, and, potentially, Mexico. Regardless of which of the three global trading blocs comes to dominate, the South American labor colony will be a target for much of the new century.

The fundamental fact dictating the Mexican and South American labor colony socialcycle is age. The population of the United States and Canada is aging, and a majority will be over the age of 40, whereas the majority of the populations of Mexico and South America are under the age of 21. Youth and poverty equate to rebellion. Political leaders of both Mexico and South America, who are essentially aristocrats and control the wealth, know that rebellion does not allow consolidation of wealth; therefore, the prag-matic politicians and aristocratic business leaders will assure that their populations are provided with jobs from North America and/or other trading blocs, that the quality of living improves, that peace and employ-ment are maintained, and that the money stays where it has always been. The compromise: allowing their youth to be colonized for labor. That is more acceptable than rebellion.

The economic powers, with their aging populations, will retain the intellectual labor pools, scientific labor pools, technological labor pools, and educational labor pools; they will abandon their own underclasses, who will be unable and unwilling to compete with the off-shore labor colonies, to permanent poverty supported with the social-political-eco-nomic compromise of welfare and entitlement programs. The labor colo-nies and global market is of far greater economic size and importance than the underclasses of North America, particularly as the underclass is, in part, kept from growing further through stringent immigration controls.

Subcycle 1: Decentralization

An outgrowth of the labor socialcycle is the need for North American companies to decentralize operations for the purposes of organizing and managing the labor colonies. The rational will always be, ostensibly, for market expansion; the real reason will be, as always, for control of labor. The precedents are clear in the sugar cane, tobacco, rice, rubber, fruit, and a myriad of other labor-intensive industries on a worldwide scale. It will be no different in the coming new century. Strength in the labor colonies will guarantee a position of strength in the three trading blocs. The strongest player wins. Historically, the winning player has had the greatest amount of labor under cultivation.

Microcycle A: *Ownership of Labor Systems*

Economies of scale and efficiency will evolve ownership of the labor systems on a continental and trading bloc basis. If there has been progress, it comes in the fact that economic powers recognize that it is cheaper and more efficient to share the costs of maintaining a labor colony than going it alone. Redundancy is not an admired attribute in the new century. Consortia of ownership of labor systems will emerge in the first half of the new century that will allow both efficiency and greater control by removing the competition for labor from the equation. Certain nations will take a leadership role in owning and providing the labor to their trading bloc partners, while other partners will emerge as the traders, the innovators, or the financiers. There will remain only the classic three components: resources, capital, and labor. Each are owned by someone.

Socialcycle VII: *Functional Cyber-Dominion*

Existing within the now mature Information Age is the primitive algorithmic decision-tree process that allows next-step actions to be initiated without analysis. Each of these next-step actions represents a pre–Information Age question that was asked by a human. In the new century, greater numbers of questions with greater depth of action will be determined by cyber-systems, thus eliminating the subjectivity of human response to increasingly complex decisions. This is artificial intelligence. The social function of artificial intelligence will not be to make better decisions, even if that is to be a by-product, but to eliminate middle- and lower-level managers from the businessphere structure, resulting in greater operating efficiency (read: profit).

The new century college graduate will not be in competition with other graduates as much as in competition with artificial intelligence systems. Meaningful, high-wage jobs will begin after the level served by artificial intelligence. Below artificial intelligence will exist only service- and labor-intensive jobs, relegated forevermore to low-wage status and existing to placate the poor, uneducated underclass. The "education ceiling," the "glass ceiling," and the "wage ceiling" will be repositioned as the "cyber-ceiling." Breaking through the limits of the cyber-ceiling will be the entry-level requirement for future wealth. By definition, this ratchets up the intelligence requirements for the management ranks of the new century. Extended across the spectrum of society's activities, artificial intelligence will have enormous effects on functionality. Much of what is accomplished through routine decision-making processes will be automated with high-function algorithmic processes approaching a state of zero error. In turn, efficient functionality assures greater profitability of business and the overarching support structures of society.

Subcycle 1: Societal Systems and Process Integration

The functional dominion of artificial intelligence will demand an extensive reordering of the organization, systemization, and processes of the holistic society. The state of integration will not be reached until the last half of the new century, but palpable change will be experienced as society undergoes significant rearrangement of its management activities. Information, in the form of written records, will gradually mutate to cyber-records; multivariate online databases will gradually replace the concept of libraries; individual histories will evolve as life begins and progresses through infancy, childhood, adulthood, and finally the retirement years, all neatly integrated and organized and instantly available. Biologic information—the core of the next major economic age—will be encoded, controlled, and adapted as necessary through integrated cyber-systems to generate either positive advance for humankind or an apocalypse of genetic superiority. But, throughout the new century, the systems and processes of society will become more organized, more recorded, more precise, more available, and more specific; that will occur as a result of the application of cyber-dominion.

Microcycle A: Heuristic Societies

With the dominance of artificial intelligence, applied through functional systems and processes of integration, society will reach a stage of heuristic development. *Heuristic* is defined as "serving to indicate or point out." This definition, by extension, can include "the elimination of free will." When all decisions of a lower order are made automatically, there exists the danger of a loss of free will and the rise, again, of tyranny. As a negative microcycle of cyber-dominion, heuristic societies will be at risk in the latter decades of the new century. Heuristic commercial societies, however, will be improved by the elimination of mediocrity of decision processes, elimination of waste of scarce resources, and the negation of poorly conceived planning. From a pure perspective of resources, capital, and labor, the heuristic development stage of commercial societies is, in all probability, a positive evolution.

Supercycle VIII: Diminution of Luxury

Each of the previous seven socialcycles has mandated a diminution of societal luxury for the new century. The lesson learned and to be applied in the next economic wave is the necessity for moderation. Individuals, families, communities, states, provinces, and national governments are about to have a bolus of moderation forced down their throats. They will choke, but they will survive through the application of an economic Heimlich Maneuver. Society will no longer be able to afford the luxury; the return to moderation is at the core of the return to the survival values necessary to maintain Western civilization.

Subcycle 1: Growth of Needs versus Wants

As the desire for luxury is quelled and, ultimately, extinguished for vast portions of society, it will be replaced with the adequacy of meeting needs, which will attain the status of an admirable trait and, therefore, philosophically and psychologically assuage the loss of luxury. During the first two decades of the new century, needs-based appeals will grow in frequency and intensity, and marketing approaches will cater to the responsibility of meeting needs in moderation. (Wal-Mart knew this before anyone else.) As an attribute, needs-based moderation will extend from the individual through the entire structure of society and come to rest squarely on the steps of government. Control of ruinous government spending and the squandering of the taxpayers' capital will end with the recapture of government by the people.

Microcycle A: Rise of Security-Based Products

Any product in the new century that enhances or relieves any of the previous socialcycles, subcycles, or microcycles will be a security product insofar as it contributes to the overall security and stability of society as a whole. Education will be a security-based product; a necessity for meeting needs. Health care will be a security-based product. Investments will be security-based products. Electronic gizmos and luxury cars will not be security-based products. Security will come to mean meeting needs with moderation and a self-sacrificing but satisfying turning away from the excesses of luxury. Society, in the new century, will begin to think about the generations ahead, a startling reversal from the denial experienced in the last half of the 20th century when, all too often, children reached the status of disposables.

Socialcycle IX: Irrelevancy of Brand

The return to moderation and security-based functionality diminishes the relevance of brand except where brand can prove itself to be a better value, a proof that, for the most part, will be difficult to slip by the wary, security-conscious, needs-motivated new century consumer. Come forward step by step from Socialcycle I and ask, "Will people be wearing designer anything in the year 2005?" The answer is "No!" Undress most things, and you find that aspirin is aspirin, corn is corn, soap is soap, leather is leather, cotton is cotton, and people are no longer buying the pap and papblum fed to them by the totally out-of-touch and increasingly irrelevant advertising agencies. The simple fact is that a diminution of luxury coupled with a rise in needs versus wants makes brand unimportant going forward, especially when accompanied by a price premium in a price-resistant environment.

Subcycle 1: Irrelevance of Mass Advertising

The socialcycles all carry with them the certainty of a growing self-reliance and self-help societal attitude. Advertising carrying a single message for a single body of society or for large segments of society will be obsolete in the new century. Intense individuation will replace mass cohesion as a fundamental of future persuasion. Accordingly, mass advertising will give way to self-directed advertising on demand. The pressures of privacy issues and environmental liberalism will also serve to moderate the use of mass, unsolicited advertising. With dispersal, needs versus wants, economic and social stresses, diminution of luxury, custom engineering, irrelevance of brand, devaluation, and the dominion of artificial intelligence and integrated information and marketing systems, there will be little purpose for mass advertising.

Microcycle A: Fragmentation of Demand and the Rise of Database Marketing

With the obviation of mass advertising, demand will fragment and increasingly de-escalate to individuation. As dispersal of wealth occurs, the only logical and efficient method for channeling demand will be through the use of integrated database technologies and multimedia portals of customer access. This will apply equally to products and services. The ultimate ascension of the participatory database in providing goods and services will take place in the first decades of the new century as more and more advanced technology delivers interactive connectivity into the dispersed homes and businesses of the productive classes of society.

Socialcycle X: Custom Engineering

The final socialcycle is one of almost total customization at the individual level, at least for those portions of society where wealth has been consolidated. Technology will make customization possible; technology will make the communication systems ubiquitous; technology will assemble and maintain the information through artificial databases that learn from individual behaviors. Undifferentiated, mass approaches in the functioning of society will be limited to the least economically beneficial segments of society, the poor. All others having the economic, political, and educational power will receive individuated responses to the provision of their needs and, to some extent, their wants, depending on their economic level. This will occur essentially because of the redistribution of wealth and the consolidation of political power in the self-directed, self-deterministic participation in a democracy of security, moderation, and concern for the future.

Subcycle 1: The Bioeconomic Age

Science will emerge as the control of individuation in the new century. The fifth major economic age of humankind (after the Hunting and Gathering, Agricultural, Industrial, and Information Ages) will be the Bioeconomic Age. Bioengineering and economics will form either a holy or an unholy alliance for the creation of good or the creation of evil. Regardless of the morality, the end creation will be a bioeconomic elitism further splitting society into a deeper polarization of haves and have-nots. Only the coin of the realm changes in succeeding economic ages.

Microcycle A: The Rise of Ethics

In the new century, and as a result of the dawn of the Bioeconomic Age, ethical questions as well as fundamental philosophical constructs will be forced upon society for resolution. With care, the world society has the opportunity for the creation of a moral, ethical, and productive architecture upon which to build the 22nd century.

These ten socialcycles describe monumental changes to the societies of the world. In tandem with the technological, economic, political, and other categorical change, it is important to keep in mind that the population of the world will increase dramatically over the next half-century. It is inconceivable to assume that the nations of today with their multiplicity of problems will be able to sustain the quality of life that has existed in the last half of the 20th century. The rate of population growth is greater than the rate of life improvement, and that essential recognition is inherent in the socialcycles.

It is also important to recognize that no single ideology is supported or excoriated in the preceding discussions of socialcycles. The provocative nature of the vision, by itself, is sufficient to be regarded as either prophetic or anathema. Which view is taken is immaterial, as long as it provokes thought and dialogue among thoughtful business leaders who are concerned about where we, as a society of North Americans and as a society of humankind, are going and whether we really want to go there. One thing is certain: wherever North American business decides to go, it will be because of a free market, the reestablishment of values, and the societal mandate for enduring good through entrepreneurship and the creation of wealth. Nothing can more effectively serve the good of a nation than pursuit of economic, technological, and societal/cultural improvement. As an important component of the North American commercial milieu, business to business direct marketing has arrived at this point in our history as a force not only for commerce but for society.

Conclusion

Business to business direct marketing has enormous opportunities and enormous concerns to be managed in the next 25 years. Where once success was a relatively simple matter of narrow focus and attention to detail, over the next half-century direct marketers will be thrust into a crucible of economic, technological, social, and cultural change.

Like the waves breaking on the shore, much of this change will be slow and some will not happen at all; over time, however, small, logical, structural changes will occur to the landscape and, over longer periods of time, permanent alterations to the land mass of the market and the business to business direct marketing industry will occur with reasonable certainty. The chief elements of cause and effect are economics, technology, and social and cultural forces. Each element will have its momentary dominion over the process of change, but each will continue to move in that unstoppable momentum that must necessarily chafe and collide with the static nature of *now*. Nothing will be again as it is now—not in a second, an hour, a year, or a century. Those business to business direct marketers who observe, think, and project constantly ahead based on economic common sense, technological advantage, and social goodness are assured the laurels of success.

Retail Direct Mail

Comes the Revolution

Murray Raphel

Murray Raphel is president and founder of Raphel Marketing, Inc., based in Atlantic City, New Jersey. He is author of six marketing and business books and has written for a variety of trade journals. His monthly column appears in *Direct Marketing* magazine.

The year was 1964. We had a little children's clothing business in Atlantic City, New Jersey. Our annual volume was so small that we could not afford conventional advertising. We did have names and addresses of a few hundred customers, so we decided to send them a mimeographed letter once a month listing merchandise on sale. For a very small cost, we doubled our business. I wrote a story about what we were doing and sent it to *Direct Marketing* magazine. The editor called, said he would buy the story, and added, "Since we believe retail direct mail is the coming revolution, would you like to write a monthly column on retail direct mail?"

"I certainly would," I replied, hung up, turned to my wife, and asked, "What's retail direct mail?"

The "coming revolution" of retail direct mail predicted 30 years ago turned out to be scattered shots by untrained marksmen using ancient weapons. Only within the past few years has there been an attempt to encourage, educate, and embolden small retailers to use direct mail in their businesses. The exceptions are the big guys from the major hotel, restaurant, and supermarket chains and the mail order arm of the department stores.

Retail direct mail remains, for the most part, an orphan to these proceedings. It is known about, sometimes mentioned, but rarely invited to the party. Anyone who doubts this fact should simply look through the program of any direct marketing convention held in the United States or anywhere in the world. Most direct marketing professionals are so busy talking to one another at these conferences that they ignore the retailer, face pressed against the window, waiting for someone to open the door and say, "Come on in." Trying to find anyone speaking on retail direct mail is searching for the proverbial needle in a haystack. This, despite the fact that more money is spent in direct mail in the United States than on magazines, radio, billboards, and T-shirts advertising the local restaurant all put together. Money is spent by catalog companies and large retailers, but not by small retailers who spend only about 2¢ out of their advertising dollar on direct mail. Surveys reveal only about 5% of U.S. retailers are doing ANY kind of retail direct mail.

Some revolution . . .

If the "business of America is business," according to former U.S. President Calvin Coolidge, surely the business of any country is business. And if you think of "business," the image that comes to mind should not be the multiconglomerate but rather the small businessmen and women who contribute up to 80% of the employment and a major share of the country's gross national revenue. But who's teaching them, showing them, encouraging them to do retail direct mail—their most valuable weapon to survive and succeed in this increasingly competitive economy?

New Directions for Retail Direct Mail

Retail Direct Mail Specialists

These specialists are companies that make direct mail for small or medium-sized retailers as easy to buy as newspaper, radio, or TV. Someone who makes you an offer (in the time-honored phrase) you can't refuse. Because you can't do it as well or as inexpensively.

Manufacturer-Retailer Partnerships

Where manufacturers realize their success depends on helping the retailer who faces the consumer. The generations-old natural antagonism between these two groups will have to disappear if both want to succeed and prosper in the future. They will co-op or pay for retailer direct mail programs to help sell their product.

Rewarding the Customer

There has to be something "extra" the retailer offers to his or her good, better, and best customers over and above the traditional exchange of merchandise for dollars. There are small glimmers of hope, however, appearing first in one country, then another, then still another. In correspondence with leading direct marketers around the world, most acknowledge there are major opportunities for retail direct marketing but very few trends to indicate that anyone (retailer, manufacturer, marketer) is doing much about it today. Here are some comments:

Italy: "In Italy, there are no examples of relevant retail DM activities."
  —Giampaolo Gasparri, DM&B Direct, Milan

Germany: "The majority of retailers in our country do not use direct mail."
  —Rolf-Dieter Holzel, Ogilvy & Mather Direct

U.K.: "The UK scene is not particularly sophisticated DM-wise for Retailing."
  —Peter Tomkins, DMMC, London

Switzerland: "I have unfortunately not heard of anybody in the retail trade who has brought forward far sighted progressive direct mail ideas which really function."

  —Helmut Hillen, Marketing Manager, Mobel Pfister

Hillen does see small glimmers of progress on the horizon. He says, "The classical advertising in newspapers, magazines, TV, radio, billboards is no longer in a position to actively influence the customer."

The once-distant sounds of the retail direct mail revolution are coming closer. Joe Cappo, editor of *Advertising Age*, says, "65% of advertising dollars now go to promotions, catalogues, special events and direct mail!" (*Tah-dah! Offstage sound of trumpets!*) One reason for this is that the consumer is no longer everyone. They are someone.

There was a time when placing an ad in one of the three major TV networks meant 90% of the population would see your product. Today, with the rapid growth of cable and the opportunity to watch up to 500 TV stations, the consumer has become selective. The task of today's retailer: find a niche and scratch it.

"Traditional mass media advertising doesn't work for the small store," says Donna Hanberry, executive director of the Alliance of Independent Store Owners and Professionals. "TV, radio and most daily papers reach a large geographic area. For the local drug store, dry cleaner, grocer or clothing retailer, it doesn't make sense when most of your potential customers live three miles from your store."

There was a time when the manufacturer was in the driver's seat. The manufacturer determined the road to take and told the retailer in the back seat, who, in turn, told the consumer farther back. Today the roles are reversed. The consumer is driving! Consumers tell the retailer what they want to buy. Retailers, in turn, tell the manufacturer what they want to sell. The times, in the immortal words of Bob Dylan, are a-changing.

One reason for this is the sudden realization of the lifetime value of a customer. Until recently, most retailers were concerned with the sale of the moment. How do they sell the customer walking through the front door and then how do they sell the next one? Little or no thought was given to customer loyalty and repeat business.

Says Hillen, "The consciousness of the value of a loyal customer or the reduction in turnover caused by the loss of a regular customer has, as a matter of fact, only become apparent in the last few years."

When the retailer finally understands the importance of the lifetime value of the customer, the revolution will begin. And the retailer should be concerned about losing any customer. Here's why: How much money does a business lose in a year if it loses one customer a day who spends $5 a week? Answer: $48,230! $[\$5 \times 7$ customers per week $\times (52 + 51 + 50 + \ldots + 1)] = (5 \times 7 \times 1,378) = \$48,230$

Stew Leonard, operator of one of the most successful supermarkets in the world in Norwalk and Danbury, Connecticut, says, "The average supermarket shopper will spend $246,000 in their lifetime. Every time a customer comes through my front door I see, stamped on their forehead in big red numbers, '$264,000!' There's no way I'm going to let them be unhappy with me."

The average business loses 20% of its customers every year. If a business could cut that figure in half, it would double the average company's growth rate.

King's Supermarkets in New Jersey, owned by Marks & Spencer in the United Kingdom, tracks its customers' shopping patterns by computer and knows which customers shopped when. If a customer has not shopped in a month, he or she is sent a "We miss you" letter with a $10 gift certificate toward food purchases the next time he or she comes to the store. Its retention rate zoomed because of this simple "reminder" direct mailer.

"Satisfying the customer is the first step toward loyalty," says Hillen. "The second step is to establish a system of a customer card with the aim of keeping their loyalty, increasing their sales and raising the value of each sale."

The Simpler the Program, the More Effective

Stan Golomb prepares monthly mailings for more than 600 dry cleaners throughout the United States. He designs one basic piece each month and sends it to each retailer for its customer database (which he maintains) and also to a few thousand additional names in the area. The results have been phenomenal, with some stores doubling or tripling their volume because of these simple but powerful direct mail pieces that average about 70¢ each for the complete job: printing, corrections, mailing.

Judd Goldfeder runs a program called, "The Customer Connection" for restaurants. His "We do it all for you" idea means just that. He collects the restaurant's current customers' names from cards they fill out while being served and sends out regular mailings to bring them back again. Now the restaurants can mail to customers on birthdays, anniversaries, or for any special promotions during the year. Says Goldfeder, "Over the past 20 years people have been eating out more frequently and the population has been growing. The number of places available for dining has grown even more rapidly. In 1970 there were 17,231 people per fast food outlet. In 1985 there were 8,432. There used to be 845 people per full service restaurant. Now there are 685—a decline of nearly 20%. How do you keep the customer coming back?" His response rate: between 10% and 25%.

A recent program with a supermarket chain in Oregon began with a list compiled from current shoppers. They had a 68% return on their first sweepstakes mailing! Their monthly mailings—a simple 8-1/2" × 11" fold-over mailing piece—average a 15% return and dramatically increased the supermarket's business.

This program has now been extended to five other supermarkets in different parts of the United States and, after continued testing, will be made available to thousands of independent supermarkets throughout the country.

Retailers who are using direct mail are making exploratory steps to find more information about their customers. By building a better database, they not only have more specific knowledge about their present customers, but they also know where they should look for future customers.

The main use by retailers who are using direct mail is to simply "drive punsters (customers) into stores," says Peter Tomkins from DM Management Consultants, U.K. Tomkins said little is being done on data gathering or closed-loop campaigns. There are exceptions: the M&S/Store Group is working on programs to identify life stage/family patterns. But these exceptions are rare. Also, says Tomkins, retailers who use direct mail use it to sell a specific product. He cites examples of companies that use their credit/ retail cards to sell financial services but do not cross-sell related products.

The concept of "One Europe" and dropping trade barriers does not necessarily extend to direct marketing, says Hillen. "It ranges from rarely to never that Swiss retailers are looking for possibilities to expand their direct mail business to other countries. As a general rule they do not know the market, the requirements, the potential customers or the competitors sufficiently and prefer to concentrate on the Swiss market."

But Hillen says there is hope. "In Europe, in general, and in Switzerland, in particular, the tendency to move from classical advertising to direct-activating forms of communication (direct mail) is increasing." (Comes the revolution?)

He cautions, however, that there are negative forces that will slow down this recent growth, including the consumer's growing reluctance to see even more messages in the mailbox: At least 5% of all Swiss householders have a "no advertisement" tab on their letter boxes, which means the mailcarrier discards all advertising mail. In some larger cities, like Zurich, that percentage is 15%. Some communities have 25% of the population asking the postman not to deliver any advertising mail that is not personally addressed.

But isn't this a benefit for the small retailer who knows his or her customer? We think so. Customers welcome mail from a retailer where they presently shop. In fact, they are insulted and feel ignored if they are not told of a special sale or the arrival of new merchandise.

For the most part, direct marketing is used by large retailers. They have separate marketing departments that have the know-how and ability. Small retailers are still using direct mail on a tentative or rare basis because they either do not know how or do not know where to go and find out. The newspaper, radio, TV station, and magazine salespeople all approach the smaller retailer with the ad already prepared. He or she simply has to say "yes" or "no" or make corrections. There are a few direct mail salespeople going to the small retailer. What is needed is some kind of program applicable to specific businesses and altered to the wishes of the individual retailer, such as the ones outlined above for small supermarkets and dry cleaners.

Here's what's happening in some of the European countries.

In Germany . . .

- Department stores and specialty retailers add inserts to local newspapers. The large catalog companies (Heine, Quelle) do well.

- Supermarkets and hypermarkets use weekly leaflets put into all letter boxes in a defined area around the outlets. Some of these leaflets are sophisticated 15-page magazines.

- One of the big four department stores (Hertie) launched a charge card to customers. They now have 350,000 card-carrying members. Members receive direct mail on an ongoing basis to generate extra traffic to the store.

(But what about the small retailer?)

In Switzerland . . .

- The well-known retailers are the bigger companies: Globus, Jelmoli, IKEA, Bally, Movenpick Wines, and Beyerler.

(But what about the small retailer?)

In an increasingly difficult economy and with more competition from traditional and nontraditional retailing formats, what role will retail direct mail play in the future?

Rewarding the Customer

In his book *How to Win Customers and Keep Them for Life,* Michael LeBoeuf says, "Winning and keeping customers depends on rewarding people for being customers." He adds, "It's the rewarded customer who tells others just how wonderful your products and services are, which, in turn, creates more customers." He concludes, "The rewarded customer buys, multiplies and comes back." (Michael LeBoeuf, *How to Win Customers and Keep Them for Life* [New York: Putnam's Sons, 1987].)

FACT: The average business in the United States spends five times as much money for a new customer than it does on the customers it already has.

FACT: 'Tis far, far easier to sell more to the customer you have than to sell a new customer.

"Marketers have a stealth weapon in frequency marketing that's unseen to competitors," says John Groman, Executive VP at database agency Epsilon, a division of American Express. A fast-growing revolution in retail direct marketing is the frequent buyer card. Businesses first saw this work successfully with airlines, then hotel chains, and finally retailers adopted the concept for themselves. How have these programs worked? In sum, rather well for the larger retailers. Some examples follow.

- In Waldenbooks' Preferred Customer Program, members receive discounts and rebates and are segmented to measure who buys what type of book. So mailers for specific books are sent to people who read those books.

- Staples, an office product discounter in the United States, gives every customer a "membership" card when he or she checks out with purchases. This card entitles the bearer to special benefits. Customers fill out a form and their names go into the computer. Recency, frequency, and monetary information is carefully computerized each time customers shop. If they have not shopped in a while, Staples calls them to find out why.

- IKEA, a manufacturer of popular-priced furniture in Europe and the United States, uses a membership card. This gives anonymous customers an identity and builds customer loyalty. Customers pay an annual fee of about $5.00 (U.S.) and receive free catalogs, use of a kindergarten play area for children while parents shop, special low-priced meals in the store's restaurant, etc.

- Some retailers are not ready to offer a card at the time of purchase. Customers must prove they are worthy of this honor (this too shall pass). The BHS Choice Card in the United Kingdom offers a "Loyalty Card" that has to be earned by a certain minimum amount of purchases, which entitles the card holder to lower prices.

- Kathryn Gilbert, program manager of Sprint, a U.S. telephone company, has this comment: "We enrolled more than three million customers since we began our Caller's Plus (customer reward) program in 1989."

Supermarkets

Supermarkets have been criticized for not paying attention to their customers. Joe Cappo asks the question: "What other businesses do you know of where the customer spends $5,000 a year and the business never says 'thank you' to the customer?"

One of the first businesses to reverse this trend was the Ukrops supermarket chain in Virginia with their "Frequent Buyer" card. They simply give the card to any customer that asks for it. The card is scanned at the point of purchase, and the customer receives special discounts. This has been adopted and adapted by many other supermarkets across the United States and in other countries as well.

An enterprising retailer, Rolf Holmberg, in a resort village 30 miles north of Stockholm, signed up 5,000 of his community's 7,000 households for his supermarket's Membership Club. (Says Holmberg, "People with a membership card spend 90% more than people without the card.")

Some U.S. supermarkets have taken a dramatic step and eliminated traditional newspaper advertising in favor of direct mail. Their reasoning: It lets them target their customers with diverse ethnic and cultural backgrounds by tailoring a specific message for each group.

Vons, California's largest supermarket chain, dramatically switched $1 million from newspaper advertising in one community to direct mail. They may take their entire advertising budget—more than $41 million—and switch it to direct mail.

Dominick's Finer Foods, Chicago's second largest food chain, switched to direct mail from newspaper advertising one year ago. In 1990, Dominick's spent more than $8 million, nearly half its total media budget, on newspaper advertising. In 1992 it spent . . . nothing. "Direct mail advertising is very effective in getting our sales message out to consumer homes," said Rich Simpson, Dominick's director of public affairs.

Advo, the leading distributor of direct mail advertising circulars, says supermarket direct mail, nonexistent with their company ten years ago, accounted for more than $140 million of their firm's $700 million business last year.

Hotels

Frequent-guest reward programs at hotels began in 1983 in the United States with Holiday Inns. They copied the idea from airlines' frequent flyer programs. The largest hotel membership club is Marriott's, with 4.5 million members. Annual cost to Marriott is about $60 million. How it works is that you receive points depending on dollars spent or nights stayed. Points can be used for room upgrades, free rooms, or even unrelated prizes: U.S. savings bonds or catalog merchandise.

Some hotels charge for this privilege. Sheraton Club International began in 1986. Members pay $25 a year to belong and receive four points for every dollar spent on rooms and in hotel restaurants. What's the reaction of the customer? "We have a 70% renewal rate," said Sheraton spokeswoman Lisa Dickson.

"We believe in honoring our customers so we set up the Hilton Honors program," says Perryman Maynard, vice president of Hilton Hotel marketing programs. They selected the customers that travel most: the individual business traveler. This group makes up only 15% of Hilton's customers but accounts for 50% of their room nights and 60% of their revenue.

They sent membership packages to enroll in this new club, and nearly 350,000 joined. Membership jumped to one million in just one year. These new Hilton Honor members almost doubled their stay the first year. Hilton's theme is "opportunity lost." Translation: "Here's what you lose if you stay someplace else." (This is one of our favorite theories: Fear of loss is far more powerful than promise of gain.)

Next: To create more excitement (and, yes, more business), they came up with a "double point" program tied in with American Express. "Use your AMEX card and receive double points." This doubled their room night business. Their latest: a triple point program with AMEX. And if you do not use your card during the year, Hilton writes offering upgrades next time you vacation and stay in a Hilton. Nearly 13% responded to that offer.

Today, Hilton has nearly 3 million members. Room nights used by this group alone jumped from 700,000 to 3.5 million, or 16% of their total rooms, up from 2.5% when they began. Bottom line: for every dollar they spend, they receive nearly $31 back.

Because success begets success and there are even higher rungs to climb up the ladder, there are clubs inside clubs. Saks started a "Saks First Club" when it discovered that only 5% of its customers brought in more than half of its business.

Hyatt has an inner-circle club of its top 1,000 customers. One feature: Don't make a reservation. Just step up to the desk, present your card, and there's always a room for you!

Some hotel groups without these programs offer, instead, "recognition awards." For example, Fairmont Hotels created a President's Club. A Fairmont terrycloth robe is sent as a gift after your third stay at one of their hotels.

Mix and Match

What happens if you offer the customer other advantages for belonging to your club? The more rewards, the more participation, the more loyalty. American Airlines ties up its Frequent Flyer program with Sheraton, Marriott, and Hilton. American also ties in with MCI, Citibank, Hertz, Avis, and investments with the American Advantage Mutual Fund. Why do companies do "partnering?"

1. "A partnership increases the value you offer your customers with no or low cost to yourself as a partner."

   —William Ross, Professor of Marketing,
     University of Pennsylvania

2. "You build long-term relationships for both companies."

   —Tim Smith, American Airlines

3. "Partnerships build brand loyalty and incremental business."

   —Ray Noble, PR Manager, Avis

Good Programs for the Big Retailers, But Not for the Small

The average small-business person, however, is concerned with the buying and selling of merchandise, the worry over personnel, the concern that what he or she has advertised will arrive in time, with who's parking where in the parking lot. Small retailers simply don't have the time to absorb daily six-inch-high stacks of computer printouts. So they ignore them. The small retailer who wants to do direct mail cannot be overwhelmed with statistics, numbers, concepts, proposals, or daily multi-page computer printouts. Here is our conclusion and the two directions they must take.

Conclusion

Retail direct marketing is growing throughout the world. In the most recent survey taken by the Postal Direct Marketing Service (PDMS) in 1992, they asked European companies if they "plan to do more direct mail in the future." Almost all said yes. Over the past eight years, direct mail has increased an average of 9% annually in Europe. It has increased in double digits in the United States and in even more dramatic figures in Australia.

Direct mail's share of the advertising budget is also growing. A few years ago, the percentage of moneys spent in direct mail against all other advertising was in the low single digits. Today, on average, 15% of the total advertising budget of European companies is used on addressed DM, and it is increasing faster in the United States.

The large retail companies, as we have pointed out, have staffs, budgets, and advertising agencies to pursue this fast-growing medium. But what of the smaller retailer? What is their future?

Prediction #1:   Manufacturer/Retailer Partnerships

"Advertising is a long-term investment that should be supplemented by promotions that reward customers."

—Ed Artzt, Chairman/CEO, Procter & Gamble

The manufacturers of goods, products, and services must realize that their customer is not just the retailer to whom they sell their products, but also the consumer who buys from the retailer. Their goal, then, must be to assist the retailer to sell more product. This is a revolutionary departure from accepted marketing/advertising but a necessary step if the manufacturer is to continue to have a source of independent small retailers. There are examples of this new enlightenment.

International Photo Group is located in Belgium, France, the Netherlands, Sweden, and Norway. They use the name brand Spector. They work with independent camera shops. They started with a new slogan for their new program: "We don't sell you prints. We sell you profit." Said Johan Mussche, Spector's marketing director, "We made our independent dealers into real business partners."

The company established a Dealer Business Management System (DBMS). This allows retailers to collect all the necessary data through computers at their registers. "It's a basic tool for our future marketing," says Mussche. "We can now identify the buyer, their preferences, their history."

Greenwich Workshop is the largest distributor of signed, limited-edition prints of American artists. It supplies the finest quality catalogs and "sell sheets" to its 1,000-plus independent dealers. But only after it prepared a "Direct Mail Handbook" for each dealer and ran a series of seminars showing how direct mail increased business for other dealers just like themselves did sales increase for the retailer and then, of course, for Greenwich.

Prediction #2: *Retail Direct Mail Specialists*

This is one of those ideas-whose-time-has-come solutions that falls into the familiar litany of, "How come nobody ever did this before?" What some enterprising entrepreneurs have come up with is merely an extension of how direct mail works most effectively for targeting your customers. Instead of offering something to everyone, they offer something to someone. By the year 2000, no matter what your business, there will be somebody (probably a group of somebodys) who will offer you a specific program for your specific business.

Prediction #3: *Rewarding the Customer*

It is no longer enough to give your customer goods for dollars. Everyone does that. Aren't all supermarkets alike? Don't they all sell food? Aren't all clothing stores alike? Don't they all sell clothing? Aren't all banks alike? Don't they all sell financial products and services? What can you do to make yourself separate from and (hopefully) in front of the competition? Reward your customer.

It begins with enrolling them in some sort of "club." It continues with the ability to have direct communication into the customer's home with newsletters, service messages, surveys, and bonus value offers—specific messages to specific customers. The concept is to provide your best customers with extra value in the form of purchasing power in your store. What you are doing is establishing "relationship marketing." People appreciate special treatment. They respond by being loyal and committed customers. Says William Ross, Professor of Marketing at the University of Pennsylvania's Wharton School, "When you reward customers, you induce them to remain loyal. Purchase behavior is habitual. If I can induce you to come to me, I can induce you to continue to come."

Despite this absolutely proven fact, it is amazing to note that nearly half the direct mail "experts" that participated in a Yankelovich, Skelly report on "Direct Marketing in the Year 2000" said direct marketing should focus on meeting short-term goals (48%), while only 42% said direct marketing should focus on establishing long-term relationships with customers.

If the "experts" believe that, then we begin to understand why, after many, many years of prophets crying in the uninhabited forests, there still remains the thinking that "retail direct mail is the future—sometime, somewhere, somehow . . . maybe."

Let your fingers take a walk through the Yellow Pages from accountants to yoga instructors and you'll find hundreds (thousands?) of small retail businesses to which the words "direct marketing" mean the catalogs they receive too many of around Christmas. It's time they knew it's a way to do business. It's time they knew it's a way to do more business. It's time they knew it's a way to stay in business!

Look through the obituary pages of the financial newspapers and see the tens of thousands of small businesses that die every year. There is one way they will not be among that number who take down their neon, fold up their retailing tent, and silently fade away. The time has come to no longer ask what your business can do for you, but what you can do for your business. The answer is: direct mail.

Listen! The sounds are getting louder! The attack has begun. Can it be the revolution has finally arrived?

CHAPTER

▼
18

Clubs

Old, Now, and New

Leon N. Graham
&
Worth Linen

Lee Graham is Executive Vice President of BMG Direct, which operates Bertelsmann's music and video clubs in the United States. Previously, he was President of Scali, McCabe, Sloves Direct and Vice President for Marketing at Columbia House. Mr. Graham is a past Chairman of both the John Caples International Awards and Direct Marketing Day in New York.

Worth Linen is the President and CEO of BMG Direct, a U.S. subsidiary of Bertelsmann A.G. and part of the Bertelsmann Music Group. Mr. Linen was educated at the Hotchkiss School, Fettes College in Edinburgh and received his B.A. from Williams in 1973. He is currently serving as a co-chairman of the Williams College Third Century Campaign.

In 1744, when Benjamin Franklin invited his neighbors to join a reading society (for an upfront fee and regular dues) in which they could read books selected from a catalog, he may have started the first direct-marketed club in the New World. Certainly, by the time Harry Schermann and Maxwell Sackheim introduced their Little Leather Library in 1916, the basic ingredients of the club concept were in place:

- Appeal to consumers with a common interest. In the case of the Little Library, it was Americans (many recent immigrants) struggling to improve themselves and their children through good books.

- Offer them product shipped to their homes.

- Give them a financially appealing deal made possible through economies of scale.

Sackheim and Schermann were successful, but only to a point. Their club depended on members' ordering when they chose to do so. Inventory forecasting was difficult, and sales volume tended to be erratic. When the two direct marketing pioneers introduced the Book-of-the-Month Club (BOMC) in 1926, they followed the Little Library formula. However, they also shipped a selection of the month automatically—almost like a magazine subscription. Again, sales were erratic and volume unpredictable because returns were frequent.

But then Sackheim had one of his legendary brainstorms: Instead of shipping books automatically every month as part of their subscription, he would give members a chance to say "no" in advance. Only if the member didn't say "no" would the selection be shipped. Suddenly, the economies of scale for the club concept were changed dramatically. Members who didn't say "no" (i.e., use their "negative option") received the editors' selection of the month. Of course, they could return it, but most importantly, the fact that members had to do something with every mailing caused the envelope to be opened. This acted as a trigger for ordering from the catalog, whether or not members took the monthly selection. Monthly sales grew substantially, inventory requirements became more predictable, and *negative option club* entered the direct marketing lexicon.

The success of BOMC spawned other book clubs—the Literary Guild remains the most notable—and soon music clubs as well. Sam Josephowitz and his brother, an orchestra conductor, began the Concert Hall Society, a classical music club. John Stevenson introduced Jazztone, the American Recording Society, and Musical Masterpieces. Each used negative option successfully but appealed to a limited market and remained small.

In 1955, Columbia Records' president James Conkling noted that these music clubs accounted for 20% of all records sold in the United States. He decided that Columbia would enter the club business on its own, the first major music company to do so. Expecting opposition from music retailers, Conkling devised a marketing scheme that allowed consumers to join the club through retail stores. This failed when retailers refused to take part, so Conkling abandoned the idea of using retail stores and invited members to join directly.

Columbia's success led RCA[1] to enter the business in 1958. Both of the music clubs were successful and enjoyed periodic growth spurts resulting from technological innovations such as 8-track tapes, music cassettes, compact discs, etc. Today the two music clubs serve well over 10 million members. (Other early music club entrants, such as the Record Club of America, have mostly fallen by the wayside.) The major book clubs— BOMC and Doubleday—serve over 5 million readers. All four clubs continue to rely on negative option as their main selling device.

So, a marketing paradigm that evolved almost by accident for books, and then evolved to music, now serves over 15 million Americans. For books, this makes sense. The club provides an "editorial function" for the member, winnowing through the dozens of possible books published each month to select the best book for the reader. Thus the monthly selection can be perceived, in the case of book clubs, as a service to the member.

However, it is questionable whether the editorial selection function works as well for records as it does for books. Most music buyers already have strong ideas about which album they wish to buy, because the content of a music album gets far more advance exposure than the content of a book. Beyond their initial choice of "listening preferences," members don't have any choice about their monthly main selection. Further, although the club has thousands of titles available, only a limited number can be listed in any monthly magazine. The selection function thus provides less an editorial service than something that limits choice, as perceived by the consumer.

This brings us to the key question for the negative option marketing paradigm in the year 2000 and beyond: Is the negative option paradigm, fundamentally a mass-market system, adaptable for the individual-service environment that will evolve in the next decade? In our opinion, negative option clubs are really a mid–20th century mass-marketing invention looking for a home in the 21st–century world of marketing to the individual.

---

[1] RCA became the BMG Music Service in 1988 when RCA Records was acquired by the Bertelsmann Music Group.

How will clubs adapt? *Can* they adapt? To answer these questions, we need to take a moment to look at the specific attributes of today's clubs and how they might be adapted for the future.

On the positive side, clubs are successful because they fill certain basic consumer needs. Here's what they do right:

- They provide access to a lot of product. (More than you can find in almost any store.)

- Clubs are a deal. Between discounts and free incentives, buying product from a club is at least the equivalent of, and maybe a little better than, buying from sales at retail stores.

- Clubs offer shop-at-home convenience, the benefits of which are obvious for any consumer who is short on time to get to a retail store.

On this last point, please note that there again is a large difference between the book industry and the music industry. While bookstores are generally perceived by most of the book-buying public as a good place to browse, record stores have evolved to target a younger audience. They have taken this to such an extreme that adults often find themselves alienated by the brash teenage environment of many of today's record shops.

On the negative side, here's what's wrong with clubs for today's consumer:

- Although most members do it faithfully, they hate sending the little card back every month.

- Club members perceive they get *too much* mail and *not enough* choice. While a club may carry thousands of titles, the physical limitations of a monthly catalog allow for only several hundred in any given mailing. Even when this is customized by listening preference (such as jazz, country, classical, etc.) for record clubs and reading preference (history, fiction, romance, nonfiction, etc.) for book clubs, members perceive that their choices are limited.

- Although for some consumers being a "member" of a club may provide some psychic benefits, it is our experience that most members perceive that club communications and structure are not adequately tailored for them. Thus the current club structure cannot serve their individual needs in a way that gives them a sense of control over their shopping experience.

An example is the old negative option myth (fast dying but still heard in some marketing circles) that one shouldn't make it too easy for consumers to say "no" to their monthly selection. (This way, one can sell more stuff whether the consumer wants it or not.) All of today's major clubs now realize that this is the antithesis of service and are racing to set up the infrastructure to make it easier for their members to communicate with them.

This sums up the basic attributes, positive and negative, of clubs as they exist today for the consumer of the 1990s. To explore what clubs might look like after the year 2000, it is necessary to look around at the current and potential technological developments that affect the world of direct marketing. To paraphrase Satchel Paige, don't look back, because some new technology is definitely gaining on you.

In our opinion, the technology that will most directly affect clubs is interactive selling. Whether this takes place in the form of television married to touch-tone phone ordering (following the developmental lines of today's TV selling systems such as HSN and QVC) or some really high-tech system of database access from in-home terminals (similar to France's Minitel system) really doesn't matter. We predict that by the year 2000, most consumers will be able to access large product databases in a format that they can see on a screen; they will have some degree of control over how they access that database and what products they choose to see on their screen; and they will have some form of consumer-friendly in-home ordering device that will be electronic rather than having to depend on a piece of paper going through the mail.

That is not to say that mail will be completely displaced. America is still "the Land of the Flashing 12." How many households have you walked into where the 12:00 is still flashing on the VCR? This shows that even though 78% of American households have bought a VCR, many (most?) still don't really know how to use it. Nevertheless, afraid of it or not, Americans do buy the latest technology sooner or later.

So to survive and prosper in the next century, clubs will have to evolve with the technology. To do that, unfortunately, we think clubs will have to literally stand on their heads to change from a mass-marketing system to become an individual marketing service. The technological demands—not to mention the potential costs—of this concept are stunning.

The big clubs all have millions of members. Each one sends each member a communication at least once a month. The response rate to those mailings is virtually 100%. Every member either: (1) orders a product from the catalog, (2) sends back a card saying "no" to the monthly selection, or (3) receives the monthly selection by not sending the card back. That last group then either accepts the monthly selection by paying for it or rejects it by returning it. In any event, virtually every member responds to each club mailing. Multiply that by the number of members and the number of mailings, and you have a huge number of annual communications. So even to support *today's* paradigm, club systems have to handle huge amounts of data and handle millions of direct mail and phone transactions every month.

Our vision is to create a marketing system that allows consumers access to virtually all of the thousands of titles carried in the club inventory, not just the several hundred selected for each mailing. It would also allow consumers to shop across any listening or reading preference. So the classical member can buy hard rock if the mood strikes. The product selection database will have to be able to be displayed visually on a screen and not just in print. Lastly, the ordering process will also have to adapt to electronic media in that it will either take place over the phone or through some other interactive in-home ordering system. This concept presents several key problems to be solved.

First, by lessening, or losing, our ability to "batch" both outbound communications (catalogs, form letters, etc.) and other inbound customer responses (orders, payments, customer service forms, etc.), we will lose many of today's operating efficiencies. Second, will relational database technology ever evolve to the point where it can handle large transaction volumes as efficiently as batch-oriented databases? Third, can we tie them to laser printing technology that can truly be customized and personalized to react to individual consumers on virtually a one-to-one basis? Fourth, will we be able to develop phone centers that can handle the huge volume of inbound communications that we now handle through the mail? (Not if we rely exclusively on live-operator systems; but will consumers accept automated-voice technology?)

We think the answer to all the above "techie" questions will ultimately be yes. It's really a matter of watching for the technology to mature and picking when to take the plunge. But to implement the solutions will involve major investments in telemarketing capabilities, customer service systems, quick access databases, highly personalized laser printing, automated product shipping technology, and more. All clubs will have to take sizable risks—not to mention profit reductions—if they're going to step up to the next round of competition.

One final, huge question involves the "bugaboo" of negative option. Whether or not consumers order main selections, the negative option system does get them to open the envelope and respond. In a consumer-friendly, automated, electronic-marketing environment, can we drop negative option and still maintain the level of member involvement? If we don't drop negative option, will 21st-century consumers put up with us?

For the club marketers of today this may seem a Hobson's choice. But we think it also presents a tremendous opportunity. If clubs can be made consumer friendly to the extent that individual members perceive that the club suits their individual needs, if members can purchase product through the club in a quick and easy manner, and if much of the baggage of club memberships goes away, then we believe that clubs will be ideally placed to serve the information and entertainment needs of consumer households for the foreseeable future and on into the 21st century.

19

Financial Services Direct Marketing

Investing for the Future

James R. Rosenfield

James R. Rosenfield, Chairman/CEO, Rosenfield & Associates, has become an international authority on direct/database marketing. His major area of expertise involves the application of direct/database marketing techniques to nontraditional environments such as consumer products, financial services, and travel. Rosenfield serves on the editorial review board of Northwestern University's *Journal of Direct Marketing* and has taught at the University of Colorado, Ohio State University, and Northwestern University.

.ddle years of the 1980s, deregulation and competition had ef-
.. cultural revolution among financial institutions: For the first time,
oegan to take marketing seriously. Product and marketing managers
oliferated, as did their programs, abetted by the boom mentality of that
now far-off period.

The cultural revolution continued through the later 1980s and into the
1990s, although in a leaner, more disciplined way. Emphasis began to shift
from customer acquisition to customer retention. Customers themselves
became more nervous, more fickle, more sophisticated, and more cynical.
Marketers began to address these realities by at least paying lip service to
the need for relationship marketing and integrated marketing communications. And some leading-edge companies actually began to do these things.

By the mid-1990s, financial services marketing had long since sloughed
off its old image as a backwater. It can be argued, in fact, that the best
financial services marketing right now is the best marketing in the world,
firmly grounded on the concepts of brand and relationship, and strongly
supported by database and telecommunications technologies.

Indeed, the best financial services marketing obliterates the obsolete
distinctions between above-the-line and below-the-line and operates appropriately for late-20th-century realities: Because all media are now interactive (the 800-number is the major facilitator of this), the best financial
services marketers always give their prospects and customers a chance to
talk to them and then keep track of what they say and do. This used to be
called "direct marketing." By the mid-1990s, it was referred to as "database
marketing." In the 21st century, it will simply be called "marketing." As the
20th century marches towards its end, any other approach to marketing
seems regressive, dysfunctional, outmoded, and ultimately self-destructive.

The Present: Financial Services Firms
and Database Marketing

Database marketing most fundamentally involves the use of customer behavioral information to create strategies, design products, and implement
communications tactics. Overhyped, misunderstood, and often misused,
database marketing by the early 1990s began reaching its first real state of
critical mass, when certain companies with a true commitment to it began
to outperform their competitors.

If a database approach is the future of marketing, financial institutions
have a definite head start: Unlike packaged goods firms, for example, most
financial institutions know exactly who their end-users are. Specific name,

address, and transaction information, of course, provides the fundamental building blocks for a marketing database. (When it comes to telecommunications—the second part of the marketing technology equation—financial institutions also tend to be relatively adept, due to the transaction-heavy nature of their business.)

Not only do financial services firms have a head start when it comes to database marketing, they also have all of the necessary preconditions for making it an optimally effective approach.

1.   *Financial services are behavior/transaction-intensive.*

Any experienced marketer knows that at the end of the day, when costs are measured and profits calculated, the only thing that matters is behavior. It's not what people say that counts, it's not what they think, it's not what they feel: It's what they do. Many financial services by their nature create lots of behavior, which turns into fuel for the database engine.

2.   *Financial services are information-intensive.*

The behavior-intensive nature of financial services throws off a great deal of information, and information is the lifeblood of database marketing. Each transaction provides a wealth of data for companies that are willing to listen: credit card use, for example, not only yields information relating to recency, frequency, and amount of purchases, but also categories of purchase. By looking carefully at categories, a bank can reinforce relationships much more adeptly than ever before, while eliminating enormous waste, for example, by targeting only travelers for travel-based loyalty and frequency programs.

3.   *Financial services are emotion/psychology-intensive.*

Nothing is more emotion-ridden and psychology drenched than money and the behavior that money engenders. Emotion/psychology-intensive products and services lend themselves much better to the relationship marketing concept than do low-emotion products. Why? Because a relationship implies depth, and there's no depth without emotion. A marketing database, among other things, is a quantification of relationships.

4.   *Financial services are protracted.*

The longer time a customer spends transacting with a company, the more opportunities open up for accumulating additional information. Financial services firms have a wealth of possibilities for this kind of data-capture:

applications, branch and office visits, telephone contacts, etc. All of these customer contact points tend by their nature to be protracted. As well as this kind of "vertical protraction," financial services firms enjoy "horizontal protraction." Even in an age of fickle and disloyal consumers, customers still tend to remain with their financial services firms for a relatively long time. (Credit cards emerged by the mid-1990s as at least a partial exception, but credit cards are a hybrid, combining some financial product characteristics with some of the traits of packaged goods.)

The Future: Marketing Redefined

To survive and prosper in the future, all financial services marketers—indeed, all marketers everywhere—need to ask themselves three questions:

- What is marketing?
- What are the marketing imperatives for the next few years?
- How will these imperatives change the way we handle organizations, products, media, and messages?

What is marketing?

In his landmark article, "Marketing Is Everything" (*Harvard Business Review*, January/February 1991), consultant Regis McKenna observes that for most companies, marketing is "selling stuff and collecting money." He's right. And that approach works perfectly well as long as categories and populations are growing. They're no longer growing, though, in late-20th-century America, and the old approach to marketing no longer works.

Marketing needs to be redefined. The narrow concepts of the past have to be abandoned and replaced with a customer-driven, whole-systems model: Marketing is the tissue that connects customers and companies, people and products. It's no longer a function, a thing, a department, or a discipline. It's a way of approaching business.

What are the marketing imperatives for the next few years?

There are four imperatives that are likely to constitute the cost of entry for successful marketing over the next few years:

1. The need to create communications corridors, enabling interactive contact between companies and their customers and prospects

2. The need to provide solutions, rather than products

3. The need to build trust

4. The need to accomplish these objectives by building and integrating both brand and database

Communications Corridors. The most important communications corridor is the 800-number. The 800-number, in fact, is perhaps the single most significant marketing phenomenon of the late 20th century. It creates dialogue, generates feedback, and is at least potentially the best database building tool available. It's also a medium that transforms everything it touches. The addition of an 800-number turns anything—a print ad, a TV commercial, a credit card, a label on a package—into an interactive direct response medium.

From a customer service and relationship marketing standpoint, the psychological importance of the 800-number cannot be overestimated. By combining high-touch with high-tech, the 800-number restores control to customers who feel they have lost control (by misunderstanding a statement, losing a credit card, encountering a situation requiring insurance compensation). Giving customers control is vital: An inner dialogue between control and fear of losing control is one of the major consumer cultural issues of the late 20th century.

Although financial services firms in general are relatively skilled at 800-numbers, there are two areas where they will need to shore up deficiencies over the next few years: automated call processing and brand building.

Automated call processing offers irresistible economies and should certainly be used. There's a problem, though. A company can potentially lose the greatest power of the telephone: its ability to create human contact. This is particularly damaging in customer service situations, where the caller might have a need for reassurance and empathy. Companies can come close to having the best of both worlds—the cost efficiencies of automated call processing and the empathy of a human being—if they let callers exit immediately to a live representative. Most systems list numerous menu options, with the exit to a live representative usually last or close to the last. It should be first or close to the first. (This is especially important with an older customer base, because technological tolerance decreases with age.)

Insensitive use of automated call processing will compromise profitability. Customers with problems will become angrier, more cynical, and more negative if they have to wade through a seemingly interminable series of options before getting to a human being. One result: greater customer attrition, which is hugely expensive. Studies done by Bain & Company indicate that in most businesses a 5% decrease in attrition translates into a 60–100% (or more) increase in profits.

A second negative result: greater turnover among customer service representatives, because customers become more negative and angrier. Hiring and training new representatives turns into a hugely significant cost.

Brand building is the other area where financial services firms have to polish their 800-number performance in the future. In a recent study, the 50 leading credit-card issuers in the United States were called on the phone and asked some unexpectedly difficult questions: "Who are you? What's your size? How long have you been in business?" Sadly, only 2 of the 50 could answer these questions. The nervous, cynical consumers of today and tomorrow care deeply about the stability of the financial institutions they deal with. You can't build trust if you can't answer these questions. (Solution: Program answers to these questions into the customer service representatives' computers, so that they can access company and brand information instantly.)

Following are some implications, recommendations, and predictions for the future:

- Financial services firms should treat all media as interactive and abandon the outmoded practice of running ads that fail to give prospects and customers a chance to enter into dialogue. Dialogue is behavior, and behavior is everything.

- For leading-edge financial services firms, the 800-number will evolve into a sustainable competitive advantage, enabling them to build perceived value and therefore charge a premium for their products and services.

- Financial institutions should allocate increasing resources into media specifically designed to build communications corridors with customers: direct mail, telemarketing, newsletters, private-label magazines, etc.

- Financial services firms should closely monitor the new interactive media, where computers, telephones, and video will ultimately converge into a single household unit (the fiber-optic-based "information superhighway").

Solutions, Not Products. No one wants or needs a financial product. People want and need solutions. In a world of parity products, the clear, simple promise of solutions is the best way to create and keep customers.

USAA is arguably the best financial services marketer with the best customer satisfaction record in the United States, if not in the entire world. One of USAA's major philosophies is to design simple products, and then keep them simple. If USAA can't simplify a product enough, it won't offer it.

This philosophy is ostensibly a bit surprising, considering that USAA's core constituency consists of military officers and ex-officers, a highly educated group of people trained to sift through complexities and make decisions. Yet even with this group, clarity and simplicity are now a fundamental consumer benefit.

It stands to reason: The world at the end of the 20th century has become a very complicated place, with exponentially more data, more stimulation, and more decisions than ever before. Psychologically, the natural reaction to an increasingly complex world is to seek simplicity.

Financial products by their nature are complicated, and financial services marketers by and large have not done a good job of simplifying things. As financial products become more competitive, in fact, the tendency is to add more complications in an effort to differentiate products. Differentiation is a good strategy. But complication is an unacceptable side effect. If you can't differentiate without complicating, don't do it.

Following are some implications, recommendations, and predictions for the future:

- Smart financial institutions will regard clarity and simplicity as sustainable competitive advantages and will begin designing materials—promotional, legal, operational, financial—to be not only user-friendly, but also "gazer-friendly," so that an increasingly post-literate audience can get the story at a glance.

- Most marketing organizations need to be taken apart and redone. In a world where solutions, not products, matter, product management is clearly an outmoded organizational style, by definition focusing the marketer on the product, not on the customer. It's the right organization for a growing, developing situation, but the wrong organization for a mature, developed environment.

Build Trust. Culturally, Americans are not very cynical people. In spite of this, consumer cynicism has become a common phenomenon of the mid-1990s. Cynicism kicks into overdrive where financial services are concerned: Few other categories have suffered from so much destabilization, so many dislocations, and so much bad press. So profound has mistrust of financial institutions become that by 1993 some once-universal clichés had virtually dropped out of the language: "You can bank on it," or "You can take it to the bank."

Trust can't be built by asking for it: "Trust me" is an invitation to cynicism. And, importantly, cynicism has destroyed much of the language financial services marketers use to build trust. The words "service," "quality," and "value" now have to be avoided, because they almost always elicit a spontaneously cynical response from consumers.

Trust can only be built by being trustworthy and by trusting the customer. The latter is often a difficult adjustment for financial firms, particularly lending and insurance companies, many of whose cultures and operating procedures are built on mistrust.

Following are some implications, recommendations, and predictions for the future:

- Smart financial services marketers will regard cynicism as an opportunity, not a problem. Cynicism is generated by disappointment, and the flip side of cynicism is a desire to believe in something. That desire provides the psychological basis for building trust.

- "Trust the customer" needs to become the financial services firm's equivalent of "The customer is always right." The only practical way, though, for many financial institutions to trust the customer is through technology: by enabling customer service representatives to access customer history immediately, and then empowering them (via decision trees) to trust trustworthy customers.

- "Solutions plus price plus value plus trust" will be the formula for every successful financial services marketer as the 20th century reaches its final years.

- A good way to lose trust is to invade customers' privacy. Financial services firms have to become hypersensitive and proactive about privacy concerns, which are gaining cultural momentum at a rapid clip. Best advice: Use information to help determine products, pricing, strategy, and tactics. But don't feed back specifics to customers unless the offer logically revolves around specific information, e.g., "Because you maintain a balance of more than $5,000, we've moved your account into the no-fee 'Five Star' category."

Conclusion: Build and Integrate Your Brand and Database. Predictions about the future are dangerous and usually wrong. The world, filled with surprises, refuses to behave in a linear fashion. Predictions, by their nature, tend to be linear extrapolations from the past.

It seems clear, though, that as we march toward the 21st century, business and marketing success for financial institutions will depend on being both psychologically acute and technologically adept. This means building your brand, the psychological part of a customer relationship, and building your database, the technological part.

With the exception of a few quite advanced companies, most financial services firms by the mid-1990s were still unbalanced: good at psychology (brand-building) or good at technology (database-building), but seldom good at both. In the relatively near future, survival and prosperity will depend on being adept at both of these elements.

To hazard a prediction a bit further out in the future—say by the year 2010—there will be no such thing as a brand without a database, or a database without a brand. They will be one and the same. Psychology and technology—at least among the best and the brightest—will be woven into a seamless whole. Everything will be integrated, and everything will revolve around relationships.

That doesn't mean that a marketing paradise is at hand for financial institutions or anyone else—that would be a naive expectation. But it does mean much less waste, much closer connections with customers, and much more sensible and user-friendly ways to go about the always challenging task of producing and marketing financial products and services.

▼
20

Book Publishing and the New Consumer

Providing Information and Entertainment for the Year 2000 and Beyond

John D. Hall

John D. Hall is currently President of Time-Life Books. Previously, he was President of Time-Life Music. He entered Time Warner as Senior Vice President, Director of Marketing at Book-of-the-Month Club, Inc.

When I was asked to write this chapter, I was assigned the topic "books and continuities," with some latitude to broaden the scope as I saw fit. I have chosen the topic given in the title because I believe that in order to compete, publishers will have to view their world in much broader terms than "books and continuities." We are in the information game and, to some extent, we are in the entertainment game.

The perplexing question increasingly is, "What will the delivery system be for this information and entertainment?" The good news is that direct marketers, if they are able to adapt, are in the right place at the right time as the pendulum swings toward more direct interaction between supplier and consumer. I have no doubt that the book format and the continuity distribution system will continue to exist, but in order to grow in the next century, publishers will have to provide information and entertainment in the form that consumers want it, and through the vehicle that they want to receive it in.

The form may be books or some interactive electronic mode or quite possibly some hybrid. The delivery vehicle may be continuity through the mail or may be viewed through the electronic superhighway on which you might subscribe to an ongoing service or order à la carte. The baby boom generation may prefer words on paper. Younger generations may prefer information electronically. Certain categories of information are obviously more appropriate for new interactive media than others. The menu of choices is going to explode, and the winners in this rapidly changing marketplace will be those that are the most nimble and the most adaptable.

Product Development

One thing that will not change in the future is the need to develop products that consumers want. This is the most difficult task of all, and it will become even more difficult because of an increasingly fragmented, rapidly changing marketplace. We will be faced with more segmented, smaller niche markets and a wider array of potential formats: books, audio, video, CD-ROM or its successor, electronically delivered through cable or phone systems. We will be faced with multiple moving markets and unprecedented capability to reach them and to target them. This will necessitate dramatic changes in the new product development process. Today, a typical direct market development process might include the following basic steps:

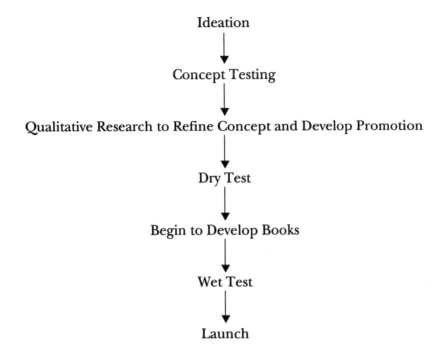

Ideation

↓

Concept Testing

↓

Qualitative Research to Refine Concept and Develop Promotion

↓

Dry Test

↓

Begin to Develop Books

↓

Wet Test

↓

Launch

This process can take six months to two years and has become ever more extensive as publishers try to minimize the risk associated with the costly development of a set of books or a book series. This will change. Because the marketplace is changing so rapidly, the research done 18 months ago may be invalid by the time a series is launched. It may be five years from the time the research is done until the time the series is finished. This won't wash. We will have to find much faster ways to determine whether we have a viable concept or not. Increasingly, the role of research will be to eliminate losers, not to identify winners (this is not new). We will need to develop faster, cheaper ways to gauge ideas. I predict that some new technology will replace dry testing—a slow, costly, inefficient mechanism.

Already, we can begin to see the potential application of new technology to testing methods. One can easily envision use of new creative software to develop simulations of advertising to test possible positioning of a product, and to develop simulated editorial content to gauge readers' reactions to different executions. Eventually, we should be able to do all of this testing on the "electronic superhighway," which should offer unprecedented testing opportunities.

Concurrently, we will have to reduce the cost of developing product (books or whatever). Technologically, the world of book production is changing rapidly, and the successful publisher will need to invest in advanced technology in order to reduce investment in manpower. Desktop publishing systems will be essential. Editorial material will be developed and stored electronically. This will result in lower costs, quicker development, and, most importantly, more flexibility. We will be much more readily able to change editorial direction. Now, that process is like changing the direction of an ocean liner. In the future, with new publishing technology, we will be much more able to change the course of major publishing projects because repackaging of this material will be much more feasible. Different executions, different formats, different configurations, and different languages will be easily reconfigured from the same base of editorial material. So, the model in future will be as follows:

1. Significantly reduced time for market research and pre-launch development

2. Faster, less costly development of books or information

3. Faster entrance of publishers into the marketplace, with less investment

4. Faster exit from the marketplace with losses minimized

5. Re-use of material in some other distribution channel or market

There is, however, one thing that will not change. Great instincts will be more important than ever. As always, the big ideas will not emerge from research, they will explode from the inspiration of individuals with their fingers on the pulse of the marketplace.

Demographics, Reading, and Their Impact on Continuity

The baby boom generation is, and will be, a book-buying group. I suspect that they will be less likely to embrace new electronic media, and that as their disposable income and leisure time increases, they will buy more and more books. Continuity series may become a less preferred delivery system for this generation, which has continually demonstrated its need for choice. Already, we see back-end markets eroding as customers become more and more experienced direct market customers. Direct marketers will need to become adept at selling in multiple configurations and will need to develop ever more sophisticated and sensitive marketing strategies to replace the back-end sales generated from continuity inertia. We will have to provide customers what they want, when they want it. Quality counts. Value counts. Convenience counts.

Projections show that future generations will read fewer books. We will need to adapt our information-providing systems accordingly (more on this later). These generations, trained on pre-teen and teenage CD club experiences, are direct market savvy. We will no longer be able to rest on inertia, certainly a factor in continuity and club sales. Increasingly, we will have to better segment (and screen), better communicate, and better configure offers to meet the needs of these consumers.

Future generations will demand entertainment mixed with their information. To a certain extent, the "interactivity" of the new electronic media will provide this entertainment. The mixture of full-motion video and 3–D animation with text will provide entertainment, but I suspect a generation raised on video games that is less prone to read "books" will demand even more. Already, we see this phenomenon in the CD-ROM materials being developed for children, where the appropriate "point and click" is rewarded with a "quack," a "bark," or a "moo."

Channels of Distribution

In the future, publishers will need to become adept at multiple channels of distribution. The line between those publishing for retail and those publishing for direct market will blur. This will happen because it is increasingly apparent that direct market advertising supports retail sales. Every day there is a new example to prove this. For a product in the direct market and at retail, it is clear that one plus one equals more than two. I'm not sure that this means that the retail customer and the direct market customer are two different people, but rather that consumers want choice (once again) to be able to buy what they want when they want. Adding momentum to this trend is the fact that retailers who have found direct marketing anathema from time immemorial are now realizing the benefits of this advertising, and the "as seen on TV" category is one of the fastest growing in retail. In order to take advantage of the retail opportunities, direct market publishers will surely need to master the broadcast media.

Broadcast skills will be important for other reasons. The impact of TV on book publishing is already apparent. "Big books" are frequently related to heavy TV exposure. In the future, the electronic superhighway will offer incredible opportunities to target customers in the broadcast media. And the skills needed to develop the new electronic media will include the ability to communicate through TV (along with programming and, most importantly—and this doesn't change—the ability to communicate with words).

New Media

At Time Warner we believe the new medium for information and entertainment will be interactive TV. Through a combination of technologies—TV, computer, and printer—the consumer will be able to order information and entertainment "on demand." The challenge for publishers in this new medium will be to provide information in an appealing, user-friendly way. If you've seen CD-ROMs, you know we've got a way to go. I suspect that publishing categories with high utility, like do-it-yourself, reference, and cooking, will migrate to the new electronic media, where you will be able to "page" through a menu of options and order the specific piece of information you need. For direct marketers, this will represent incredible change in the way we offer products. Rather than offering hundreds of thousands of customers one book every four to six weeks at $15.00 or more, we will be moving to a world of millions of transactions in the $1.00 to $3.00 price range where customers will order specific pieces of information they need.

New media will not replicate the tangible, collectible nature of books. We are not solely in the business of providing information. We provide objects of value to be displayed, treasured, and passed on to new generations. Direct marketers will be forced to come up with new offers. In this new world of infinite choice, we will have to determine offer configurations that will optimize lifetime value. The lines will blur between continuity, club, and catalog type offers. In short, we will need to become more versatile both in developing product and in direct marketing it.

Books will survive. In all of media history to date, new media have added to the marketplace rather than cannibalized or obliterated other media. Radio did not obliterate newspapers. TV did not obliterate radio. Interactive media will not obliterate books. All in all, this is an exciting place and an exciting time for direct market publishers. We will continue to provide time-honored objects of knowledge and value, and there will always be psychic rewards for that. And we face an explosion of possibilities in the new world of information with more opportunity than we've ever seen. Interactivity will mean the most direct link between marketer and customer. We have managed this relationship better than most marketers. If we can develop innovative, communicating products and offers for this marketplace, we are in a position to lead the way into the new frontier.

▼

21

Finding the Direct Marketers of the Future

Accomplishments and Challenges

John D. Yeck

John D. Yeck, a partner in Yeck Brothers Company, a major direct mail/ marketing agency in Dayton, Ohio, has been active in direct marketing for over 50 years. He is a member of the Board of Directors of the Direct Marketing Association and its Business-to-Business task force and chairman of the Direct Marketing Educational Foundation.

Where will future direct marketers come from? Not just "people," but those special ones—the bright, capable, skilled individuals able to cope with and conquer the increasingly complicated problems and opportunities posed by twenty-first century marketing. Let's just call them the *good* people.

At the heart of this question are others: "How and why will they choose direct marketing for their careers?" and, even, "What can we do to help more good people come to a direct marketing career?"

Conditions That Prevail

Before trying to answer those questions, let's briefly analyze the direct marketing condition.

It's clear that advertising and marketing people are moving toward greater use of the *direct marketing method*. This is true not only in the traditional channels of direct order, direct response and tightly targeted mail or phone advertising, but in general advertising as well.

That method includes:

- Strong emphasis on careful **selection** of ever-narrower segments of prospects

- Crafting effective **messages** that appeal directly to those segments

- **Testing** to improve the effectiveness of those messages, delivery formats, etc.

- Careful **measurement** of results of those tests to allow

- **Accountability**

- And, finally, **applying** the learning process to produce future improvement.

The direct marketing method almost always involves the construction and use of databases and a great deal of computer work as well, so it's clear that the need is for many, many different kinds of skills.

The explosion of direct marketing in the past 30 or so years has multiplied the need for good direct marketers tremendously. While there is always a "shortage" of the best skills in any field, a look back to the 1950s and earlier shows why it is becoming more pronounced. The number of direct order firms has multiplied as have the channels of communication and distribution. Where there were a mere handful of direct mail agencies then, over 1,000 direct marketing agencies are members of the Direct Marketing Association now. They all need good people.

In addition, as the whole field of marketing and advertising increasingly uses elements of this direct marketing method, more and more CEOs ask their marketing departments not only to account for results-per-dollar spent but to improve those results. "Now that we can have accountability in our advertising and marketing," they say, "let's get more people on board who know how to do it right!"

More Demand

But there aren't enough highly skilled, trained, productive "direct marketing" people to meet today's demand, let alone tomorrow's, as the need expands. As more and more companies and agencies accept the disciplines of the direct marketing method—target, test, learn, and improve—its use will continue to grow. Naturally, more and more good people with various direct marketing skills will be required.

People skilled in direct marketing will come from ad agencies, of course. Direct marketing calls for many of the same skills as advertising, once the understanding and appreciation of database marketing, the skill of one-on-one communication, and the discipline of accountability have been accepted and acquired. But those sources will never meet the demand.

Where will the talent come from in the future?

In the past, hundreds, probably thousands, of direct marketing companies started on kitchen tables. Most of them failed, but some grew to become the leaders in the field.

Some say the kitchen table is passé, that you now must have millions just to start a direct marketing business. Not entirely so. As a freshman at the University of Texas a few years ago, Michael Dell tackled the "impossible" task of selling personal computers direct, without millions to invest, because he didn't know any better. He changed the marketing habits of the whole PC industry. Since he didn't have a kitchen table, he used his dorm room and was soon selling $50,000 worth of PCs a month out of his room and the trunk of his car. After that, his "direct" business just grew and grew. In less than a decade, he was not only selling over $2 billion worth of computers each year but had driven major manufacturers of computers into direct order too.

Dell, while the most visible success, is not the only example. Direct marketer "from-scratch" entrepreneurs pop up everywhere. Others will come from apprenticeships as they always have—promising young people taken under the wing of a master and trained by counsel and example.

Some will just stumble in, discover they were made for direct marketing, and stay. Richard Sears was a telegrapher who stumbled upon a cheap source for good watches; John Patterson, father of business-to-business mail, was a coal merchant who figured that the new-fangled cash registers that helped his retail business could help others if he could tell them about them by mail. No one can be sure whether L.L. Bean's success came from his ability to make a better pair of boots or from the fundamental honesty that led him to refund money to a purchaser when his first batch of boots didn't perform as well as expected.

The vacuum will be filled in various other ways. Some new employees will come from other fields that aren't growing as rapidly. We're certainly living in an era when older people change careers more often than they used to, either from choice or circumstance.

Most new direct marketers, however, will be young people. Since virtually all bright people can go to college today if they wish—and most do—we'll find almost all of the new direct marketing recruits in the colleges and universities. No question. While it's long since been proven that you don't have to go to college to be smart and successful (and vice versa, I guess), the percentage of bright high school graduates attending college is pretty high. That's the place to start.

There are many bright young people in geology departments or with degrees in botany or horticulture. Because the world is a strange place, some of them may be direct marketing stars of the future. But don't bet on it. When we look at the characteristics that distinguish direct marketing from other occupations, we know that some fields of knowledge and skills will produce more of the kind of people who will succeed in and improve the field. Young people who understand the values of good communications, and major in communications, who relate to people and are drawn to sociology or psychology; those who have an interest in business and economics, even accountants and statisticians; artists and writers, computer-literate problem solvers who relish the mysteries of database; these are the young people who have already determined that they are interested in the kinds of skills that lead to success in direct marketing.

So direct marketing will need more young people trained in communications, computers, creative problem solving, and management skills, among others.

But the Information Age is creating tens of thousands of new jobs that require communication, computer, creative problem solving and management training everywhere. Other fields want those same *good* people, too.

So in the years ahead, the same key skills needed for direct marketing will be in demand across *many* future job areas, not just those in marketing.

They are now.

Competition for competence is hot and gets hotter every day.

Short Supply

At the same time there appears to be a widespread decline in basic skills. Test scores in the schools keep dropping. Illiteracy skyrockets. Put those trends together, and it's clear that if nothing changes there simply will be more jobs requiring outstanding ability in our required skills than there are young people to fill them.

As the economy grows and the Information Age expands, direct marketing will be in direct competition for skilled people across the board, as the gap between job requirements and worker abilities widens. Not only that. With increased "worker training" emerging as a national priority, possibly subsidized under a government "industrial policy," competition for smart kids will be even more formidable. For the government is not likely to subsidize training of the best students for direct marketing jobs.

So we'll have to do that ourselves.

How Can We Attract Them?

We need to develop and implement a strategy that will not only interest bright young people in direct marketing, but also get them good jobs and move them toward success. Then we must create conditions that make that strategy work.

The first step in such a strategy is to interest and inspire bright, talented, capable young people into learning about and identifying with direct marketing and get them *excited* about a direct marketing career.

The second is to develop better methods to help them over the gap between preparation and first job within the field so the good prospects aren't lost and so that their energies and abilities can be put to work quickly. Recruitment.

Finally, once they are working in some segment of direct marketing, they need opportunities to *learn more* about it and how to truly *excel* in the field. Continuing education.

First Step: Develop Interest, Excitement

The marketing field must support and encourage greater interest in educating young people in the art and technology of the direct marketing method. The Direct Marketing Educational Foundation (DMEF) is an example of a single-focused effort to increase and improve the teaching of direct marketing in the colleges and universities.

The Foundation has made considerable progress in generating interest and excitement since it began in 1966. In "Where Shall I Go To College To Study Direct Marketing," DMEF lists about 175 colleges and universities with at least one course in direct marketing. Master's programs with direct marketing concentrations are offered at Northwestern University and University of Missouri, Kansas City, along with certificate programs at other schools.

Since 1980 at least 2,000 professors have had contact with some kind of a DMEF program, i.e., the Institutes, Advanced Programs, Educators' Conference, College/Career Days, or Collegiate Echo Competition. About 300 professors and as many as 2,000 students actively *participate* in DMEF programs each year. (That doesn't include exposures to promotional messages or enrollment in those courses where direct marketing is all or part of the curriculum.)

DMEF's roster of programs and services for professors and students now includes: Professor's Institutes, Educators' Conference, Textbook Authors' Seminar, Seminar for MBA Candidates, Collegiate Institutes, Agency-hosted Seminars, National Internship Program, College Days, Hammond Career Days, Collegiate Echo Competition, career booklets and informal career guidance. These are all designed to develop interest in and knowledge about the field.

Second Step: Employment

While it's important to interest and excite young people in direct marketing, that effort is wasted if they can't get a job.

Getting an excited new graduate into his or her first direct marketing job . . . recruitment . . . is currently direct marketing's weak spot. We know from experience that very bright, capable students can, and do, become very interested in direct marketing careers and are eager to find jobs in the field. In addition, once they are employed in direct marketing, they tend to stay and to grow within it. That seems clear.

Unfortunately, job hunters and job openings don't always appear at the same place at the same time, late in the spring, for example. But, of course, that's the challenge. Direct marketers certainly met the challenge in developing interest in the field with the DMEF. Bringing job hunter and job together can be viewed as simply another challenge.

The DMEF, while not acting as an employment agency in any sense, does what it can to help students by acting as a clearinghouse for resumes of Collegiate Institute graduates. Any firms interested in high-quality, entry-level employees may visit a Collegiate Institute for interviews with the most promising students, as some DMA members do regularly. One DMA member who makes a practice of hiring such students reports that 11 of the 12 hires over the years became successful employees.

The fact is, more and more companies are finding it profitable to hire young people who have some academic background in direct marketing. Companies that host DMEF Collegiate Institutes report a substantial savings in the cost of selecting a new Collegiate Institute graduate or one from a school with good direct marketing courses compared to recruiting and training a young person from scratch. Even a little background in the basics of direct marketing helps cut recruiting and training costs.

The DMEF also acts as a facilitator of summer internships. It searches, each spring, for DMA members who will accept one or more student interns during the summer. Next, it compiles a directory of the type and location of counselors and direct marketing professors. They alert their best students and work to match ability and geography between job and student. The students then independently apply direct to the firm and meet with the DMA members if invited. Actual job arrangements are made between employer and student.

Some students work for class credit and receive little or no pay; most receive at least nominal wages. The key objective of the more serious students, however, is actual experience in direct marketing and a credible reference to put on their resumes, plus the confidence gained by being able to talk about "real" direct marketing experience when they go after their first "post-graduate" job. And that first job often is where they interned because they've had a chance to prove their worth.

While most DMA members look on internships as a way to help students, many get tangible value out of the relationship, too. Since the DMEF's effort to locate interested students is heavily weighted toward those with a real interest and some academic experience in direct marketing, DMA members get help that's a cut above average. In addition, the student's fresh outside viewpoint often contributes ideas that are profitable for the firm. In any event, the program adds to the supply of bright young people coming into the field and helps them greatly in getting their foot in the door.

To help the member make the internship more valuable to the student, the DMEF provides supplemental material for study during the internship period. This gives the interns, who naturally receive a limited range of experience in any short period, a broader picture of the direct marketing field. Internships are also sponsored independently by some direct marketing clubs. Sponsors also include individual firms like Bob Jurick's Fala Direct Marketing, which has interned up to 10 students at a time for a half dozen or more years.

While helpful, all these efforts are limited, of course. Jobs can't be invented or legislated and they are entirely under the control of employers. The young graduate laments "I can't get a job without experience, but I can't get experience without a job."

If we are going to have a larger and better pool of experienced people in the future, we need an increase in entry-level jobs right now. The interesting point is that this needn't be seen as a sacrifice. With the blooming of the Information Age, kids just out of college with "no experience" in direct marketing are so much sharper in the field of electronics and the like that instead of being a training burden, they often turn out to be indispensable employees very quickly.

Continuing Education

Developing a future supply of top-grade direct marketers is up to the current generation. In every craft, the Masters of the past selected Apprentices, trained them to be Journeymen, who then became Masters on their own.

So, too, the "Master" direct marketing practitioners of today determine the level of skill tomorrow. Historically, this "craft" has been served well. It needs continued and, probably, increased commitment to meet the growing challenges and stiff competition of tomorrow.

Continuing education in the field is in good and growing supply. The DMA Professional Development and Training Department provides both "public" and "in-house" seminars and institutes. That program is constantly expanding. In 1985 it served an estimated 3,100 people; in 1995 an estimated 3,500 and it's capable of continuing expansion as the demand increases.

Although the oldest, the DMA's efforts to educate practitioners are far from the only ones. Many direct marketing clubs cooperate with local universities and junior colleges to offer Continuing Education classes. Numerous individuals and seminar organizations offer both public and in-house programs.

Not too long ago you could count the number of direct mail books on the fingers of one hand. Now there are scores of them. A few years ago, there was one major magazine serving the field. Now there are many.

However, use of these educational helps is left pretty much up to the individual and to promotion by the seminar management and publishers.

Chances are that deliberate industry efforts to encourage more educational activity by young employees would increase the skill level and the retention of professionals.

Summary

What's needed for direct marketing is a "field of dreams." Not a baseball diamond, but the development of a smooth, recognizable pathway to progressively responsible and challenging jobs in the direct marketing field. Although the "playing field" is different, the directive for the direct marketing field is the same as the movie: Get to work. Just have faith. Build it and they will come.

Fortunately, the stars of direct marketing have always been willing to share information gladly. As a result, young people with serious interest are able to learn through books, articles, attendance at conferences, seminars and institutes about successes and pitfalls.

That spirit of sharing spawned the DMEF.

In 1965 Lew Kleid, a successful list broker, made the initial gift to what was to become the Direct Marketing Educational Foundation with the words, "Direct mail has been good to me. I'd like to help pass along some of that knowledge to help younger people get interested in it too."

Look at how the Direct Educational Foundation has followed the lead of Lew Kleid and his generous thoughts. Recall how Ed Mayer and scores of other individuals, clubs, agencies, and companies have joined in the education effort.

The activities of the Foundation are only part of the story. They concentrate almost entirely on the organization charter, "to increase and improve the teaching of direct marketing in colleges and universities." The Foundation is doing an increasingly good job. It has focused primarily on that first big step of developing *interest* in and *excitement* about in direct marketing among better students. It aims to entice them into investigating and choosing some phase of direct marketing as a career.

In general, that second critical step of getting smart, talented young people into the business does not currently get the broad attention and organized effort necessary. This is the next challenge for the industry.

The Past, Present and Future of Direct Marketing

Bob Stone

Bob Stone, Chairman Emeritus of Stone & Adler, Inc., has contributed greatly to the direct marketing community through his writing and teaching. He has authored two books. *Successful Direct Marketing Methods* and *Successful Telemarketing,* and has conducted *Advertising Age's* direct marketing column since 1967. A professor of direct marketing at Northwestern University and the University of Missouri–Kansas City, Stone is a member of the Direct Marketing Hall of Fame.

If the past is prologue to what lies ahead, we are at the right place at the right time. The all-star team of direct marketers who have preceded me has provided snapshot after snapshot of what we might expect to see in our respective futures.

Our Rich Heritage

I can say with certainty that our futures wouldn't be so bright if it were not for our present and our past. None of the distinguished authors who have contributed to this visionary book would advocate killing the past to make room for new rules for the future. Instead, the suggestion is that we play off of all that is good in the present and meld that knowledge and technology with dynamic plans for the future.

So let's take some snapshots of what we have inherited.

The Credit Card

Sears recognized the need in the early 1900s. Diners' Club and American Express came along in the 1950s, followed by a spate of new commercial cards. Credit cards, in one form or another, won't go away.

Lead Generation

John Patterson, founder of National Cash Register, invented lead generation in the 1880s. Qualified leads shall continue to be the common denominator for sales efficiency.

Clubs

It's only a little over 50 years ago that "Book-of-the-Month Club" was conceived as a way to spread selling cost over the sale of a series of books. That concept spread to records, tapes, CDs, movies, food, coffee, and scores of product and service categories. Clubs will always be with us.

Telemarketing

Toll-free 800 phone service was first introduced in 1966. It's been a boon to direct marketers as an efficient way to get inquiries, to get sales. The 900 number, illicit uses aside, has proved to be efficient way to sell services and to solicit contributions.

Videocassettes

Videocassettes have proved to be a medium with the impact of television without the time cost of TV. The medium has proved ideal for demonstrating cars, selling cruises, capturing lectures, and demonstrating technical developments. Just as it is predictable that, come the year 2000 and beyond, we'll get movies of our choice on our TV sets by telephone command, it is likewise predictable that we will get videocassette tapes on our TV sets by command.

Print Advertising

In the late 1950s, mass-circulation magazines first made regional editions available to direct marketers. This made it possible to test at less than full-run costs. In 1965, newspaper inserts came on the scene. This made it possible to enjoy the same quality of printing in a newspaper as indirect mail. Print advertising will always be with us.

Broadcast

Direct marketers got into TV early on. But the big breakthroughs have come with the advent of cable. Cable, not unlike radio, offers the opportunity to select stations whose programming format fits the product and service being offered (news, sports, entertainment, health, etc.). And the opportunities don't end there. There are Prodigy, TV Answer, and CompuServe, which are bringing interactive TV to fruition. It is estimated that by May 1994 about 500 television channels will be available. Talk about market segmentation!

Then there is the emergence of infomercials, the equivalent of 30-minute commercials, which seem to be here to stay. Add to all this the millions of people who watch and respond to home shopping shows, and we have to be enthusiastic about the future of broadcast.

Catalogs

The demise of the Sears big book in no way spells the demise of the catalog. Instead the Sears decision reinforces a long-standing trend toward specialized catalogs that better serve today's consumer niches. I predict that America's long-standing love affair with the catalog will continue well beyond the year 2000.

The tools that have brought us to where we are, are only part of our rich heritage. The other part of our heritage is the body of knowledge we have gained as the result of testing. There are certain principles that have proved to be true time after time—after time.

The 30 Timeless Direct Marketing Principles

Over my career in direct marketing I have identified 30 principles that prove true better than 90 percent of the time.

1.   All customers are not created equal. Give or take a few percentage points, 80% of repeat business for goods and services will come from 20% of your customer base.

2.   The most important order you ever get from a customer is the second order. Why? Because a two-time buyer is at least twice as likely to buy again as a one-time buyer.

3.   Maximizing direct mail success depends first on the lists you use, second on the offers you make, and third on the copy and graphics you create.

4.   If, on a given list, "hotline" names don't work, the other list categories offer little opportunity for success.

5.   Merge/purge names—those that appear on two or more lists—will outpull any single list from which these names have been extracted.

6.   Direct response lists will almost always outpull compiled lists.

7.   Overlays on lists (enhancements) such as life-style characteristics, income, education, age, marital status, and propensity to respond by mail or by pone will always improve response.

8.   A follow-up to the same list within 30 days will pull 40–50% of the first mailing.

9.   "Yes/No" offers consistently produce more orders than offers that don't request "no" responses.

10.   The "take rate" for negative-option offers will always outpull positive-option offers at least two to one.

11.   Credit card privileges will outperform cash with order at least two to one.

12. Credit card privileges will increase the size of the average catalog order by 20% or more.

13. Time limit offers, particularly those that give a specific date, outpull offers with no time limit practically every time.

14. Free gift offers, particularly where the gift appeals to self-interest, outpull discount offers consistently.

15. Sweepstakes, particularly in conjunction with impulse purchases, will increase order volume 35% or more.

16. You will collect far more money in a fund-raising effort if you ask for a specific amount from a purchaser. Likewise, you will collect more money if the appeal is tied to a specific project.

17. People buy benefits, not features.

18. The longer you can keep someone reading your copy, the better your chances of success.

19. The timing and frequency of renewal letters is vital. But I can report nothing but failure over a period of 40 years in attempts to hype renewals with "improved copy." I've concluded that the "product"— the magazine, for example— is *the factor* in making a renewal decision.

20. Self-mailers are cheaper to produce, but they practically never outpull envelope-enclosed letter mailings.

21. A pre-print of a forthcoming ad, accompanied by a letter and a response form, will outpull a post-print mailing package by 50% or more.

22. It is easier to increase the average dollar amount of an order than it is to increase percentage of response.

23. You will get far more new catalog customers if you put your proven winners in the front pages of your catalog.

24. Assuming items of similar appeal, you will always get a higher response rate from a 32-page catalog than from a 24-page catalog.

25. A new catalog to a customer base will outpull cold lists by 400–800%.

26. A print ad with a bind-in card will outpull the same ad without a bind-in up to 600%.

27. A direct response, direct sale TV commercial of 120 seconds will outpull a 60-second direct response commercial better than two to one.

28. A TV support commercial will increase response from a newspaper insert up to 50%.

29. The closure rate from qualified leads can be from two to four times as effective as cold calls.

30. Telephone-generated leads are likely to close four to six times greater than mail-generated leads.

The Future of Integrated Communications

Yes, we do have a rich heritage to build on. But, as this book has forcefully demonstrated, direct marketing strategies continue to evolve. And the strategy of the future, in my opinion, is *integrated communications.*

Integrated communications puts direct marketing on a par with general advertising, sales promotion, and public relations. The strategy dictates that direct marketing be a part of a total campaign when direct marketing can contribute substantially to accomplishing the total campaign objective.

All of this makes eminent sense. But there are those (sometimes referred to as "direct marketing hard-liners") who vigorously resist the integrated communications concept. The reasons they give are many. "We'll lose our identity." "Direct marketing will end up with the short end of the total budget." "We'll lose track of total direct marketing dollar volume." Then there are those who argue over whether the marketer or the agency should determine what percentage of total budget for a campaign should go to general advertising, direct marketing, sales promotion, and public relations.

Strangely, none of these negatives refers to consumer good or the objective of producing cost-effective campaigns. Deep down, as I see it, it's a battle over turf. Only management can resolve turf battles. The sooner management takes a strong hand, the sooner integrated communications will reap the benefits of the concept. Ultimately, integrated communications will surely prevail.

The Future of Direct Marketing Education

Assuming continuing growth in direct marketing—a good assumption—the question arises: Where will future direct marketing talent come from? I predict that by the year 2000, over 50% of entrants to direct marketing will be college trained.

This prediction is based on the success record of the Direct Marketing Educational Foundation, which has been instrumental in getting direct marketing taught at over 300 colleges and universities nationwide.

The prediction of college-trained job entrants is reinforced by a masters program being taught at Northwestern University's Medill School of Journalism. Its program meshes exactly with the concept of integrated communications. The full curriculum appears in Figure 1.

FIGURE 1

Integrated Advertising/Marketing Communications: The curriculum quarter by quarter

Quarter One (4 credits)

A. Core Courses
    Financial Management Strategy
    Marketing Management
    Consumer Behavior

B. Students may pick one of the following:
    Advertising and Sales Promotion Theory
    Corporate Public Relations/Media Relations Strategy
    Direct Marketing Fundamentals and Strategy

Quarter Two (4 Credits)

A. Core Courses
    Integrated Communications Strategy Development
    Integrated Creative Strategies
    Marketing Communication Research

B. Students may pick one of the following:
    Advertising/Sales Promotion Strategy
    Direct Marketing Circulation Planning and Management
    Employee Relations and Communications Management

Quarter Three (4 Credits)

A. Core Courses
    Organizational Structure and Management
    Analytical Techniques

B. *Students may pick two of the following:*

Advertising/Sales Promotion Decisions
Advertising/Sales Promotion Media Planning
Direct Marketing Strategy: Formation and Implementation
Direct Marketing Database Management and Application
Marketing Public Relations
Investor Relations Management

Quarter Four (3 Credits)

Professional residencies on or off campus

Quarter Five (3 or 4 Credits)

A. University Electives at the Graduate Level or electives at the Kellogg
   Graduate School of Management (one or two)

B. Professional Practicum (one)
   Typical examples from past years:
   Advanced Scanner Data
   The Creative Product: Its Impact on Integrated Marketing
      Communications
   Advertising Effects
   Consumer Satisfaction, Dissatisfaction and Complaining Behavior
   Direct Marketing Programs and Strategies
   Marketing Crisis Management—Communications Solutions
   The Management of Quality Improvement: Communications Issues

C. *Students may pick one or two of the following:*

Advertising, Sales Promotion Theory
Pricing and Sales Promotion
Fundamentals of CPR and Media Relations
Marketing Public Relations
Public Affairs/Issues Management
Direct Marketing Fundamentals and Strategy
Direct Marketing Consumer Acceptance

About the Contributors

Toni L. Apgar

Toni Apgar has been an Editorial director of *Direct Magazine* and *The Cowles Report on Database Marketing,* both published by Cowles Business Media. Database marketing and customer lifetime value are two subjects that became her specialty while working at *Direct.*

Toni is currently the Editorial Director of *Vegetarian Times,* a property of Cowles Magazines, Inc., where she is focusing on both the core magazine and ancillary products.

Prior to *Direct,* Toni was executive editor of *Folio:* magazine, also published by Cowles Business Media. Before that, she was the editor of *The Marketer,* published by Act III Publishing, and, prior to that, the directing editor of several marketing and small-business newsletters published by The National Institute of Business Management. At the Institute, Toni gained insight into the powerful role of data in acquiring and retaining profitable subscribers and how an editor can use that data to fine tune his/her editorial product.

Drayton Bird

Drayton Bird has 34 years' experience as copywriter, client, creative director and as Vice Chairman & Creative Director of Ogilvy & Mather Direct.

Direct Response Magazine said he had "made an impact on UK direct marketing unlikely to be matched by any other individual." Advertising legend David Ogilvy says he "knows more about direct marketing than anyone in the world. His book about it is pure gold." Drayton Bird is a celebrated speaker, having entertained and instructed audiences in 32 countries.

Ron Bliwas

As President/Chief Executive Officer of A. Eicoff & Company, a division of Ogilvy & Mather, for the past 12 years and an employee of the agency for more than 20 years, Bliwas has established himself as the country's leading authority on television direct response and trade support advertising. He has introduced many organizations to these television advertising strategies and provided them with the tools to make them effective.

Under Bliwas's leadership, A. Eicoff & Company has grown to become one of the top 15 agencies in Chicago. Its client base has greatly expanded, including companies such as Sears, Beltone Electronics, Rodale Press, Time-Warner, Banc One, Meredith Corp., Campbell Soup, Duracell, and American Express.

Ron is a member of the worldwide Chief Executives Organization (CEO), the Young Presidents Organization, and the World Presidents Organization.

Thomas M. Collinger

Tom Collinger's direct marketing background began at age 13 in the warehouse of his father's direct marketing firm in St. Louis, Missouri, where he got a taste of the "backend" of the business. Once Tom earned his Bachelor of Science Degree from the University of Colorado, he joined Bowers and Associates, a sales promotion agency in St. Louis. Following a two-year stint there, Tom rejoined his father's firm, Marketing Associates of America, where he worked in the marketing department for four years.

Tom entered the advertising agency business in 1981, as V.P./General Manager for Ayer Direct, where he stayed until 1983, when he was made General Manager of Ogilvy & Mather Direct, Chicago. Almost five years later, in 1987, Tom joined Leo Burnett Company.

Stephen A. Cone

Steve Cone currently serves as chairman of Epsilon, a wholly owned subsidary of American Express. Based in Burlington, Massachusetts, Epsilon is a leader in providing state-of-the-art marketing database services.

Prior to being named Epsilon's Chairman, Steve served as Senior Vice President of Direct Marketing for five years at American Express headquarters in New York.

At AMEX and Epsilon, Steve has been the driving force behind bringing supercomputers into the world of direct marketing and using advanced technology to greatly enhance customer service and satisfaction.

William K. Duch

Bill joined Rodale Press in 1984 where he served as Database Marketing Manager and later as Marketing Services Director. In that capacity, he was chairman of the Database Marketing Committee. Bill joined CCX Network, Inc. (now Acxiom Corporation) in 1988 as director of Consulting Services. In Novermber 1989, he was promoted to Group Executive, Consulting Services.

In April 1993, Bill joined Cowles Media Services and Consulting as Senior Vice President. In that capacity, he also serves as the Executive Director of the Center for Database Marketing.

Bill has been a frequent contributor to the direct marketing and trade publishing press and is a frequent speaker at industry conferences. He has been active in the Direct Marketing Association for over ten years. In 1991, Bill was included on the *Target Marketing* magazine list of the 200 most influential people in the direct marketing industry for the fourth year in a row and is included in the 1993-94 edition of *Who's Who in the East.* In 1992, he was elected to a second three-year term on the DMA Ethics Policy Committee.

Leon N. Graham

Lee Graham is Executive Vice President of BMG Direct, which operates Bertelsmann's music and video clubs in the United States. Previously, he was President of Scali McCabe Sloves Direct and Vice President for Marketing at Columbia House.

Mr. Graham is a past Chairman of both the John Caples International Awards and Direct Marketing Day in New York.

John D. Hall

John is the current President of Time Life books. For the previous three years he was President of Time Life Music. He entered Time Warner as Senior Vice President, Director of Marketing at Book-of-the-Month Club, Inc. Previously, he managed the only direct marketing business at Johnson & Johnson—Johnson & Johnson Child Development Toys. Prior to that, he worked as an Account Supervisor at Ogilvy & Mather Direct. He began his career at *Country Music Magazine* as its first Circulation Director.

Jack M. Klues

Jack Klues joined Leo Burnett's media department after his graduation from the University of Illinois in 1977. He rose to Media Supervisor in 1979 and was promoted to Media Director in 1985. He was named a Vice President the same year.

Mr. Klues recently solidified a plan to help Burnett more effectively negotiate within the competitive magazine market. He also serves as the company's direct marketing liaison.

A Senior Vice President since February 1993, Mr. Klues currently oversees media for the Amurol, Nintendo, Samsonite, and Tropicana accounts.

Herschell Gordon Lewis

Herschell Gordon Lewis heads Communicomp, a Plantation, Florida, direct marketing creative source. He is a direct response writer and consultant, with clients throughout the world. Among the organizations for whch Mr. Lewis has written copy are the United Nations Children's Fund, Transamerica Insurance. Mutual Assurance, National General Insurance, Commerce Bank, Cowles Business Media, Royal Copenhagen, Reader's Digest Travel Club, Colonial Williamsburg, Consumers Union, Southern Bell Telephone, QVC Network, St. Jude Children's Research Hospital, and the United States Historical Society. He also has written copy for many consumer and business catalogs, including Stark Bro's Nurseries and San Francisco Music Box Co.

Among his books are *Copywriting Secrets and Tactics, Direct Marketing Strategies and Tactics, Big Profits from Small Budget Advertising, Herschell Gordon Lewis On the Art of Writing Copy, Direct Mail Copy That Sells,* and *How to Write Powerful Catalog Copy.* Together with Mr. Ian Kennedy and Jerry Reitman, Mr. Lewis is producer of the recently-issued "100 Greatest Direct Response Television Commercials."

Lewis writes the monthly feature "Creative Strategies" for *Direct Marketing Magazine* and is the copy columnist for *Catalog Age.* He also writes "Copy Class" for *Direct Marketing International,* and is the "Curmudgeon-at-Large" for *Direct.* For years he has conducted the copy workshop at the International Direct Marketing Synposium, Montreux, Switzerland, and he appears frequently at the Pan-Pacific Symposium in Sydney, Australia.

Donald R. Libey

Mr. Libey is president of The Libey Consultancy Incorporated, a marketing and strategic planning consultancy and seminar production firm.

Mr. Libey publishes a series of newsletters—*The Libey New Century Letters* as well as *The Libey Letter*—with over 1,000 readers. He also is author of four books, *The Libey New Century Library.* With a background in domestic and international direct marketing that includes consumer, health care, financial, investment, non-profit, business-to-business, and publishing, Mr. Libey has been associated with major international direct marketing corporations and Fortune 500 companies in positions from marketing to the board of directors.

Worth Linen

Worth Linen is the president and C.E.O. of BMG Direct, a U.S. subsidiary of Bertelsmann A.G. and part of the Bertelsmann Music Group.

Prior to this appointment, Mr. Linen was Vice Chairman of Wunderman Worldwide, one of the world's leading direct marketing agencies.

Mr. Linen has also been active in the direct marketing industry and pro bono causes. These have included serving as program chairman for Direct Marketing Day in New York and as General Chair of the Caples Awards. He has also spoken frequently at DMA events and lectured at New York University's Direct Marketing program. Under his direction, BMG Direct is sponsoring the 1993/94 Collegiate Echo competition.

Mr. Linen was educated at the Hotchkiss School, Fettes College in Edinburgh, and received his B.A. from Williams College, in 1973.

Linda McAleer

As Executive Vice President at Millard Group, McAleer heads the Publishing and Non-profit Group in the Brokerage Division. Working with clients within this category she is adept in the sophisticated techniques of circulation analysis, computer modeling, and universe analysis required for successful direct mail planning.

Mc Aleer is past President of the New England Direct Marketing Association, the Women's Direct Response Group, and the Washington D.C. DMA. She also serves on the operating committee of the DMA's Circulation Council.

Professor David M. Messick

David Messick is the Morris and Alice Kaplan Distinguished Professor of Ethics and Decision in Management at the J.L. Kellogg Graduate School of Management at Northwestern University. His research areas deal with decision making in social evironments.

Messick has authored more than 100 scientific papers and books. He has received awards from the Fulbright Foundation (for research in The Netherlands), from the National Science Foundation, and from the national Research Council (for research in Hungary). He was the co-organizer of the 12th International Conference on Subjective Probability, Utility, and Decision Making in Moscow, USSR, in 1989. His most recent edited books are *Contemporary Issues in Decision Making*, 1991, (with K. Borcherding and O. Larichev) and *Social Dilemmas*, 1992, (with W. Liebrand and H. Wilke).

Carol Nelson

Carol Nelson is Executive Vice President of Communicomp, based in Plantation, Florida. Previously, she was General Manager and Creative

Director for Cohn & Wells, Chicago, a full-service international direct marketing agency. She also has held staff positions in both general advertising and direct marketing agencies and has written and created advertising campaigns for a variety of consumer, business-to-business, financial and fund-raising clients. She is author of *Integrated Advertising, Women's Marketing Handbook,* and *How to Market to Women.*

Lisa A. Petrison

Lisa A. Petrison is an adjunct professor at Northwestern University, and is currently working on a Ph.D. in marketing at Northwestern's J.L. Kellogg Graduate School of Management. She has held marketing and communications management positions in the banking and video-game industries and is the co-author of *Sales Promotion Essentials,* 1991 (with Don E. Schultz and William A. Robinson).

Murray Raphel

Murray Raphel is a seasoned marketing professional. He speaks annually at the Direct Marketing Symposium in Montreux, Switzerland, the Food Marketing Institute's annual convention, and the Pan Pacific Marketing Symposium in Sydney, Australia. He has served as a consultant for the Food Marketing Institute. Mr. Raphel is the author of such books as *Customerization, Tough Selling for Tough Times,* and *Mind Your Own Business,* among others. He is the president of his own marketing firm, Raphel Marketing, Inc.

Ernan Roman

Ernan Roman is President of the New York-based Ernan Roman Direct Marketing Corporation (ERDM). Mr. Roman has been a pioneer in developing the conceptual framework and operational requirements for integrated direct marketing campaigns. ERDM's clients include numerous divisions of AT&T, Hewlett-Packard, IBM, Citibank, Motorola, and Bell Atlantic.

Recognized by the industry for his contributions, Mr. Roman was awarded the first Marketing Leader Award ever given by the Direct Marketing Association for a telemarketing campaign. He has also earned a prestigious DMA Echo Award for consumer direct mail for Christie's Art Auctioneers, and an Echo Leader Award for an integrated direct marketing campaign for AT&T General Business Systems.

James R. Rosenfield

In his 24-year career, James R. Rosenfield has become one of the world's most respected marketing and direct/database marketing authorities. His major area of expertise involves the application of direct/database marketing techniques to non-traditional environments, such as consumer products, financial services, and travel.

Rosenfield serves on the Editorial Review Board of Northwestern University's *Journal of Direct Marketing,* and has taught at the University of Colorado, Ohio State University, and Northwestern University.

He writes regularly for publications in the United States, Europe, Asia, Australia, and South America, and has published over a hundred articles and monographs. He authored the book *Financial Services Direct Marketing,* published by Sourcebooks, Inc., in 1991. His new book, *Why Marketing and Advertising Are Obsolete . . . And What to Do About It,* is scheduled for publication in 1993. Among other activities, he is in charge of direct marketing training and consulting for MasterCard International and handles direct marketing training for IBM (Asia/Pacific). He is Chairman of Rosenfield & Associates and Rosenfield/Dentino, Inc., and is a graduate of Columbia University.

Alan Rosenspan

Alan Rosenspan and his teams have won over 100 international, national, and regional awards for advertising results, including 18 DMA Echo Awards, a Gold "Effie," and several Best of Show Awards from New England DMA.

He is an instructor at Bentley College and The Boston Ad Club; the author of the chapter "Psychological Appeals" in the 1991 edition of *The Direct Marketing Handbook,* published by McGraw-Hill; and the creator of the "Direct Marketing Shoestring Awards" held in New England, and soon to be held in Seattle and Chicago.

Mr. Rosenspan is also a regular speaker at international conferences, and has given dozens of presentations and seminars in Switzerland, Holland, Africa, Australia, and throughout the United States. He is currently a Senior Vice President/Creative Director at Bronner Slosberg Humphrey in Boston.

Hershel B. Sarbin

Hershel Sarbin is chairman and CEO of Cowles Business Media, a diversified knowledge-based enterprise with interests in magazines, database marketing and management, print and electronic newsletter, books and conferences. In his 30 years in the communications industry, he has gained recognition as an innovative executive with broad experience in every phase of publishing. He was president and COO of Ziff-Davis Publishing company from 1974 to 1979, where he was responsible for 50 special-interest consumer magazines and business publications. Born in Massillon, Ohio, he graduated Phi Beta Kappa from Case Western Reserve University and received a JD degree from Harvard Law School.

Don E. Schultz

Don E. Schultz is presently a Professor of Integrated Advertising/Marketing Communications at the Medill School of Journalism, Northwestern University.

Following his graduation from the University of Oklahoma with a degree in marketing/journalism, Schultz began his career as a sales promotion writer for trade magazine publishers in Dallas. From there, he moved into publication sales and management and was advertising director of a daily newspaper in Texas. He then joined Tracy-Locke Advertising and Public Relations in Dallas in 1965. He was with the agency for almost 10 years in its Dallas, New York, and Columbus, Ohio, offices as branch manager. He served as management supervisor for a number of national consumer product, service, and industrial accounts.

In 1974, Schultz resigned as Senior Vice President of Tracy-Locke to launch a career in academia. He obtained his Masters Degree in Advertising and his Ph.D. in Mass Media from Michigan State University while also teaching in the MSU Department of Advertising. He joined the Northwestern University faculty in 1977.

Schultz is a director of the Promotion Marketing Association of America and Chairman, Accrediting Committee, Accrediting Council in Journalism and Mass Communications. He also has served as Director, Institute of Advanced Advertising Studies. He was selected the first Direct Marketing Educator of the Year by the Direct Marketing Educational Foundation. He is a member of the American Marketing Association, American Academy of Advertising, Advertising Research Foundation, Association for Consumer Research, Business Marketing Association, International Newspaper Marketing Association, International Newspaper Advertising and Marketing Executives Association, Direct Marketing Association, and the International Advertising Association.

In addition, Schultz is president of his own marketing, advertising and consulting firm, Agora, Inc., in Evanston, Illinois. He is author of several books, including *Strategic Advertising Campaigns* and *Integrated Marketing Communications* (with Stanley Tannenbaum and Robert Lauterborn), numerous articles on advertising, direct marketing, and integrated marketing communications. He currently is editor of the *Journal of Direct Marketing*.

Jayne Zenaty Spittler

Jayne Zenaty Spittler is Vice President and Director of Media Research at the Leo Burnett Company in Chicago. She supervises tracking and projecting the performance of all media vehicles; producing major agency guidance documents and points of view; developing procedures and systems for better media planning and buying; and monitoring and evaluating media research studies and sources.

Spittler is the agency's representative on several industry committees, such as the Media Research Committee of the American Association of Advertising Agencies and the Agency Media Research Council, which she chairs. She also is the current chair of the Video Electronic Media Council of the Advertising Research Foundation. She is on the Academic Committee of the American Advertising Federation.

Prior to joining Burnett in 1981, Spittler was a professor of telecommunications at Indiana University in Bloomington, where she taught courses in audience research, computer technology, and telecommunications regulation. She has published papers in several scholarly journals and conducted research for the Federal Communications Commission and the Corporation for Public Broadcasting.

Spittler holds a doctorate in Mass Media, with an emphasis in telecommunications and systems science, from Michigan State University. During her graduate studies, which focused on non-broadcast technologies, she served as chief computer programmer for a National Science Foundation experiment on two-way cable in Rockford, Illinois. Her B.A. is from Clarke College in Dubuque, Iowa, in chemistry and computer science.

Maxwell Sroge

Since its founding in 1966, the Maxwell Sroge Company has grown to become the 10th largest advertising agency in Chicago. Mr. Sroge, president of the company, has since expanded the agency's services to include catalog creative development, catalog marketing consulting, and acquisition and merger services.

Mr. Sroge has authored and co-authored a number of books on catalog marketing including *All About Mail Order, Best in Catalogs, 101 Ideas for More Profitable Catalogs* and *The United States Mail Order Industry*. He has also held seminars on mail order marketing and given speeches to Direct Marketing Clubs at colleges and universities throughout the United States.

Bob Stone

Bob Stone, Chairman Emeritus of Stone & Adler, Inc., has contributed greatly to the direct marketing community through his writing and teaching. He has authored two books, *Successful Direct Marketing Methods* and *Successful Telemarketing,* and has conducted *Advertising Age*'s direct marketing column since 1967.

A professor of direct marketing at Northwestern University and the University of Missouri/Kansas City, Mr. Stone is the recipient of several awards including the Direct Marketing Association's Best of Industry award and two Gold Echo awards. He is also a former president of the Chicago Association of Direct Marketing and is a member of the Direct Marketing Hall of Fame.

Paul Wang

Paul Wang is an assistant professor in the graduate direct marketing program at Northwestern University and is the technical editor of the *Journal of Direct Marketing.* He specializes in database and direct marketing issues, and serves as a research consultant to a variety of companies interested in database marketing. His Ph.D. is in communications studies from Northwestern University. He is author (with Robert Jackson) of *Strategic Database Marketing.*

H. Robert Wientzen

A graduate of George Washington University, H. Robert Wientzen joined Procter & Gamble's general advertising department in 1967. Since then, he has served on the boards of several organizations, including Advanced Promotion Technologies and the Direct Marketing Association. In November 1991, *Target Marketing Magazine* named Mr. Wientzen one of the 200 most influential people in direct marketing.

John D. Yeck

John Yeck came to Dayton, Ohio, in 1934, shortly after graduation from Miami University, as an assistant Boy Scout Executive. In 1938, he established his direct mail organization and, a few years later, was joined by his brother, Bill. Yeck Brothers Company, a major direct mail/marketing agency in Dayton, has been active in direct marketing for over 50 years. The firm's business-to-business and financial programs have won many national awards, all based on results obtained. Mr. Yeck is currently a partner in the firm.

Yeck is a member of the Board of Directors of the Direct Marketing Association and its business-to-business task force. He is chairman of the Direct Marketing Educational Foundation, has received direct marketing's Miles Kimball award, the Ed Mayer award for leadership in direct marketing education, and is one of the few active DMA members in the Direct Marketing Hall of Fame.

Author of many articles and two books, *Planning and Creating Better Direct Mail* and *How to Get Profitable Ideas Through Creative Problem Solving*, Yeck has spoken to audiences in 10 countries.

His organization provides turn-key direct marketing programs for such well-known firms as Federal Express, John Deere, Pitney Bowes, The Bell System, Frigidaire, Citicorp, Chase Manhattan Bank, Household International, Mead, and American Express.

INDEX

Aburdene, Patricia, xiv
ActMedia, 152
Addressable television, 86-87
Advanced Promotion Technologies (APT), Inc., 155-156
Advertising
  and entertainment/events, 91-92
  in magazines, 100
Advertising agencies, 35
Advertising mail, environment and, 51-52
Agencies. *See also* Direct marketing agencies
  advertising, 35
  conglomerates and, 39
  integration and, 37-39
  role of, 161-162
  sizes of, 37
Aging, labor and, 188
Airlines, frequent flyer programs of, xv, 58-59
American Express, Epsilon marketing database software from, 64
Analog signals, 82
Anderson, Richard, 28
Apgar, Toni, 97-105
APT Network, 155-156
Artificial intelligence, 174, 176-177
Artzt, Ed, 206 Asia
  labor in, 188
  market in, 168, 186
Automated call processing, 221
Automation, order/information flow and, 73-74

Batching, 214
Behavioral segmentation, 8
Big Six, 34
Bird, Drayton, 21-31
Black boxes, 72
Bliwas, Ron, 159-164
Book clubs, 210-211. *See also* Clubs
Book-of-the-Month Club (BOMC), 210
Book publishing, 227-232
Bork, Robert, 47
Bove, V. Michael, Jr., 88

Brands
  database integration with, 224-225
  financial service marketing and, 222
  irrelevance of, 192
Broadcast media, 245
Bush, George, 129
Business cycle, 166-167
Business to business direct marketing, 165-194

Cable television, 82, 84
Canada, 168
Caples, John, 110
Cappo, Joe, 198, 203
Carol Wright program, 125-126
Catalina Marketing, 153
Catalogs, 131-137, 245-246
Cato, Johnson, 35
Central memory repository, 64-65
Channels. *See* Distribution channels
Charities, consumer privacy and, 53
Citicorp, 153-154
Clubs, 209-215
Collinger, Tom, 33-42
Collins, Tom, 90
Communicating, copywriting and, 110-114
Communications, integrated, 37-39
Communications corridors, 221-222
Communications superhighway, 84-85
Compensation, of list brokers, 75-76
Competition, global, 167-168
Competitiveness, of magazines, 99-100
Competitive users, and international marketing, 30
Compression, electronic, 82-83
Computers. *See also* Technology
  electronic direct marketing in-store and, 152-153
  time, speed, and, 62-68
Computer software, catalogs on, 136
Cone, Stephen A., 57-68
Consortium databases, 72-73
Consultants, services of, 34
Consumer(s). *See also* Customer
  battle for, 36

building trust in, 223-224
database, 7
responses to telemarketing, 142-145
Consumer goods companies, 150
Consumer privacy, 45-46, 117-118, 154
addressing concerns of, 53-56
list brokers and, 72
relationship violations, 52-53
Consumer Privacy Act, 129
Consumer research, 151
Continuing education, 240-241
Copywriting, 110-114
Costs, in international marketing, 30-31
Cray, Deborah, 85
Creative messages, 109-114
Creativity, in direct mail, 119-123
Credit card, 244
Cultural differences, in international
markets, 26, 31
Culture. *See also* Social/cultural changes
Cummings, John, 36
Custom engineering, 193
Customer. *See also* Consumer(s)
rewarding, 207-208
satisfying, 198-199
targeted, 7-8
Customization, 39
Customized mass marketing (CMM), 8-12
Customized print, 85-86
Cyber-technology, 174-180, 189-191.
See also Artificial intelligence;
Virtual reality

Damart, 28
Dapper, Steve, 41
DARPA (Defense Advanced Research
Project Agency), 62
Database(s), 16, 114
for customized mass marketing, 8, 9
inappropriate usage of, 47-51
integrated, 175-176
lists and, 72-73
and media companies, 103-105
speed, memory, and, 63-68
for telemarketing 143-144
Database companies, 34
Database electronic marketing systems.
See also Direct marketing,
electronic
Database marketing, 146, 150, 192. *See also*
Direct marketing
financial service firms and, 218-220

future of, 116-118
Debt, inflation and, 172-174
Deceptive Mailings Prevention Act, 129
Deceptive mail practices, 129
Demand, fragmentation of, 192
Demographics, 86
book publishing and, 230-231
Desktop publishing systems, 230
Devaluation, 185-186
Digital storage, 83
Digital switching, 83
Digitization/compression, 82-83
Direct mail
creativity and, 119-123
environmental impact of, 128
future of, 115-130
as relationship medium, 123-124
retail, 195-208
Direct Market Educational Foundation
(DMEF), 237-239
Direct marketers, in future, 234-241
Direct marketing. *See also* Consumer
privacy
business to business, 165-194
changes in, 33-42
electronic, 149-156
evolution of, 3-13
of financial services, 217-225
growth of, xiv-xv
inappropriate activities and, 49-51
international, 21-31
media in, 90-92
principles of, 246-248
status and future of, 243-250
Direct marketing agencies. *See also*
Agencies
guidelines for future, 40-42
horizontal integration and, 34
managing, 34-42
Direct Marketing Association, consumer
privacy and, 46, 55-56
Direct response TV, 159-164
Discount pricing, 169-170, 182
Discount retailing, 135
Distribution channels, 82-83. *See also*
Media
for book publishers, 231
DMA Mail and Telephone Preference
Service, 46, 55
Donnelley, R.R., 85-86
Donnelley Marketing, Carol Wright
program of, 125-126

Donnelley Marketing Information Services (DMIS) National TV Conquest, 86
Duch, William, 97-105

Echo Award, 122
Economics, and business to business direct marketing, 166-170
Economic stress, 182 Economy, 172-174
Education, 248-250
    continuing, 240-241
    marketers and, 237-238
800 numbers, 124, 221, 244
Electronic direct marketing, 5, 149-156
Electronic media. *See also* Media
Electronic superhighway, 88
Ellis-Brown, Gordon, 25
Employment, in direct marketing, 238-240
Entertainment/events advertising, 91-92
Environment
    advertising mail, wastefulness, and, 51-52
    direct mail impact on, 128-129
Epsilon, 64-66. *See also* Right Time Marketing Ethics, 193-194
    list brokers and, 72
Europe
    Common Market in, 185-186
    consumer privacy in, 117
    direct retail mail in, 200
    labor in, 188
    market in, 168
Events advertising, 91-92
Execution, 135-136
Exporters, 28
Exurbanization, 187-188

Failing, Bruce, Sr., 152
FCB Direct, 39, 41
Fiber optics, 83-84, 89
Financial services, direct marketing of, 217-225
Fragmentation, of demand, 192
Frequent flyer programs, xv, 58-59
Frequent-guest reward systems, 204
"Full Service Network," 84

Gasparri, Giampaolo, 197
Germany, direct retail mail in, 201
Gilbert, Kathryn, 203
Global competition, 167-168
Global economic stress, 182
Global markets, fragmentation of, 183

Goldfeder, Judd, 199
Goldstein, Mark, 38
Golomb, Stan, 199
Government
    communications regulation by, 84
    deceptive mail practices and, 129
    MPP and, 62
Graham, Lee N., 209-215
Great Marketing Turnaround, The, 90

Hall, John D., 227-232
Hal Riney and Partners, 35
Hanberry, Donna, 198
Heuristic societies, 190-191
High-ticket items. *See also* Direct response TV
Hillen, Helmut, 197, 198, 200
Hillis, Danny, 62
Holmberg, Rolf, 203
Holzel, Rolf-Dieter, 197
Home shopping services, 91
Hotels, retail direct mail and, 204-205
Hyperinflation, 186

Iacocca, Lee, 141
Inflation, and debt, 172-174
Infomercials, 90-91, 161
Information. *See also* Consumer privacy; Database(s)
    automation and 73-74
    optimizing vs. distorting, 110-111
In Search of Excellence, 40
Inside-out marketing, 5
In-store direct marketing, 152, 155-156
Integrated communications, 37-39, 248
Integrated database, 175-176
Integrated Direct Marketing (IDM), 141, 142
Integrated marketing (IM), 3-13, 15-19
Integrated marketing communications (IMC), 3-13
Integrated telemarketing, 139-147
Integration, 17-18, 37-39
Interactive databases, 72
Interactive direct response, 163
Interactive media, 88-89
Interactive selling, and clubs, 213-214
Interactive technology, 76-77
Interactive TV, 232
International direct marketing, 21-31
    catalogs and, 135
    foreign market sophistication and, 28-29

principles for success, 25-31

Jobs, in direct marketing, 238-240
Junk mail, 128-129

Kennedy, Ian, 109
Kleid, Lew, 241
Klues, Jack M., 79-95

Labor, 188-189
Land's End, 28
Language, and international marketing,
    27
Larson, Eric, 116
Lead generation, 244
Learning channels, 161
Legislation, consumer privacy and,
    47
Leo Burnett Company, 35
Leonard, Stew, 198-199
Lewis, Herschell Gordon, 109-114
Libey, Donald R., 129, 165-194
Linen, Worth, 209-215
List brokers, 69-77
    as consultants, 75
    paid prospects and, 126
Lists, 4-5. *See also* Mailing lists
    consumer privacy and, 48
    for international marketing, 29-30
    prices of, 70
    selections on, 73
Little Library, 210
Long-form TV ads, 90-91

Magazines, 97-105
Mail. *See also* Consumer privacy;
    Environment
    advertising, 51-52
    clubs and, 213-214
    costs of, 70
    direct retail, 195-208
Mailers. *See also* Mail; List brokers
Mailing lists, 4-5. *See also* Lists
    paid prospects and, 126-127
Mail-order businesses, ownership of, 135
Manufacturer/retailer partnerships, 206-
    207
Marcus, Stanley, xiv
Margin erosion, 182
Market awareness, 114
Marketing
    cyber-domination of, 174-176

defined, 220
in future, 220-225
Marketing database
    memory and, 64-65
    speed, memory, and software, 63-68
"Marketing Is Everything," 220
Marketing objectives, setting, 12
Marketing program, direct response
    advertising in, 163
Markets, protectionist hemispheric, 168-
    169
Mass advertising, irrelevance of, 192
Mass consolidation, 183-184
Massive parallel processing (MPP), 62-68
Mass marketing, 6
    customized, 8-12
    defined, 35
Mass media. *See also* Media
Mayer, Ed, 241
McAleer, Linda, 69-77
MCI Friends & Family plan, 117-118
McKenna, Regis, 220
McNutt, Bill, III, 27
Media
    in direct marketing, 90-82
    distribution channels and, 82-83
    interactive, 88-89, 232
    magazines, 97-105
    place-based, 92-93
    planning for, 79-95
    targeting with existing, 85-87
    telemarketing and, 145
Media neutrality, 101
Memory, database and, 64-65
Merge/purge, 74
Messages, 109-114
Messick, David M., 45-56
Mexico, 168
    labor in, 188
Modeling, list brokers and, 74-75
Monetary reform, 186
Moss, Gary, 37-38
MPP. *See* Massive parallel processing
Multilevel relational databases, 72 Multiple
media, 144 Music clubs, 210-211.
    See also Clubs

NAFTA. *See* North American Free
    Trade Agreement
Naisbitt, John, xiv
Naked Consumer, The, 116
Needs vs. wants, 191

Negative option marketing, 211-215
Nelson, Carol, 15-19
New marketing, 6, 7
900 numbers, 162
Noble, Ray, 205
Nonstore setting, retail sales in, xiv-xv
Nordstrom's, 42
North America, inflation, debt, and, 172-174
North American Free Trade Agreement (NAFTA), 168
North-South America trading bloc, 168-169, 184
 labor in, 188

O'Brien, Mike, 153
Odyssey (group), xiii-xiv
Ogilvy & Mather (O&M) Direct, 37, 38, 39, 40, 42
Ombudsman, to integrate campaign, 19
Orders, automation of, 73-74
Ownership, of mail-order businesses, 135

Pan-Asian satellite TV network, 87
Partnerships, 76
 manufacturer/retailer, 206-207
 among media companies, 93-94
Patterson, John, 236, 244
Personal computers, 152
Personal service, technology and, 57-68
Personnel
 for direct marketing, 234-241
 for international marketing, 31
Peters, Tom, 40
Petrison, Lisa A., 45-56
Pickholz, Jerry, 40, 42
Place-based media, 92-93
Point of Purchase Advertising Institute (POPAI), 151
Political stress, 183
Polk, Sol, 135
Popcorn, Faith, 36
Pricing
 discounting, 169-170, 182
 whole price, 170-172
Print, customized, 85-86
Print advertising, 245
Printing, technology and, 214
PRISMS (Personalized Individualized Selections of Merchandise), 134
Privacy. See Consumer privacy
Private databases, 72

Process integration, societal systems and, 190
Product(s)
 for international markets, 26
 magazine advertising and, 100-101
 security-based, 191
Product development, book publishing and, 228-229
Professionalism, 114
Prospects, paid, 126-127
Protectionism, 183-184
 in hemispheric markets, 168-169
Psychographics, of media preferences, 142-143
Publishing
 books, 227-232
 magazines, 97-105
Punctuation, in copywriting, 112-113

Radio, 87
Raphel, Murray, 195-208
Rapp, Stan, 90
Rapp Collins Marcoa, 39, 41
Rating sources, 86
Reader/s Digest, 99
Recombinant marketing, 172
Regression analysis, 74-75
Regulation, 84
Reinhard, Keith, 39
Reinventing the Corporation, xiv
Reitman, Jerry, 109
Relational database technology, 214
Relationship medium, direct mail as, 123-124
Relationships, consumer privacy and, 52-53
Religion, in international marketing, 29
Research tools, for media, 86
Retail direct mail, 195-208
 size of retailer and, 205-206
Retailing, 151
 direct retail mail and, 195-208
 in nonstore setting, xiv-xv
Return on investment (ROI), and incremental income flows, 12
Right Time Marketing (American Express/Epsilon), 59-61
Riney, Hal. See Hal Riney and Partners
Roman, Ernan, 139-147
Roman, Murray, 141
Rosenfield, James R., 217-225
Rosenspan, Alan, 115-130

Ross, William, 205, 207

Sackheim, Maxwell, 210
Salesmanship, 114
Sales promotion, and trade incentives, 149-156
Sarbin, Hershel, 97-105
Satellite transmissions, 82, 87
Schaeffer, Rebecca, 47
Schermann, Harry, 210
Schultz, Don E., 3-13
Sears, Richard, 235-236
Secrecy, databases and, 72. *See also* Consumer privacy
Security-based products, 191
Segmentation, 36, 39, 81
Selective binding, 85
Service, list brokers and, 71, 77
Share wars, 183-184
Slosberg, Mike, 118
Smith, Tim, 205
Smith & Hawkins, 128
Social/cultural changes, 194
Socialism, 184-185
Social productivity, 184
Social stress, 183
Software, MPP (Epsilon), 64-68
Software business, strategic alliances in, 125
South America, market in, 168-169
Spar, Laurie, 37
Spittler, Jane Zenaty, 79-95
Sroge, Maxwell, 131-137
Star TV, 87
Stone, Bob, 116, 243-250
Storage, digital, 83
Strategic alliances, 76, 124-126
Successful Direct Marketing Methods, 116
Sugarman, Joe, 124
Supercomputers, 65-66
Switzerland, direct retail mail in, 200, 201

Targeted (customized) new marketing, 6-13
Targeting, 81, 114
  with existing media, 85-87
Target markets, 104
Taxation, 173, 185
Technology, 4, 5
  business to business marketing and, 174
  catalogs and, 132-134

direct response TV and, 162-163
  interactive, 76-77
  interactive selling, 213
  for list brokers, 71-77
  media and, 82
  personal service through, 57-68
Telemarketing, 244
  integrated, 139-147
  resistance to, 142-143
  technology, 214
Telemarketing firms, 34
Telephone, future uses of, 221-222. *See also* Telemarketing
Telephone companies, consumer privacy and, 117-118
Television. *See also* Interactive media
  addressable, 86-87
  direct response, 159-164
  infomercial and, 90-91
  targeting with, 86
Time-Warner Inc., 84
Timing, 59-61
  MPP and, 62-64
Tomkins, Peter, 197, 200
Trade associations, for international marketing, 26-27
Trade incentives, sales promotion and, 149-156
Trading blocs, 168
Trust, building, 223-224
Two-way messaging, 83

Universal product code (UPC), 151
USAA, 222-223

Value added tax (VAT), 174 VCRs, 82
VideOcart, 154-155
Videocassettes, 245
Video games, 177
Virtual reality, 174, 177-180

Wang, Paul, 45-56 WATS lines, 141
Whole price, 170-172
Wientzen, H. Robert, 149-156
Wright, Carol. *See* Carol Wright
Writing techniques. *See* Copywriting
Wunderman, Lester, 41
Wunderman Worldwide, 35, 39, 41

Yeck, John D., 233-241

Ziff, Bill, 98, 100

TITLES OF INTEREST IN MARKETING

SUCCESSFUL DIRECT MARKETING METHODS, by Bob Stone
PROFITABLE DIRECT MARKETING, by Jim Kobs
INTEGRATED DIRECT MARKETING, by Ernan Roman
BEYOND 2000: THE FUTURE OF DIRECT MARKETING, by Jerry I. Reitman
POWER DIRECT MARKETING, by "Rocket" Ray Jutkins
CREATIVE STRATEGY IN DIRECT MARKETING, by Susan K. Jones
SECRETS OF SUCCESSFUL DIRECT MAIL, by Richard V. Benson
STRATEGIC DATABASE MARKETING, by Rob Jackson and Paul Wang
HOW TO PROFIT THROUGH CATALOG MARKETING, by Katie Muldoon
DIRECT RESPONSE TELEVISION, by Frank Brady and J. Angel Vasquez
DIRECT MARKETING THROUGH BROADCAST MEDIA, by Alvin Eicoff
SUCCESSFUL TELEMARKETING, by Bob Stone and John Wyman
BUSINESS TO BUSINESS DIRECT MARKETING, by Robert Bly
COMMONSENSE DIRECT MARKETING, by Drayton Bird
DIRECT MARKETING CHECKLISTS, by John Stockwell and Henry Shaw
INTEGRATED MARKETING COMMUNICATIONS, by Don E. Schultz, Stanley I. Tannenbaum,and Robert F. Lauterborn
GREEN MARKETING, by Jacquelyn Ottman
MARKETING CORPORATE IMAGE: THE COMPANY AS YOUR NUMBER ONE PRODUCT,
    by James R. Gregory with Jack G. Wiechmann
HOW TO CREATE SUCCESSFUL CATALOGS, by Maxwell Sroge
101 TIPS FOR MORE PROFITABLE CATALOGS, by Maxwell Sroge
SALES PROMOTION ESSENTIALS, by Don E. Schultz, William A. Robinson and Lisa A. Petrison
PROMOTIONAL MARKETING, by William A. Robinson and Christine Hauri
BEST SALES PROMOTIONS, by William A. Robinson
INSIDE THE LEADING MAIL ORDER HOUSES, by Maxwell Sroge
NEW PRODUCT DEVELOPMENT, by George Gruenwald
NEW PRODUCT DEVELOPMENT CHECKLISTS, by George Gruenwald
CLASSIC FAILURES IN PRODUCT MARKETING, by Donald W. Hendon
HOW TO TURN CUSTOMER SERVICE INTO CUSTOMER SALES, by Bernard Katz
ADVERTISING & MARKETING CHECKLISTS, by Ron Kaatz
BRAND MARKETING, by William M. Weilbacher
MARKETING WITHOUT MONEY, by Nicholas E. Bade
THE 1-DAY MARKETING PLAN, by Roman A. Hiebing, Jr. and Scott W. Cooper
HOW TO WRITE A SUCCESSFUL MARKETING PLAN, by Roman G. Hiebing, Jr. and Scott W. Cooper
DEVELOPING, IMPLEMENTING, AND MANAGING EFFECTIVE MARKETING PLANS, by Hal Goetsch
HOW TO EVALUATE AND IMPROVE YOUR MARKETING DEPARTMENT, by Keith Sparling and Gerard Earls
SELLING TO A SEGMENTED MARKET, by Chester A. Swenson
MARKET-ORIENTED PRICING, by Michael Morris and Gene Morris
STATE-OF-THE-ART MARKETING RESEARCH, by A.B. Blankenship and George E. Breen
AMA HANDBOOK FOR CUSTOMER SATISFACTION, by Alan Dutka
WAS THERE A PEPSI GENERATION BEFORE PEPSI DISCOVERED IT?, by Stanley C. Hollander and Richard Germain
BUSINESS TO BUSINESS COMMUNICATIONS HANDBOOK, by Fred Messner
MANAGING SALES LEADS: HOW TO TURN EVERY PROSPECT INTO A CUSTOMER, by Robert Donath, Richard Crocker, Carol
    Dixon and James Obermeyer
AMA MARKETING TOOLBOX (SERIES), by David Parmerlee
AMA COMPLETE GUIDE TO SMALL BUSINESS MARKETING, by Kenneth J. Cook
AMA COMPLETE GUIDE TO STRATEGIC PLANNING FOR SMALL BUSINESS, by Kenneth J. Cook
AMA COMPLETE GUIDE TO SMALL BUSINESS ADVERTISING, by Joe Vitale
HOW TO GET THE MOST OUT OF TRADE SHOWS, by Steve Miller
HOW TO GET THE MOST OUT OF SALES MEETINGS, by James Dance
STRATEGIC MARKET PLANNING, by Robert J. Hamper and L. Sue Baugh

For further information or a current catalog, write:
NTC Business Books
a division of *NTC Publishing Group*
4255 West Touhy Avenue
Lincolnwood, Illinois 60646–1975 U.S.A.